To Phil
Hope you enjoy it!
With best work

GW00787778

About the author

As a businesswoman who co-founded a travel dot-com at the turn of the millennium, and before that sold (and repaired) the first portable computers and the first laptops in the UK, Helen Hallpike has extensive experience at the forefront of technological change in the workplace. She has been employed as a strategic analyst for a number of blue-chip companies and has also worked in Germany and Japan. She won the Clothworkers' Exhibition to Somerville College, Oxford University, where she was awarded a 1st Class Honours degree and the Heath Harrison Travelling Scholarship; she also holds a PGCE from Cambridge University, the Diploma of the Chartered Institute of Marketing and an MBA from INSEAD European Business School, to which she won the Louis Franck Scholarship for Finance.

Author's note

With thanks to the statisticians at the Office for National Statistics and many other helpful sources of useful and astonishing data, and to Laurinda Quinn for advice on Human Resources issues, Sarah Horrell for feedback on market trends, and Mike Quinn, for advice on IT in business, as well as to my mother as my dedicated proof-reader, and, for insights into publishing, to authors Roz and Dave Morris. Above all, for the inspiration to research this subject and for his irrepressible support I dedicate this book to my husband, William.

Career Crunch!

The 25-year career vs. the 100-year life

by Helen Hallpike

ISBN 978-1-4457-6176-3

First published by Lulu Enterprises, Inc. 2010

email: Helen.Hallpike@career-crunch.com

Website: www.career-crunch.com

Career Crunch!

<u>Contents</u>

Career Crunch!

Introduction

White-collar 'odd-job-men'

Even before the Credit Crunch began in 2007, professionals in their mid-to-late forties were leaving their jobs and setting up as consultants, interims or non-executive directors. However, far from successfully pursuing two, three or more sequential careers in one working life, or happily choosing to downscale to a less demanding 'portfolio career', as management theory has suggested[1], in reality the redundant professional cobbles together a role as the *'odd-job-man'* of the white-collar workforce, constantly pitching for temporary assignments with companies which need experienced experts, but no longer want them permanently on their books. New laws to encourage even longer working lives[2] are up against the new phenomenon of the twenty-five year career.

Across the globe, even in centrally-planned economies such as China, fit and healthy workers in their forties are being unceremoniously booted out by their employers. Commercial and demographic needs are pulling in different directions. In the workplace, specialist training, mostly of younger employees, is displacing generalist experience as the primary qualification for career advancement, and traditional management roles are becoming redundant as corporate hierarchies are flattened and streamlined by a combination of technological advances and global competition. Meanwhile, the workforce is propelled by two powerful demographic trends: firstly, increasing longevity, which enables, but also compels older people to work; and secondly, a bulge of aspirational baby-boomers trying to squeeze into the remaining middle-management positions.

This book is written for businesspeople who are skilled, hard-working and adaptable, and need to earn a regular salary beyond the age of forty. In a global market of decreasing product and industry life cycles, and increasing sources of competition, this book takes a wry, detached look at the global business and demographic forces driving our emerging career patterns, with some pragmatic suggestions for what to do about it.

John Maynard Keynes famously joked about the division in Economics between the long term and the short term: "In the long term, we're all dead". The big problem today is - *we're not.*

So will your career come to a halt before you do? Read on ....

Chapter One

Cut off in your prime: *The 25-year career*

Eight students are in the London Head Offices of a major international company recruiting for next year's graduate intake. They are debating vigorously.

"I deserve to stay in the balloon because I'm only eighteen years old so I'm too young to die!"

"I agree! You can't throw her out of the balloon – her life is all before her, you'd be cutting her off in her prime!"

"Well, what about me? I'm thirty-five years old and have fifteen years' experience in Marketing. I'm hard-working and experienced, and I've *proved* I'm useful."

"Yes, but you're getting old. You've had the best part of your life. Move over and make room for someone else!"

And with that the 'thirty-five-year-old' is unceremoniously bundled out of the balloon, to the amusement of the observing company managers.

This true incident was an exercise in the form of a 'balloon debate' which took place in the 1990s, but those middle-management observers would not have been so amused had they realised how the jobs market was going to develop in another ten years. Even Senior Management, competing ruthlessly for the top positions, traditionally pause to welcome the new graduate intake so many years beneath them on the rungs of the career ladder, with a gracious charm born of the knowledge that these young things in their early twenties are no threat, and never will be, to the established company giants aged fifty plus. Yet the situation is changing, and a manager or director cannot be sure of remaining in employment until his pension pays out at age sixty-five, let alone expect to hold a portfolio of lucrative but undemanding non-executive directorships until he is well into his seventies. Since the dot-com boom and bust, the decline of rising stars has been ever more immediate and dramatic. What happens to them then?

Age perception partly depends on life stage: A sixty-year-old new mother courtesy of IVF treatment can't afford to think about old age – although to the media it is the key fact about her. To a grandmother at forty, a forty-five-year-old mother still going to junior school parents' evenings is *ancient.* What about working life? Does age perception here, too, vary according to what you are doing when?

The four ages of working man/woman

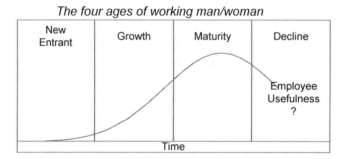

What numbers would you put along the bottom of this graph?

Professional e.g. Accountant:
- *New entrant* into the market at graduate level, aged 21?
- *Growth* once fully qualified as a professional, say aged 25-40?
- *Maturity* aged 40-60? Would you reluctantly concede that some people might start to...
- *Decline* a little from their peak aged 61 onwards?

Service industry specialist e.g. Hairdresser:
- Suppose you go to work as a hairdresser at age 16 with day release from college.
- You practise as a fully fledged hairdresser aged 18-26, at which point you set up your own salon, taking on all the responsibilities of payroll,

paying the rent, attracting the customers and keeping your staff coming in on time.

- At 30 you open a second salon ('Maturity') and spend more time on management.
- By the age of 40 you have 4 salons and are thinking of taking a bit of a back seat, and maybe selling up when you're about 48 – you retire from your working life before 'Decline' sets in?

Entertainment/Sports Personality e.g. .Footballer/Pop star:
- 'Growth' age 17-20
- 'Maturity' at age 21-26
- rapid 'Decline' at 30

Business Tycoon e.g. Bill Gates:
- Drop out of college
- Become a billionaire by the age of 31
- Retire at 52

Footballers and business tycoons may be at the extreme end of the scale, but new workers *do* enter the market at any age from sixteen to twenty-five if they have studied for degrees, MBAs and other professional qualifications, (or even later in countries such as Germany where students can fritter away many years on their first degrees) and leave the permanent jobs market aged anywhere from forty-five to sixty-five-plus. This means that a normal 'working life' can *vary in length* by twenty-five years! Bill Gates has no doubt put by the pension he needs for his early retirement, but what about the rest of us? Meanwhile the cases of surviving stars such as the clean-living Sir Cliff Richard or the never-satisfied Rolling Stones recently ignited a debate about Copyright Laws – artists are outliving the copyrights on their performances, highlighting the issue that in the past they were not expected to live more than another fifty years at most.

So what is the length of a typical career? According to a major study by the management consulting firm Booz & Company[3], the average age of a *departing* CEO in Europe in 2006 was only fifty-four years! And how long had he been in his job? Was this the *end* of his career? Since the average total length of job tenure of a CEO is under six years in Europe[4], this implies that ambitious employees can, on average, expect to get the top job in their late forties, no doubt dashing the hopes of a number of rivals - how many ambitious, thrusting employees will want to stay, or indeed will be kept on, if they have been passed over in favour of a boss nearly ten years younger? Such youthfulness is confirmed by Robert Half, the specialist financial recruitment agency, who found that the *average* age of a FTSE CEO was only fifty-two[5]. This is not reassuring for people who need to stay in work as long as possible, when average age and average job tenure do not add up to a job through to normal retirement. It may not be of concern to the executives themselves, since they will no doubt have amassed sufficient pension and savings for a comfortable retirement, but it sends discouraging signals to the rest of the workforce that a successful career is shorter than a normal working life.

Of course there are some older CEOs, such as the Chief Executive of Citigroup, Sandy Weil, who was seventy when he relinquished that role in 2003, and then stayed on as Chairman until 2006. The oldest Standard & Poor's Global 100 CEO in 2008 was a venerable seventy-six[6], but this was in Japan, where the average age of CEOs on the Nikkei Index (sixty-two years) is higher than the rest of the world. In China, in contrast, with its proliferation of new businesses, the average age on the Shanghai Index is only forty-seven. Life is also more precarious at the top now than it was a decade ago[7]. Mainly because of poor performance or disagreements with the Board, nearly one in three CEOs worldwide who left office in the ruthless working environment of 2006 did so involuntarily. A decade earlier they were much more secure - only one in eight could expect to go up and then straight out. A further one in five recent departures worldwide were the result of mergers or buyouts, so overall more than half of CEOs can expect to be thrown, or at least firmly nudged, out of their positions: Chief Executive Officers are not expected to 'die in their beds'. The career pattern has moved on from '*up-or-out*' to '*once you are up, perform to order, or you're out anyway*'. This indicates a large company focus on short-term profits and share price, which may originally have been conceived as healthy performance-optimisation, but in practice results in the distortion of the long-term strategy of the company to support the CEO's personal short-term targets and objectives, with all that this implies for the interests of shareholders, staff and customers.

One rung down the corporate hierarchy the picture is even more disjointed. This is illustrated in Marketing, the function the most associated with a youth culture, and here the senior management move on even faster. According to the leading executive search consulting firm, SpencerStuart[8], in 2006 the average FTSE Chief Marketing Officer (CMO) had been in office for only just over three years, and in the US this was even shorter, at just under two years! According to the research, whilst respondents felt that a CMO should remain in his position for at least three annual business cycles, they felt that it was unusual for him/her to stay in office for more than five years.

So where can a senior marketer go after that? A lot of the movement is due to "churning" as Marketing professionals are recycled round the industry – but some end up each time on the waste pile, as younger marketers are promoted. SpencerStuart also reported that marketers were perceived as suffering from the "silo effect", narrowly focusing on brands, budgets and staff, and lacking general business skills and understanding, and indeed this charge of limited vision is often levelled at ambitious specialists in all functions who try to move up into general management.

The case of the career Marketer, targeted with short-term quick hits and allowed no time to train for broader skills, focusing on bottom line results, or, even worse, on top-line sales or only on consumer awareness, is an extreme version of the dilemma facing all functional specialists. With the path to CEO blocked by narrow professional focus, typically compounded by a history of regularly changing companies, the senior marketer has no obvious career route upwards. SpencerStuart confirm this perception in a report published in 2009[9] in which they confirm that: "CMOs rarely (if ever) get promoted to CEO in the same company". They, too, blame the short average job tenure as one of the reasons why marketers find it harder to progress to general management and thence to the top position[10]. With their upward path blocked, marketers have led the way in turning to consultancy and interim assignments in the latter part of their careers. As other company functions embrace increasingly rapid changes in their products, working practices and global competition, so a two-tier structure is emerging which divides permanent staff, who enjoy pensions and security, from temporary staff, who come and go as needed. This employment pattern is used as a stop-gap in the private sector, but as a structural device in the public sector, where inflexible employment arrangements for permanent staff can be offset by more expensive but disposable interim employees.

Employee Life Cycle – Myth or reality?

There is a perception that decline sets in towards the end of a working life, so an official retirement age is also the final marker of an employee's official decline in usefulness – perhaps starting from five years before retirement. The employee life-cycle is not much documented but it is endemic in recruiters' thinking. Marketers track the life cycle of *products* through growth and maturity to decline, but companies have remained coy of clarifying their view of their most valuable resource, namely, their *staff*, and how they assume that the staff develop, mature and decline in usefulness over the course of their working life. As with all unstated views, it is difficult to refute an accusation that no-one wants to make explicit.

Of course employers, colleagues and even academics have preconceptions about older job candidates. Psychologists such as Abraham Maslow have suggested that human beings ultimately aspire to self-fulfilment, or 'self- actualisation', and older workers who are keen to do a "worthwhile" job are often *more* dedicated than other employees to the tasks they are given, as they seek personal fulfilment through their work. But going to work for self-fulfilment sounds self-indulgent to their profits-driven rivals or bosses, who already assume that as employees rise up the hierarchy they lose their early drive. A middle-aged worker faces the assumption that she is looking to consolidate her position at work, relying on existing contacts and familiar business activities, and that when she feels secure in her job and has only a short time to go before retirement she will start to coast, living off a reputation established years ago. These preconceptions about employees' attitudes at different stages of their careers help to determine who gets onto the short-list for redundancy or for recruitment/promotion, so in a competitive economic environment, older employees are neither free to focus on self-fulfilment, nor sufficiently secure to coast towards retirement.

The harsh reality is that it is more common for any employee approaching fifty to be permanently nervous of redundancy and looking over his shoulder to see who is gunning to replace him, staying on longer hours at work to try to establish his indispensability. There is an increasing divide between those who can anticipate a relaxed retirement, in the knowledge that they have final salary pensions, and the rest, who are worrying about whether their retirement savings will pay the gas bills. As a result, the world of work for the over-fifties is divided between those with secure pensions who plan either to have fun in their retirement or to "give back to society" - perhaps by doing charity work when they retire - and those who are grimly hanging on in there to earn another year's pension contributions before they are booted out. The myths of second and third genuine careers within one lifetime are mainly in the theory books and re-training leaflets, not in the office.

Figures from the Office for National Statistics[11] confirm this trend, showing that in the two years heading into the Credit Crunch up to December 2008 the number of workers over the age of fifty claiming Jobseeker's Allowance for up to six months rose by 84%, a huge figure, but not dramatically higher than the number for workers aged between twenty-five and forty-nine. However, it was then over half as difficult again for a person over fifty to find a *new* job: whilst there was a 39% increase in people unemployed for between six and twelve months who were aged twenty-five to forty-nine, this figure rose to a 64% increase amongst those over fifty. Furthermore, these figures understate the total of unemployed over-fifty-year-olds because they are reluctant to "sign on" as they generally gain no financial benefit from doing so. The Labour Force Survey[12] , which includes unemployed people who are not claiming benefit, more accurately reflects their situation. This broader measure shows that whilst amongst the younger group of workers there was a 21% increase unemployment for less than six months, for the over-fifties this deterioration was twice as bad, at 43%, and remained so: after six months the younger group started to find new jobs, but the numbers of unemployed over-fifties increased by nearly 40%! So the older employees are vulnerable, and they know it.

Nevertheless, in some professions the situation has become more favourable for older candidates, with certain roles tending to be reserved nowadays for older people. When William Wilberforce and William Pitt were first elected to the House of Commons in 1780 they had both just turned twenty-one years old, and that year one hundred MPs aged under thirty were elected! In contrast, in 2005 there were only three MPs who were so youthful. William Pitt "the Younger" then famously went on to become Prime Minister at a mere twenty-four years old, whereas more recently William Hague and David Cameron were considered young to become Leaders of the Opposition at thirty-six and thirty-nine respectively, and at the age of forty-three Tony Blair became the youngest Prime Minister since Lord Liverpool in 1812! As in the world of work, however, just as the lower age of entry is rising, so an *upper* limit seems to have been set with the resignation of Menzies Campbell, aged sixty-six years, as Leader of the Liberal Democrat Party, in 2007, because he was thought to be too old to lead the party into the next election. This political coup highlighted the phenomenon that ageism is also predictive, since it was his anticipated *future* state of health that militated against him. Age was the hottest topic linked to him prior to his resignation, which shows that even a mild, well-mannered political party would rather accept ageism than political decline.

Instead of commanding respect for their wisdom and experience, however, older political leaders are blamed for all the ills of society, and their generation is held accountable by indignant younger adults for appearing to abandon their stated ideals. Consider the youthful support for Green issues and Fair Trade (*the greed of previous generations all but destroyed the planet*). The duty of government to care for the population from cradle to grave was only established in the UK after the Second World War and yet it is proving harder to maintain now than to introduce back in 1947 when its champions had only limited resources but limitless zeal and commitment. This is perceived as another failure of the generation currently in power. To counteract age prejudice the term "Older Workers" has been coined as the polite, politically correct term for employees over the age of fifty, yet if anything this patronising euphemism makes matters worse – making the group sound superannuated and underprivileged rather than an experienced integral part of the workforce.

Perhaps respect for one's elders was always more a precept than a reality. The nomadic lifestyle of the Bushmen of the Kalahari did not allow them to take their ageing relatives with them when they moved on, so older tribespeople who began lagging behind would be provided with supplies and shelter, and left to the hyenas; even the Japanese reverence for longevity was overridden in poor rural communities by the alleged practice of 'obasute' - carrying your elderly relative into the mountains, and returning without them. Unlike trips to the Dignitas clinic in Switzerland today, this practice was only tacitly acknowledged rather than publicly debated. Historically, and in certain regimes to this day, the strong incentive to show respect to your elders whilst they still wielded power was based on the literal imperative of survival. If you displeased the King, he didn't just make you redundant - he might well behead you. If a daughter disliked her father's choice of husband, then Shakespeare had her condemned "To death, or to a vow of single life"[13]. If in Dickens' time your employer sacked you, that could mean the workhouse for you and your family – there was little job mobility and minimal social welfare. Back in the eleventh century, in revenge for the disrespect shown to him whilst he was besieging the town of Alençon, William the Conqueror, or 'William the Bastard' as he was known in France, had a selection of its citizens skinned when he took the town[14]. In history, the genuine power of life and death was unsurprisingly effective at instilling respect for authority.

In the modern world, however, unquestioning respect for mature professionals has been eroded as the population has become more educated and able to question their competence. League tables enable us to compare the performance of public bodies, ranging from examination results in schools to death rates in hospitals. Why should anyone pay an accountant a fortune to complete their tax return when they can complete it themselves online with free software from the Inland Revenue - and get an instant rebate? Why did the rich and powerful investment bankers receive rewards for failing their shareholders and nearly destroying the economy? The public feels empowered to protest against official errors and professional malpractice, urged on by legions of popular campaigning organisations.

The change from the "we" generation to the "me" generation has been comment upon from the West across the world to China[15]. Each individual is fighting for survival, and older people need expect no special consideration, on the streets or in the workplace. Radio phone-ins and TV chat shows complain that no-one is willing to stand up for the old, weak and vulnerable any more, and that children are less dutiful towards their parents and grandparents, but meanwhile members of the older generation are often less practically involved with their children and grandchildren. The traditional family network provided social support and childcare, but relocation in search of jobs means that for many grandparents their family role is reduced to that of purveyors of tea and old-fashioned food in musty houses without hi-tech toys at Christmas. Alternatively, for those pensioners who have adopted the 'spend it while you've got it' approach, they are no longer around themselves – at Christmas the children have to go to Spain to see their grandparents.

Mirroring the rise of the '60s baby-boomer generation, society has adopted a youth culture. A youthful appearance is an obsession, Botox and face-lifts the norm for glamorous figures - no ageing gracefully for them. Television presenters only exceptionally keep their jobs until normal retirement age. The BBC, like any other entertainment organisation, is subject to fashion and appearance. Attractive presenters pull in bigger audiences. Young people want to see presenters like themselves. So old presenters are out, as in the much-debated removal of Arlene Phillips, "Strictly Come Dancing" judge. Even the photos of newly-appointed Chief Executives in companies' Reports and Accounts are grinning and friendly. Compare the venerable portraits of yester-year with those of the recent leaders of church and state – most of them manifest the same informal approachability, none of the stiff aloofness of former years.

A youth culture in the workplace was well-established in the creative industries such as fashion and entertainment by the 1960s, and moved rapidly through the Advertising industry to Fast Moving Consumer Goods (FMCG) companies, where the Marketing department was key and household-name brands in the 1980s were commonly managed by twenty-four-year-olds; from there the whole of Marketing increasingly became a young person's function. The Chartered Institute of Marketing produced a paper on Ageism[16] in 2007 lamenting the prevalent attitude that if a marketer hasn't made it to a senior position by his early forties, then his career is seen to be over. The marketing profession was one of the first to become notable for significant numbers of consultants and interim employees, generally earning their living from temporary assignments through necessity, having been supplanted from their permanent positions by younger or more specialised employees. This pattern of work is still barely acknowledged in Britain, yet it has been typical of many Japanese industries for decades. In Japan, as early as the mid-1980s, I observed first-hand the two-tier employment structure, with major companies employing permanent full time workers called "salarymen", serviced by small companies whose workers are called on as needed. Yet 'salarymen', far from taking their security for granted, still work long hours to hold onto their increasingly hard-to-come-by full-time employment.

Extending this pattern to all forms of work in his book "*The Brave New World of Work*"[17] Ulrich Beck predicts a society in which lifelong employment is replaced with less stable work, where jobs regularly disappear and old skills are devalued. As this pattern is more characteristic of developing countries, he calls this development the "Brazilianization of the West". This pattern is becoming more and more pronounced in Japan, where recently even the secure 'salarymen' are beginning to lose what had always been jobs for life, pressurised to "volunteer" for redundancy once they reach that doom-laden age of fifty. Here in Britain, this change is also being unintentionally spear-headed by forty-to-fifty-year-olds in larger corporations, who are losing their jobs and having to find new skills and work. Their plight is only obliquely recognised by the government, which has set up a plethora of training schemes, most of which are simply at too low a level or too general to be of specific use to these redundant managers.

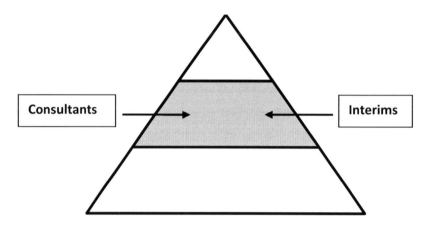

The 'odd-job-men' of the white-collar workforce: displaced older generalists circle hungrily outside the flatter structures of the big name companies, seeking interim roles or assignments as consultants.

Advertising Executives are expected to be young so they can form the communication channel between major corporations and their youthful consumers. But the fallacy of this attitude is evidenced all around us: firstly, the baby bulge of young, cash-rich consumers is itself slowly ageing, so those trendy young advertising executives who so well understood its needs and desires twenty years ago are *still* the same age as the major group of their clients' customers now. Secondly, there is no evidence that younger advertising executives, recruited to target a new generation, also naturally empathise with the interests and motivations of *older* consumers with their grey pounds. If they do, then why do adverts to the over-fifties generally feature soft-focus smiling wrinklies with laughing grandchildren and immaculate lawns – surely this is more representative of the youthful marketers' stereotypical view of their parents and grandparents than of the older generation's increasingly go-getter self-image! Look at the adverts for standard lamps in the back of the Sunday Times. A little old man hunched in a cosy armchair needing '50% extra light' to read by because his ageing eyes are tired. Did you realise that was meant to be _you_?

An older applicant faces an uphill struggle to answer these unspoken prejudices, not only when applying for a new job but also to gain a place on in-house training schemes or to survive the latest round of staff redundancies.

"But I'm only forty-four - I'm in my prime! And anyway, ageism's illegal now, so my age can't count against me...can it?"

Unfortunately it will. Listen for the head-hunter code:

"The CEO is very _young_ and he's looking for someone to fit into the company _culture_" (_actual words used_)

"How would you feel reporting to someone with so much less... _experience_ than you?" (_actual words_)

Other examples include:

- _Wouldn't this job be a step down for you?_
- _You won't be satisfied in a position like this for long_
- _Aren't you used to having far more staff than this?_
- _You haven't done any front-line selling for a number of years._
- _Will you have the energy?_
- _Will you fit the culture?_

In the UK, as in the US, there are interview questions that it is illegal to ask a candidate. For example: if she is planning to start a family soon, what his religion is and, now, how old she is. Yet even before candidates are invited to interview, a candidate's CV gives indicators of her age. In theory it is not a requirement to put any dates on a CV, but how many recruitment consultants would pass on such a CV – their immediate assumption would be either that the candidate's age was somewhere the wrong side of ninety, or that each job on the CV lasted only a few months. So before the candidate applies for a job there are screening criteria for anyone who chooses to pay heed to them in the phrasing of the advertisement. Job adverts cannot legally use age as a selection criterion, but phrases such as: "the company is seeking a rising star" or: "a recent graduate/MBA" are still very common in UK job advertisements. An oft-rejected older candidate may decide to stop wasting her time and ink, printing off another application letter, when she can read between the lines that the odds are already stacked against her. Since autumn 2006 this is of course illegal: in a case brought in Northern Ireland against timber firm James McGregor & Sons Ltd, Mr Terence McCoy successfully claimed that the use of the phrase "youthful enthusiasm" in their job advertisement and various age-related questions in the course of his interviews demonstrated ageism which may have prevented the fifty-eight year-old candidate from getting the job[18]. Meanwhile the publisher, Felix Dennis, lost a case for making a promotions director aged fifty-five redundant, because the employee's replacement and his former team, none of whom were considered for redundancy, were all at least twenty years younger than him[19]. It didn't help Felix Dennis's case when the frank quotation from his own book featured below was read out in court to illustrate his views on the high cost of older employees.

What other subtle ageist indicators are there on a job application? The trend-setting and controversial book on economics "Freakonomics" by Levitt & Dubner[20] lists pages of American names that reveal social class and colour, and this can also be applied to age. A special report by the UK's own Office for National Statistics confirms your secret suspicion that it is unlikely that a batch of British girls called Florence, Doris, Edith and Dorothy (some of the most popular names in 1904) are as young as Margaret, Jean, Joan and Patricia (1934), and they in turn are clearly distinguishable from Susan, Julie, Karen and Jacqueline (1964) and from Chloe, Megan, Jessica and Sophie (1999).[21] Jack and Chloe, the most popular names in 1999, were not in the top fifty in 1984 and in 1974 they were not in the top 100 names. A recruiter may only subconsciously prefer the idea of a trainee teen-fashion sales-assistant called Lauren to one called Susan, without even realising that his subconscious has diligently analysed these names and those of hundreds of people he has met, and concluded that it is statistically likely that Susan is about forty-five whereas Lauren is straight from school.

Ageist attitudes are commonplace, but despite legislation and public exhortation, there is little attempt being made inside British companies to tackle ageism at work or to analyse and manage inter-generational relationships. One danger of anti-ageism legislation is that age becomes an unmentionable topic associated mainly with industrial tribunals. So, privately, have you actually ever considered how you are viewed by your younger and older colleagues, both up, down and across the hierarchy? The following matrix shows a traditionalist positioning for positive relationships between people of different ages:

My positioning for a positive relationship:

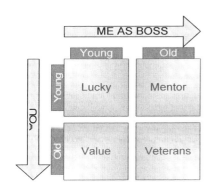 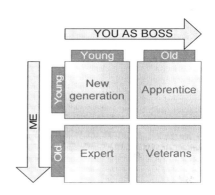

In the traditional role, the older boss could play the wise mentor to his or her younger staff, whilst remaining a jovial but slightly distant fellow-veteran to contemporaries who hadn't made it. As a young boss he could not afford to let respect for his elders put them in a superior position – he could show them he valued their experience, but had to retain decision-making responsibility. As a young boss to her contemporaries she could position herself as the lucky one to have her talents recognised early on - there would be plenty of time for the roles to reverse later. For the young new employee, how better to position himself than as the older boss's apprentice? As an older subordinate, he could not afford to be seen as a threat - better a diligent and committed expert to be consulted when necessary. When boss and employee were both veterans they showed mutual respect from years of common experience, and finally, a young Turk emphasised what he or she had in common with the young boss, as the first of the new generation to succeed where others hoped to follow. You can probably fill in the equivalent matrix for traditional *negative* relationships for yourself, but if you are uninspired think of the Emperor Nero's relationship with his mother (he had her murdered - twice) or with his tutor, the revered philosopher Seneca (obliged to commit ritual suicide). Compare this with the heroic positioning of Yoda, the fictional mentor in "Star Wars", who retires to a cave in a swamp on an obscure planet, and has to be found, pursued and pleaded with before he will impart the most esoteric advice. Post-2006, in a now officially ageless work environment, there can in theory be no concessions to age, but will the generations mix seamlessly as a result?

As you get older you realise that Ageism is not all bad

Age discrimination is evident all around us, and a lot of older people enthusiastically support it. If you are inclined to doubt the political correctness or even question the legality of this statement, think about insurance: how many protesters do you see outside the offices of insurers offering favourable rates for careful drivers over the age of fifty? Or against Saga who specialise in holidays for the older client? It is similar to the prevailing attitude towards sex discrimination: there are no feminists protesting outside women-only companies such as the all-female taxi firm whose drivers are apparently unusual in that they are unlikely to rape and murder their passengers, or outside those companies that treat female drivers as a better insurance risk. So is prejudice good or bad? Apparently it depends on whether the group in question is perceived to be in some way disadvantaged and therefore deserving of special treatment, and whether the group is benefiting from the discrimination, even if this may be to the detriment of other, less well-defined, less indignantly vocal groups. Above all, it depends whether the group benefiting/suffering from the prejudice includes *you*.

Career Crunch!

These are all examples of the kind of prejudice that economists refer to as *strategic discrimination* i.e. taking what is perceived to be the average performance of a group as an indicator of the merits of any one individual member. This practice, as illustrated above, is abhorrent to that group – unless it is to their benefit. But at least it is in theory possible for one individual to demonstrate that his performance is better than the average for his group through qualifications or a faultless driving record, for example. Not so with the other form of discrimination, *taste discrimination,* for example, choosing to recruit people you *like* rather than those who are best qualified to do the job. This underlies some of the popular excuses for not recruiting older workers: the phrase "...not sure that he would fit with the culture..." is impossible to contest. Should the older candidate act young – ensure he mentions his Facebook profile and throws in a reference to contemporary music – or claim, as a benign avuncular figure, to "admire young people today"? Either approach risks the interviewer's scorn.

The prejudiced recruiting manager should not be painted in too dark a light, however: he may only have a mild preference for younger recruits. An academic called Thomas Schelling demonstrated in 1971 that nothing more than a mild preference to live near to a majority of similar people could create racially divided ghettos. This pattern is also shown amongst British or Americans when they go to work abroad and choose to move into areas with a supportive ex-pat community, perpetuating the centuries-old tradition of foreign quarters in major cities around the world. A similar pattern can be applied to ageist recruitment in the workplace. A manager may have a mild preference for working with people of his own age, which is then tempered by his need to ensure that he does not recruit potential rivals, so he will rationally recruit workers who are slightly younger and less well-qualified in his own core skills, and complementary to the weaknesses he perceives in himself, though above all not obviously better-qualified than him to do his own job. For the older job applicant this translates as a series of disappointing rejections, whilst the recruiting manager complains that he cannot find recruits who are adequately qualified. Ageism may be illegal, but it is even more insidious if it is swept under the carpet.

Career Crunch!

Prejudice is still prevalent in many areas of work as a decision-making short-cut. Yet this behaviour, pragmatic as it may be, is short-termist. *Chapter Four* examines the economic implications of ageism in recruitment, but suffice it to say that it is cutting off your nose to spite your face to refuse to interview anyone over the age of forty-five and thus lose the benefit of their experience, just because you expect that they are boring and turning grey. Tactically, ageist recruitment might be adequate in the short term but it will lead to strategic problems in the longer term, both for individual enterprises and for the national economy as a whole. The UK State Pension is based on a historical forty-year working life, and a life expectancy of less than the Biblical "three score years and ten", but how representative is this today and will it be in the future? A career lasting twenty-five years will not usually have earned sufficient pension for a tolerable retirement. Indeed, based on historical precedent, why should it? A fit healthy worker has historically been expected to work until just before they dropped – just because the baby-boomer generation are expected to "drop" later, and had been rather looking forward to a retirement dedicated to energetic frolics, does this change the principle?

Moreover the latest UK government pension policies assume that our working lives will gradually get longer. Yet how can that principle be applied if those with employment positions in their gift choose to give them systematically to a younger group of candidates? Employees who would in the previous generation have continued to work until they were sixty-five are now being made redundant at forty-five, and were until recently routinely given early retirement at fifty - are there also structural forces at work?

Company-Internal changes

Pay scales and Pensions:
Older employees at work are often locked into much more generous pensions and pay schemes, for example, traditional airline pilots. This creates resentment and a practical problem. To get rid of outdated pay scales can take complex and costly negotiations with the Unions, and develop an unfair two-tier structure within the same company (for those who joined before and

after the new agreement). The only way out is redundancy or retirement. Even within the same pay scale, internal company salaries tend to rise over time in recognition of experience, (or simply as a result of inflation-related pay-rises which may not be reflected in the salaries of younger recruits), but the question now being asked is whether twenty-five years' experience is worth more than ten? Is long experience countered by smugness or inertia? Would a younger person with ten years' experience not do the job just as well and expect less money for it?

The alternative is to pay a lower guaranteed salary for the job, but with bonuses linked to performance. City bonuses are currently particularly unpopular, mainly because their most notable beneficiaries are identified as the cause of the global recession, but in normal circumstances they are much more economically sound than layers of senior employees all locked into six-figure salaries until they retire on massive pensions or are made redundant. Bonuses, when genuinely awarded for *enduring* value created, are transparently calculated and results-driven – no long-term profit, no bonus: the perfect economic arrangement.

Career development:
Management training was traditionally provided by blue-chip companies such as Shell and BP, as well as the American Procter & Gamble or Mars whilst specialist professional qualifications were awarded by the firms of accountants and lawyers, who still take on the cream of the bright graduates and work them into the ground on relatively low pay for several years, before they progress to reaping the conspicuous rewards of partnership in these illustrious organisations. One of the most extreme examples was until recently that of the junior doctors, who had to undergo patient-endangering sleep-deprivation to earn their stripes. The older incumbents didn't see why the younger doctors should not have to endure the same conditions that they had to, and, not surprisingly, they felt their early suffering had earned them a steady income and a secure lifestyle, conveniently protected by the intellectual and physical endurance barriers to new entrants - a complete

change from the thrusting work ethic on which they had prided themselves in their twenties.

From the 1950s through to the 1970s the paternalistic Shell/BP/Procter & Gamble model applied to many major firms, with its career-planning and regular job-changing to broaden and develop employees on the fast track to senior management. In this system, it did not become apparent who was going to make it to the very top, given this wealth of experience and talent, until late in their careers. The system saved face and preserved aspirations, and created a feeling of solidarity and identification with the company as a whole, as well as providing job fulfilment as new skills were learnt.

But from the 1980s structured career management was replaced by a more hire-and-fire model, where employees do not expect to stay with the same company all their careers, and therefore companies do not invest the same career management and training into them. The 'unwritten contract', that employees who were committed and loyal would in return be looked after and stay in employment, was broken. Suddenly, however hard you worked, you could still be made redundant. So following the employers' lead, employees became less loyal and more likely to 'jump ship'.

The impetus for this may have been economic: for example, in the mid-late eighties, as the price of oil dropped by about two-thirds, back to pre-1973 prices, and then stayed low throughout the nineties, a number of Shell employees, who were anticipating staying with the company for life, were ejected into the functional-specialist jobs market to make the best use they could of their functionally-broad but company-specific experience. Nowadays jobs have in theory been opened up to the best candidate, internal or external, but at the expense of a structured and planned career as a long-term employee. Just one symptom of this change is the decline of "milk-round" recruitment, when major companies used to do the rounds of a wide range of universities to recruit for internal graduate training programmes designed to prepare the top management of the future.

Career Crunch!

Nevertheless, if you go to the doctor, would you rather see a big toe specialist for your bunion, or a whole body generalist? A holistic approach, it is true, might convince you that you wish to remain corporeally complete, but if you do decide to operate, you'd prefer someone who knows a thing or two about bunions. So where does this leave the self-actualisation of the bored but highly sought-after bunion specialist? Does he need a good hobby or a pre-planned change in career? Or will the challenge to keep up with constant innovations in bunion-removal keep him intellectually committed to his work right up to and beyond normal retirement age?

Company-External changes

Demographic:

Faced with an ageing population, management and government literature is encouraging workers to anticipate longer working lives to fund their pensions for a longer retirement, but the academics have reckoned without the new phenomenon of the twenty-five-year career. Managers are reaching the age of forty and starting to worry about whether they will have a job for much longer. Just when we need even older people to stay in work, people are leaving full-time permanent employment at an earlier age – retiring early, made redundant, becoming consultants or interims. How has this come about? Surely the demographers have been warning us about the imminence of a gerontocracy, where the elderly voters hold all the cards. This may be the situation in the future, once the 'sixties babies retire, from around the year 2025, and use their grey vote to requisition tax revenues to focus on care of the elderly, but this is not the case right now, where those forty-something baby-boomers are still raising their families and pursing their careers.

When the baby-boom was first identified it looked as if baby-boomers would be held back in their careers by the older, longer-living generations before eventually themselves clogging up the rungs of the corporate ladder, holding back the new entrants. Instead, with the flattening of the corporate hierarchy, it is those very middle and senior managers just ahead of the first baby boomers who are finding themselves jobless, as a new generation of young specialists works its way up within its functional area and bundles the generalist middle management unceremoniously out of the corporate balloon. This is the vanguard of the huge bulge of maturing mid-late '60s babies, driving its way into management positions and clearing all before it. It now comprises a broad swathe of the population, motivated by increasingly convergent middle-class aspirations, and swollen with the largest proportion of working women in peacetime. In its turn, it is under threat from the very pattern it has created, as succeeding generations of a new breed of hands-on specialist managers follow its youth-orientated lead.

Global and technological:

Yet just as a large new generation reaches management age, traditional management roles are becoming redundant as corporate hierarchies are streamlined and flattened by technological advances. Faster communication has led to greater empowerment at lower levels of the hierarchy. As a new sales rep. before the advent of mobile phones I used to scour the country lanes or dodge the city traffic wardens to find a public telephone box so that I could phone in to the office and reassure my bosses that I was on the road drumming up sales. In contrast, the 21st century sales rep, armed with a lap-top and mini printer, types up a new contract straight away, gives a copy to the client and emails a copy to Head Office, as does the dishwasher repair man with his invoice, and their boss can track their movements on GPS at any time. In the office, PCs long ago enabled staff to type their own presentations and letters, cutting out armies of secretaries and assistants, whereas back in the 1980s one of my first bosses refused us permission to type our own letters on our new desktop PCs, insisting we continue to write them out by hand and leave them in the secretary's in-tray, where they remained until she had nothing more important to do. (That boss went on to become the CEO of a leading UK financial services provider.)

The academics have labelled this substitution of computers for people Skill-Based Technological Change (SBTC), but there is now debate as to whether the new computer-based jobs really require a high level of academic study – you need training and practice to use a computer competently, but you do not need a degree – look at the results that any fourteen-year-old can produce. Now you might argue that some of those fourteen-year-olds are of a calibre of mind that will go on to get a degree *later on* – that does not alter the fact that they do not *need* that intensely academic style of training to get results out of computers that many adults with university degrees regard with envy.

From the travel industry to insurance and banking, fragmented industries are merging to form large consolidated global players, leaving no room for layers of middle managers in charge of independent business units. Companies produce one central statement of mission and goals, and invest in centralised service functions: one central IT system (though it still may not work quite as the staff would like) and one central Personnel System (ditto). As a result of flatter organisational structures there are no longer clear paths to senior general management. The new career model, as predicted by the management guru Charles Handy as long ago as 1989, in his book "The Age of Unreason", is to work up the flattened hierarchy within a specialist function. The present problems come, however, at the final and dangerous stage, when a functional expert, having climbed to the top of his specialist plateau, checks over his shoulder to see who is pushing him from underneath to dislodge his toehold, whilst he simultaneously attempts the daring leap across the chasm to begin to scale the dizzy heights of general management.

Figures highlighting CEO company loyalty show that CEOs of major corporations are more often than not drawn from the internal ranks. Loyalty pays off: the recruitment consultants SpencerStuart analysed company tenure[22] and found that the top 100 S&P CEOs had been in their company for an average of nineteen years, and nearly one in ten had been with the company for over thirty-five years! So for the redundant CEO, or the disappointed CEO-in-waiting, a move to a new company may not be the answer – after all, there will be plenty of internal candidates, and a former CEO will not usually be considered for a lower-ranking role in the hierarchy.

Limited entry points to major corporations

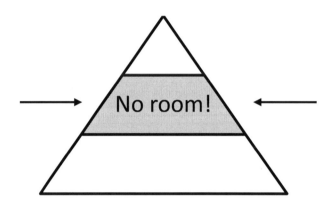

No room in the middle. Traditional entry points reduced....

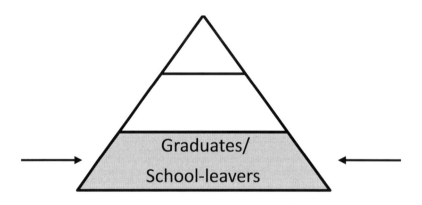

.......and restricted to the young

Career Crunch!

For functional specialists there is no room at the top:

Vertical progression blocked

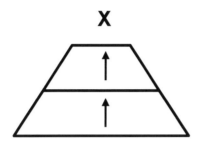

And whilst a top position may become available if a company subdivides into business units:

Subdivision vs. Consolidation

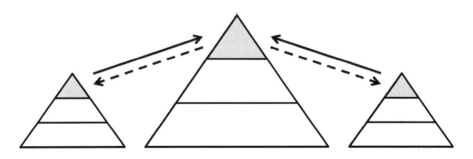

... instead of subdividing they are increasingly consolidating and reducing management opportunities.

Yet even with rapid upward internal career progression, the very top jobs may still not be accessible to the successful employee. Whilst a large proportion of CEOs have spent long years with the company, advisors who have worked with the Board as management consultants or financial specialists are also often brought onto it from outside the company, demonstrating to all but the most dedicated of middle managers that there is no long-term career route up the company hierarchy. Impatient employees observe that they have more chance of short-term career advancement by switching companies, and the reason for the current career "promiscuity" can be traced back to the reward and career structure within the company, which sends clear signals to its employees, either consciously or inadvertently, through its promotion and recruitment policies.

Furthermore, the new career path via a functional specialism also comes with an intrinsic contradiction: to follow the pattern of the legacy career structure and become a general manager you have to relinquish your unique specialist value to your employer. As a former specialist becomes a department manager she focuses on delegating and organising, checking, censuring and otherwise motivating her staff, and takes on outward-facing roles attending company-wide and company-external meetings on behalf of her department. Whilst she gains profile with other departments and the more senior general managers she also relaxes her grip on developments in the day-to-day functions within her department. Younger employees do the doing she once did.

The industry however has all the time been subtly evolving. Her old skills are still relevant but all a bit shabby and old-fashioned. She still understands the principles of her department's work, but is not up to speed with the day-to-day detail. She needs to retrain or consciously to interact with her junior staff on a daily basis to keep up to date. It is really up to her to ensure she doesn't get left behind. This situation cannot simply be observed and accepted – each individual is responsible for updating their own skills base.

Career Crunch!

Managers gradually stop using and updating their functional skills

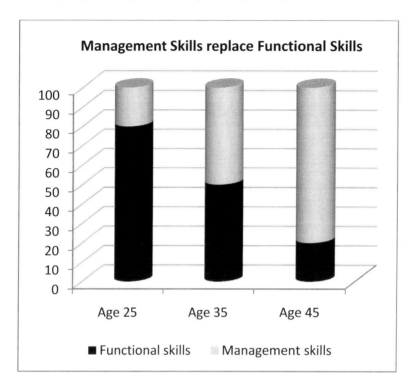

Schematic indicator of relative functional to management skills at different ages

Managers are short of time to keep up their practical skills, but they are also unmotivated to do so, wary of undermining their promotion by remaining too useful on the lower level "doing" side of the company. Take the extreme but true case of the well-established director who had never developed Excel or even PowerPoint skills, because she had always been able to delegate this work to her support team. Any younger employee or even any contemporary would have been horrified to discover this, and concluded she was a candidate for the scrap-heap, not just because of her lack of skills but her attitude. How could she have let twenty years' development pass her by and not show enough curiosity to learn exactly *how* her staff did what they did? From her perspective, though, this was completely rational – why should she use her leisure time learning to do something that she had staff to do for her?

Career Crunch!

Then there's the expert on Oracle who never got to know Windows because he did not trust it to be sufficiently stable to support sophisticated IT applications – and is still reluctant to acknowledge that it has become the standard for many applications. It is incumbent upon every manager and even every employee not only to update old skills and keep up with new innovations in their current job, but to predict and pre-empt the way their old job will change and be substituted by new skills sets.

Furthermore, at the same time as managers are promoted and acquire the trappings of career success, such as a higher salary, possibly a company car, longer holidays and a private office, so ironically they become more vulnerable to redundancy. They now embody the company cost-cutter's typical target: they are physically separated from day-to-day company business by their partition walls and absence from the office attending external meetings and on longer holidays, and yet visibly costing the company more money than before. The general assumption about their usefulness is summed up by Felix Dennis in his revealing book, 'How to Get Rich', which is essential reading for all would-be entrepreneurs, in which he bluntly explains the current process of promotion and redundancy:

"By the time talent is in its mid-to-late-forties or fifties it will have become very, very expensive. Young talent can be found and underpaid for a short while, providing the work is challenging enough. Then it will be paid at the market rate. Finally, it will reach a stage where it is being paid based on past reputation alone. That is when you must part company with it." [23]

Managers continue to be promoted until they are expendable and too expensive. The resentful redundant manager may ask why his employer offered him a higher salary and then afterwards complained that he was too expensive. The 'Peter Principle', revealing when it was devised, has become hackneyed through abuse: you have been promoted to the level of your own incompetence, and are now paying the price. You are in an illegitimate position, overpaid and underperforming, so you have to go. Overpaid redundant Pete spends his days wondering where he went wrong.

Career Crunch!

But the real question is: what expectations underpin the company career hierarchy? An aspirational employee expects promotion and longer service to be rewarded with higher pay, whereas employers, along with envious subordinates, tend to assume that managers are not as useful as "hands-on doers". With some justification, senior managers are not thought to be willing to "get their hands dirty". Some of the previous generation, secure in their jobs and generous pension schemes, gave the impression that a job near the top was a sinecure for fat cats who had worked hard for the company in the past. Times have changed, and a "market correction" is taking place: now higher reward means higher risk of losing your job. (This kind of trade-off is not without historical precedent: in the reign of Henry VIII, becoming Queen or being promoted to the position of Minister was a seriously risky business[24].)

Older middle-managers now enter the Career Value Gap, where they are perceived to be too expensive.

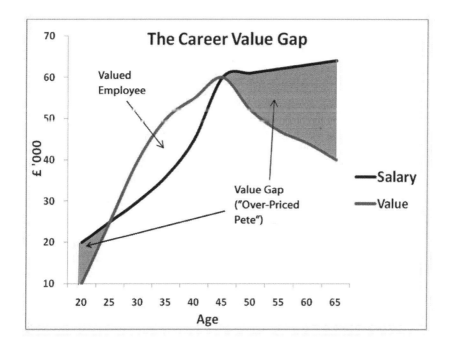

The chart above illustrates the situation of a middle-manager whose perceived value to his company has been greater than his salary for most of the early part of his career, till it peaks at the age of forty-five. After this, his salary continues to grow gently, through inflation and general pay awards, but his perceived value declines for all the reasons discussed above. From this point on he is vulnerable to redundancy, and when it happens he will not understand why.

The only point earlier in his career when his perceived value also falls below his salary is when he first joins the company, for example, as a school-leaver or on a graduate training scheme. But we noted earlier that such schemes are becoming fewer and farther between. This is the reason why. With a new emphasis on outsourcing for flexibility and transparency of costing, what would be the logic in training up a graduate who may then leave, when a company can hire in a suitably qualified, slightly older recruit at the market rate? The danger here is that no company wants to provide training, and the graduate is either obliged to muddle along, learning on the job without any structured training, in the old-fashioned and inefficient style of an intelligent amateur, or to fund formal vocational training for himself, or finally to fight for a one of the few remaining places where he can work as a glorified apprentice until he has proved his worth.

Salary is a Personal Price-point

With hindsight, Pete's strategy of sitting in his well-paid job waiting for his pension appears less prudent once he has been made redundant. Pete has a price on his head - or rather he prices *himself*, according to his most recent salary, and *not* his price on the open market. In his advanced economy everyone has the same attitude, so the economy as a whole remains stubbornly high cost. Is this sustainable? The prices he pays for goods and services have been kept low by unskilled labour entering the global marketplace at the bottom end of the world-wide price range, whilst efficiency has been increased by technical innovation and global economies of scale.

So it has been possible in the short-term for the population to ignore the logic that to maintain or increase standards of living requires a demonstrable basis (valuable natural resources, highly educated workforce, innovative industries). Otherwise individuals need to reduce their salaries just as their home currency needs to drops in value on the financial markets. Over-Priced Pete embodies this paradox. He cannot increase his income or even continue to earn the salary he has earned for the last ten years when his worth in terms of global employee skills is declining. Either he must lower his cost (i.e. his salary) or he must skill up to a new level to merit his high salary. There is no alternative. The only question is: how?

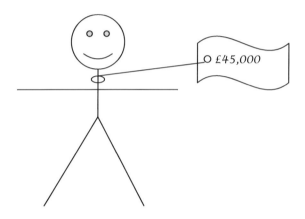

Once he reaches a middle-management salary, Over-Priced Pete's career problems are just beginning

One reason why employees cannot afford to take a drop in salary is because this will impinge on their final salary pensions. Another reason is the principal recruitment screening criterion used by agencies and employers themselves, who assess an employee's worth in terms of his *last salary*. As a result, even if he has the financial flexibility to take a salary hit in the short term, he will be reluctant to undermine his long-term salary and career prospects by accepting a lower paid job just to remain employed. The entire workforce in the affluent West has become a nation of 'Over-Priced Petes', wedded to their present occupations and salaries and expecting these to continue to progress ever upwards until they retire.

Career Crunch!

Getting to be a "manager" has always been a career goal for businessmen and women, but now it may be a career death knell. The bulk of British society now considers itself to be middle-class, and whilst the original classifications defined social class by type of employment, so that middle-class equated to professional, managerial and other white-collar roles, now 'middle class' is more a statement of values and aspirations. If the traditional C_2 group of blue-collar tradespeople include themselves in the middle class, then it encompasses the vast majority of the population, with the result that nowadays marketers have had to invent new lifestyle categories to reflect more tightly-defined consumer groups. Baby-boomers are eschewing apprenticeships as electricians and plumbers, and the result has been an excess of aspiring managers now in their forties.

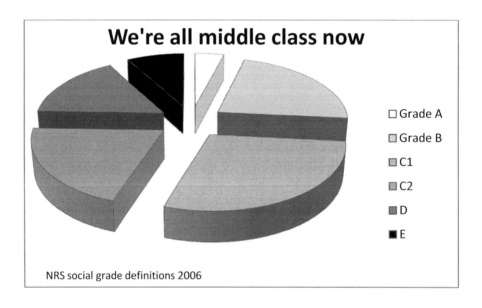

NRS social grade definitions 2006

Can anything be done about ageist discrimination when there is a constantly renewing source of it – don't young people prefer to be with people of the same age? It is self-created, and with the advent of a huge group of young people who have dominated society since the mid-'60s, it is endemic. The UK government had already brought out the big guns to deal with discrimination on the grounds of sex, race or disability, and in October 2006 it enacted legislation to address ageism. This is starting to produce results, at least in the form of cases brought before employment tribunals. In the first six months following its introduction, 972 age discrimination claims were brought, according to the website of the Employers' Forum on Age. Internationally, in the Netherlands and Lithuania, age claims account for 30% of all discrimination cases, and in the USA, age claims, which are limited to those over forty, represented over one in six of all complaints filed in 2006. In the UK, recruiters have responded either to positive exhortations or to government threats by largely excising age limitations and length of service requirements from their job advertisements.

Major demographic movements have created a youth-culture, and, although this will be a passing phenomenon, ruthless corporate streamlining has used it to re-shape our present career patterns. There are wider business factors involved, too, and *Chapter Two* looks at how the global markets have influenced Western career prospects.

Career Crunch!

Chapter Two

Rise and fall: *career cycles in global businesses*

In response to the seemingly insatiable world demand for steel, the German company ThyssenKrupp is expanding. One of its latest projects is to build a new steel mill in Sepetiba Bay in the state of Rio de Janeiro in Brazil[25] to produce five million tons of steel per year, employing 3,500 people, and creating another 10,000 jobs indirectly. This type of investment illustrates the virtuous circle of increased world trade, but also raises concerns in Europe, not only about environmental damage, but also about the future of existing jobs. The workers in the industrialised countries see old, established industries relocating to emerging economies, whilst new industries rise and decline ever more quickly in each location, as a yet cheaper source of labour is discovered in another part of the world, which has already developed equally good levels of education and infrastructure.

Flexibility to adapt to this new world order and benefit from the new opportunities will be essential to any successful 21st century economy, including those already established at the top of the ladder, whose vulnerability has been highlighted by the Credit Crunch. How is globalisation affecting the course of a career in business, and are we doing enough to adapt to it?

Just as a new company is founded by a thrusting entrepreneur, who makes up the rules and methods as he goes along, cuts corners and learns from his mistakes, so a new industry also develops initially in any way it can. At first it needs to grow rapidly, grabbing customers and creating product and brand awareness. The Internet has not quite come to the end of its rapid Growth phase, and is often described as the Wild West, internationally minimally regulated and "unregulatable", (unless regulation promises new customers, as in the case of China, where Google initially found a way to send its principles to the recycling bin and censor the Internet, if censorship enabled it to access those billion plus future users).

New Industry Life Cycle

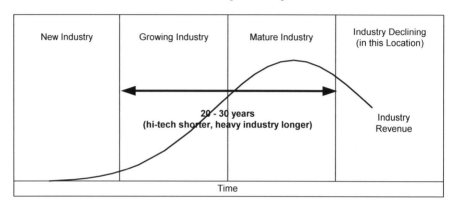

At the beginning of the Growth phase of an industry, rival companies emerge offering similar products, often with rival technology, and compete intensely. Videos originally came in two different formats, Betamax and VHS, which competed in the late seventies and through the eighties to become the standard; in the eighties Personal Computers ran on different rival operating systems, including CPM as well as Microsoft's MS DOS and Apple Mac's OS. At this Growth stage there is an urgent need for staff in all functions. Companies are recruiting and growing rapidly. School-leavers and graduates see the business potential and pile into the industry.

Then a new phase begins. One of the competing companies wins out and industry standards are agreed, and the industry enters Maturity. Once the industry is standardised, the companies in the industry develop a more fixed organisational structure and adopt operational procedures; salesmen become more benefits/safety/price orientated.

Recruitment into a New Industry
(or a Newly Introduced Industry)

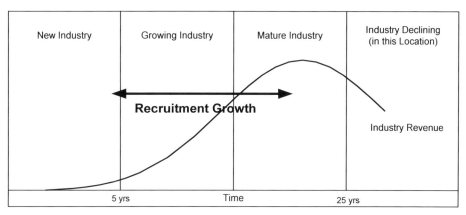

At the same time governments may well step in to regulate the worst excesses of the new industry, as in the current debate about Internet regulation. The industry itself, its products and its workforce are all mature. The only growth is from repeat or multiple purchases and, increasingly, from service contracts. Earnings are stable.

Now what has happened to the mature managers in these industries? They joined the industry in its early rapid growth phase and are now in their forties. As we saw in the previous chapter, they have moved away from their old skills and concentrated on keeping the show on the road. The company now enters a decline, along with the entire industry within the country, which is being attacked by cheaper, literally hungrier nations. So dead wood is sought. Who stands out? Over-Priced Pete, the highest paid manager, who has now been caught up by the next wave of ambitious employees ten years younger and cheaper and with skills more in line with the current industry requirements. He has de-skilled at exactly the stage at which his industry is down-sizing, and this is not a coincidence. He is made redundant, and it is only a few years before the whole industry moves abroad to find cheaper labour, and the pattern of redundancy is extended to the entire industry on a national scale.

Career Crunch!

Career Plans don't include Redundancy – But Business Plans do

Management text books often refer to "The Art of War". This approach to defining company strategy is essential for survival. Senior management play the game, like chess. Their pawns are expendable, in fact so are the expensive Knights even the Queen - as long as the King is safe, nothing else matters. Over-Priced Pawns don't need to take the initiative. They just get moved from one square to the next till they're taken out of the game and discarded.

The tragedy that is redundancy and unemployment is glibly dismissed. The text books airily tell us that the workforce must become more flexible, must accept periods of unemployment – but how does that square with your children's feet growing? A new pair of leather shoes or over-priced trainers can't wait till you next get a job in six months to a year's time. Try telling a father of three that he is redundant again, only a few months after getting a job with your company. On the LIFO basis (Last In First Out) this is fairest to the longer-term employees; the accountants approve because his redundancy is cheapest; but his life is destroyed. When he breaks down in your office and asks how he is going to pay his mortgage, just hand him a management text-book and tell him we all have to be flexible these days.

What about the employee you were told to make redundant the day you joined your new company? He writes to you regularly assuring you brightly that he is updating his skills and keen to meet up. He can no longer be contacted at his old address - the house has had to be sold - and when you meet he doesn't refer to his wife or kids - it seems they have gone back to her mother. But he knows that this is the way things are these days, and we have to adapt. He smiles all the time and talks about his plans for the future, but you can't help noticing that his suit looks worn and his shoes are wearing thin beneath the shiny polish. Just before he leaves, he earnestly asks you to think of him if a position comes up - really, he'll take anything, even if it's a demotion - you no doubt remember what a good worker he is. You assure him you'll keep his CV on file, though you have nothing at the moment. His face falls.

Career Crunch!

Redundancy is a financial and emotional shock. It is the lucky few who welcome redundancy as the chance to gain a lump sum pay-off and leave a job they were thinking of quitting anyway, and even for these people the benefits of the lump sum may soon be outweighed by the unanticipated difficulty of finding new work if they have remained for many years with the same employer. Redundancy therefore means financial hardship, at least in the short term.

One major difference between blue-collar redundancy and white-collar redundancy is that with white-collar redundancy, despite assurances to the contrary, *it's personal.* When a factory closes, the entire workforce is laid off. There is widespread hardship in the local community, but at least everyone knows it wasn't your fault. In the UK particularly, manufacturing industry has been less successful than service industries at extending its life by moving to new life-cycle higher-added-value products, so the industry has declined at the same rate as the outdated skills of its workers, and they all, literally for ship-builders in the north-east of the UK, 'go down with the ship'. When a company lays off white-collar workers, it selects them carefully, taking out dead wood and expensive employees along with those whose skills are simply no longer required.

So, much as you can blame it on bad luck, there is always a suspicion that it wasn't just unkind fate – that you were to blame. Like global warming and obese children, all our problems now seem to be of our own making, and we are to blame for them. A redundant mine-worker can apply for new jobs with his head held high: a loyal worker shabbily betrayed. A redundant white-collar employee has to work on his excuses.

Redundancy is not limited to the UK or even to affluent Western economies. China's restructuring has led to massive unemployment. Between 1993 and 2001, 43 million urban employees were laid off, or about a quarter of the urban labour force. There are least 19 million unemployed and tens of millions more unaccounted for, such that some commentators put the true unemployment figure at nearer 100 million. The Chinese Government needs to create up to 20 million jobs per annum and continue to grow at around 8%, its average rate over the past decade, just to keep unemployment at its present levels. Chinese women have been particularly affected in industries such as textiles. In a official move that is ironical in the light of Western government attempts to raise the retirement age, and of the ageing profile of Chinese society, the official retirement age for women in Chinese industry has been reduced from fifty-five to fifty.[26] Many workers have no employable skills, their education disrupted by the political turmoil in the late 1960's "Cultural Revolution", and by the Communist government policy or forcing urban dwellers to work on the land. This in a society which until recently assumed such an all-encompassing level of responsibility for the employment of every citizen that it allocated jobs to each graduate when he/she left university, and, albeit inefficiently, set out to ensure that the "iron rice bowl" was always able to feed every citizen.

Redundancy is traumatic, but no-one in the West is at risk of starvation. For anyone tempted to hark back with nostalgia to a time in history when a man could do an honest day's work on the land, untroubled by the wider economy, it may be worth contemplating life in the Middle Ages. They had their fair share of commodity price shocks and international disasters. When harvests failed, people in the UK simply starved to death; and during the recurrent outbreaks of the Black Death in the 1300s the population halved, the shortage of labourers to work the land inflated food prices, and even the country priests abandoned their churches to seek their fortunes elsewhere. The government were quite firm about wage restraint in those days, though – in 1381 King Richard II personally addressed the revolting peasants demanding higher wages, agreed to their demands until the crowds dispersed, and then hanged or otherwise exited the leaders. Quite cynical for a thirteen-year-old boy – and they say today's youth is desensitized by computer games!

In feudal England the social hierarchy was rigidly fixed, with serfs and villeins at the bottom not much better off than slaves; further afield in India the caste system similarly provided an ever-renewing, never-progressing

Career Crunch!

underclass to support the economy and insulate it from the inflationary by-product of progress. Without such effective means at their disposal to control wage inflation, more recent social systems have used other ways to keep wages low at the bottom end of the market and standards of living high at the top. Even by the Victorian era attitudes had not changed much, with the dramatic inequalities between the "rich man in his castle, the poor man at his gate", still justified as God's will, despite the changing reality of an emerging middle class creating new wealth from industry; today migrant workers fulfil that function inside Western European economies right up to the present day, whilst cheap labour is still exploited in sweat-shops abroad.

Yet the new message must be that the redundant mature employee is a product of his time. Jobs for life only exist, if at all, in the public sector. In theory, employees who are laid off are making a contribution to the economic welfare of the country, inasmuch as they are part of a new flexible workforce, constantly retraining, keeping up with the latest world business trends, adaptable and energetic, mobile and willing to take a salary cut. Being made redundant is absolutely the norm; spending a year looking for work after redundancy or after staying at home with children is not at all unusual; never getting another *permanent* job after the age of fifty is quite common (even if it is possibly due to now illegal ageist recruitment practices). However, for a redundant employee never to work again after fifty because he thinks no-one wants to employ him is not an option if the Western economies are to survive the dual perils of an ageing population and the rise of competition from LEDCs (Less Economically Developed Countries).

This point is made in a recent book about the American pensions problem with the self-explanatory title: "Working Longer: The Solution to the Retirement Income Challenge".[27] The authors' proposed measures do not appear draconian - raising the retirement age from the current average of sixty-three to sixty-six years - but they argue that this change could solve the problem in the US. The problem for all of us remains as to how to achieve a higher retirement age in practice.

Unemployment is the result of structural changes, whether you are one of at least forty million redundant Chinese or the only employee made redundant from your company. There are many reasons why an older employee's job disappears or an older returner is no longer desirable: his skills-set is no longer required; there are too many specialists in areas of work superseded by technology or fashion; there are also too many non-specialist general managers in ever-flatter organisation structures. There are younger, more recently-trained and, above all, cheaper workers who are desperate to make their mark and if necessary take on another, less hungry, employee's job as well. The older employee may have made enemies amongst the more politically astute or ruthless, or his demonstrable experience or status within the industry may be seen as a threat by rivals who have now reached political ascendancy.

Furthermore, there are both unskilled and skilled migrant workers, who have come to the UK solely to work hard and earn a lump sum of money, and in addition are actually enthusiastic and grateful for the relatively high wages they can earn in this land of plenty.

A proven solution to unemployment
Where will the up to 100 million unemployed or underemployed Chinese all end up? Germany in the 1930s had a practical solution that worked rather well in the short term: use the excess workforce to build up infrastructure, weaponry and the armed forces, thus investing to stimulate the economy. The Second World War was also beneficial to the United States: it was the additional manufacturing for the war effort that finally brought about its recovery from the Great Depression. Let us hope this is not the solution the Chinese come up with: the Chinese standing army already numbers over two million, compared with the UK's 100,000; if it expanded to take up the under-unemployed slack, the army would be larger than most countries' populations – and that would be quite intimidating.

Matching new requirements

As business conditions become more cut-throat, employees in the private sector are valued like a cabaret act at an audition – 'what can you do for *this* run of *this* show', with at best a glance at your CV: 'Does your career history support what you say?' Instead of a fixed career progression (blot your copy book and your career prospects are finished), there are now multiple opportunities. There are also multiple competitors for each job, and multiple chances to lose the job you've just managed to get. This should in theory be good news for jobseekers, offering the opportunity to re-enter the workforce by opening up competition, but only if recruiters adopt the practice of viewing applicants' CVs as evidence of a skills-set developed over time, rather than the concluding pages of a rambling or too-predictable narrative.

Technology and fashion are moving too quickly for a craftsman to sit back with his Masterpiece. Professionals in Law, Accounting or Medicine keep constantly up to date by scanning their respective trade press, attending conferences and seminars, reading up new government reports and keeping an eye on the Internet. Unskilled labourers, taken on and given rudimentary training early in their careers, are not accustomed to having to predict and adapt to change in their industry; up till now this has been the responsibility of their employers, ironically often in the face of opposition from their Trade Unions.

So, across the nation, Over-Priced Pete has two active options: increase his value to the world or reduce his price point. Reducing his price point does not just mean reducing his salary: it means reducing all the extras we expect in a rich economy - health care, social support for the weak, pensions, public amenities, clean air. The only luxury that we can be allowed to take to our economic health farm is education - if we are to remain affluent and influential in the world, education is the one area in which we cannot afford to compromise, since that is where most added-value derives. And to be effective, education must be embraced more enthusiastically and with more dedication than is the case at present. The stark alternative is that the nation of Over-Priced Petes, spending more than they are collectively worth, will be made redundant: the "British disease" has not yet run its course.

In the West, as wages get higher and life more comfortable, the nation becomes complacent, assuming its leading position will continue as its right, like the ancient Roman Empire caught up in its own intrigues at the centre, no longer looking over its shoulder towards the "Barbarians at the Gate". Imagine the frustration felt by Petrus, a Roman army officer. Following in the footsteps of his father and grandfather, he's finally got a nice villa in Roman Britain – modern under-floor central heating and lovely easy-clean mosaics, reasonably competent slaves and a prestigious career, doing *exactly* what his family have always done. So why does life feel insecure? Supplies of olive oil have been unreliable for a long time, but now the army is late with its wage payments. His men aren't managing to fight off the barbaric raids from Angles, Saxons and Jutes, and finally in desperation he sends an urgent message to HQ in Rome requesting reinforcements, along the lines of: "Hear the groans of the Britons..." The reply eventually comes back: "Sorry, mate. We've got problems of our own. You might have Angles, Saxons and Jutes but we've got Huns, Goths and Vandals. Someone was meant to have sorted out your P45 but it's been a bit hairy here. Afraid you're on your own now." Petrus wonders where he went wrong.

Career Crunch!

Interim Employment

If we want jobs to be allocated throughout the population, then the only way to restructure the workforce this drastically is through the painful procedure of replacing expensive, inflexible hierarchies with staff who are more competitively-priced or more flexible, or both, for example, on temporary employment contracts. Is this happening? The Credit Crunch has already brought about hundreds of thousands of redundancies, but are those still in employment any more flexible? Certainly, in the wake of the Credit Crunch salaries have been renegotiated, with blue and white collar workers alike taking pay cuts and reduced hours to keep their jobs. Even the stultified public sector employment practices are under threat, though here work vacancies still *grew* by over ten thousand in late 2008 whilst in the private sector vacancies *shrank* by even more. But in the distant future when employment begins to rise, will new work structures already be in place, or will everything go back to the way it was before? Are there any signs of change – for example, are there more temporary workers nowadays or not?

It is true that with jobs in short supply most employees would prefer to take a "permanent" job if they can, but figures suggesting that there are fewer temporary workers today do not tell the whole story. The figures track the story of the disappearance of a larger group of lower level white-collar workers: the traditional 'temp' – usually a female secretary or clerk, catered for by large chains of temping agencies. Their once-familiar shop-fronts still exist on some high streets, and indeed Kelly's places over 21,000 temporary staff every week, according to their website, but they have less physical presence than previously, the low level administrative roles filled by their 'temps' often taken over by computers, and the female temps' need for flexible work to fit round the children's hours and holidays often catered for by the increased availability of part-time work and job-sharing, particularly in the public sector.

So the gradual decline of the twentieth century female 'temp' masks the rapid rise of the male[28] middle-management 'interim'. They are fewer in number and slower to place, but fall into a much higher income bracket[29], as senior managers, with fees ranging from about £500-£1,500 per day. Over the last ten to fifteen years this whole sector has grown rapidly from an almost non-existent base. Interim agencies have recently featured in several of the lists of fastest growing companies: the agency Interim Partners, set up only five years ago, came 13th in The Sunday Times Fast Track 100[30] in 2008, and Green Park Interim and Executive Resourcing, which was only founded in 2006, had pre-tax profits **of** £2.2 million by 2008 and ranked amongst the Business XL 50 fastest-growing entrepreneurial companies in the UK[31]. Interim employees need to be "suitably overqualified" (to quote one recruitment consultant), so they will nearly all have held very senior posts in large companies before moving into interim management. Why did they leave their permanent employment? What will they be doing in five years' time?

Plus Ça Change – How much have we really changed the way we work?

Dramatic changes in technology over the centuries have been the main drivers for fundamental changes in the way people work. There is no documented evidence of the conversations taking place around the introduction of the flint spear-head, but you can be sure not all macho cave-men welcomed this new-fangled idea – wasn't it a bit namby-pamby to be sitting outside your cave banging bits of rock together when real Neanderthals were out wrestling woolly mammoths with their bare hands?

We do, however, all know about the Luddites who smashed up the machines introduced into the UK textile industry in the Industrial Revolution, because they said they were taking their jobs. We used to ridicule them in history lessons, but they did have a point. What with 'Enclosures' driving people off the land, and unskilled work on factory looms taking over their skilled cottage-based spinning and weaving, huge numbers of people were displaced to the cities looking for work, where, of course, they found jobs in the factories, and so their need to find work was caused by the Industrial Revolution, and then itself fuelled it.

Career Crunch!

Eventually, even agriculture was mechanised, driving more workers from the land worldwide, most conspicuously the southern black cotton-pickers in America, displaced in the 1940s by machines that could do the work of fifty men. They migrated north to the industrial cities such as Detroit, as a cheap, unskilled new source of labour. Then factories across the western world automated still further, with sophisticated robots taking over the basic production lines, and again the labour force needed to move on.

Finally the service industry, thought to be irreducibly labour-intensive, also began automating. From the 1980s we saw computers take over the work of administrative staff; through-the–wall ATMs have replaced behind-the-counter real live 'tellers' counting out cash in the banks; online bank accounts can be operated electronically without the need for a customer to go into a branch or even speak to anyone on the phone; checking-in at the airport can be done directly into the system; tickets for the cinema or an international flight can be researched and purchased online. Innovation in working practices further reduced the need for staff – more efficient Just In Time and Total Quality Management techniques from Japan further shortened the chain of command in manufacturing, reducing the need for middle managers, increasing efficiency, and empowering the workforce to take decisions and propose innovations.

Yet where are the new fundamental lifestyle upheavals that normally accompany great movements in wealth and labour? The information age is streamlining and globalising work, with fewer intermediaries and more rapid responses, but is the style of working fundamentally different? People can work from home some of the time – what is so different about that? The Luddite weavers were, after all, working from home. They sat at their spinning wheels and looms; modern workers sit at their computers and telephones – is it so very different? So have we reached the limit of workforce development, and is it inevitable that work will constantly migrate towards the cheapest supply of workers with a given level of education – if this continues to happen, almost every nation in the world will get the chance to be top dog for a few years, before their costs rise and another hungrier nation steps in. But apart from spreading around some affluence, and communicating ever more intensively, will anything fundamentally change? And faced with nothing more inspiring than cost-competition, can advanced nations retain their global hegemony and defy the cyclical rules of economic gravity?

The same process that applies to industries, products and people applies to entire nations. Like individual employees who are overpaid compared with the new market going-rate, nations, too, can be overpaid and living beyond their genuine earning capacity. It is as difficult for nations as for individuals to readjust belatedly to the market conditions and face unemployment and declining purchasing power and credit-worthiness.

Britain has slowly begun to recognise that it is in this position, along with most of the Western nations. On a positive note, this was the thinking behind the "Cool Britannia" campaign – to rejuvenate the British 'brand' that was perceived as behind the times. Apparently the young Chinese admire and emulate the British and to our great embarrassment have high expectations for our opening ceremony to the Olympic Games in 2012. However, being admired and copied is flattering, but not sufficient. The ancient Romans admired and copied the Greeks for their civilisation, their culture and their learning – so they invaded them and brought them back as slaves to teach their children. (Do not read anything predictive into this parallel.)

In pure economic terms, Britain's determined independence from the Euro did allow it, albeit involuntarily, to adjust its income downwards as a response to its weak position after the Credit Crunch. As Sterling dropped in value, this immediately repositioned the entire economy, both discouraging the British from spending money on the now expensive foreign holidays and imports, and also encouraging foreign tourists to come to Britain and raising demand for the now cheaper British exports. This was in bleak contrast to Ireland, for example, whose financial crisis and rapidly increasing unemployment could not trigger a devaluation of its currency because it was tied to that of all other fifteen countries in the Eurozone, none of which was as yet suffering as deep a recession. Perhaps we could learn from the way the US copes with the same situation? It is, after all, a geographically, economically, culturally and ethnically diverse nation with approximately the same number of inhabitants as the Eurozone. As all the states share the dollar, one part of the country going through a hard time cannot devalue its currency to makes itself cheaper and therefore more attractive to investors or visitors. However, when we consider the neglect of poor areas such as New Orleans, which only came into the spotlight in the aftermath of Hurricane Katrina, it is clear that there are disadvantages along with the economic benefits of a single currency.

UK plc and its future – a National Product Life Cycle?

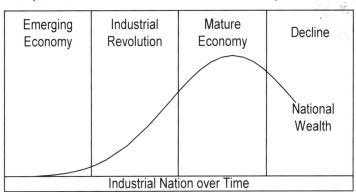

Even before the Credit Crunch, UK plc was in decline – it needed to invest in its image and re-apply for a world role. Which new "jobs" has it applied for? World leadership roles in Specialist High Finance (now reeling from the global recession), Telecoms, Nano-technology and Bio-chemistry, with forays into controversial and therefore leading edge technologies such as genetic modification and stem cell research - high value-added sectors deemed appropriate to our mature economy with its claims to an educated work-force and its expectations of a continuing high standard of living. There also remain the well-established sectors such as travel & tourism which are significant, but not net earners of foreign currency; manufacturing, which though declining, has profitably moved into value-added service contracts, and business services across a wide range of activities. Differentiation is increasingly the key to global markets: just as a product requires a Unique

Selling Proposition to differentiate its benefits, and a job candidate needs to stand out from the crowd, so a country increasingly needs areas of recognised specialisation and expertise. But even if British firms can succeed in developing lucrative new technologies, will these be scalable or employ many people? We may have a historical advantage here, but can we become an entire nation of mad scientists?

An unsentimental policy of abandoning declining primary and secondary industries in favour of more sophisticated service industries was ruthlessly and effectively driven through by Margaret Thatcher in the 1980s. It was a kind of "up-and-out-and-roundabout" strategy, getting out of old outmoded activities and moving roundabout to new ones suitable for the future. This policy was very successful in the 'out' phase, but the tricky challenge still remains: where should the roundabout lead to? Questions are now being asked as to whether a ruthless move into services, abandoning manufacturing and primary industries which were no longer viable on a purely economic basis, did not limit the UK's strategic options and skills-sets for the future.

Up-and-out-and-roundabout strategy –
should you move on once your industries get past the top?

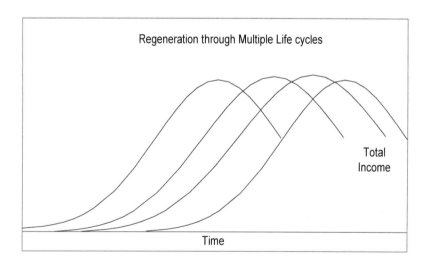

Career Crunch!

Like individual mature jobseekers, companies and industries, so countries, too, need to spot the life cycle of each industry, and know when to abandon the declining sector in which they are operating and move on to the next. This "Up-and-out-and-roundabout" strategy needs to be informed by government and directed by industry leaders such as the CBI.

Yet what is becoming uncomfortably clear? That with vision and determination expressed as investment and dedication, it only takes one generation committed to education and supported by a well-established educational infrastructure for a substantial group within the next generation to be as advanced as any other in the world – a couple of hundred years can be caught up in a generation. As a result, call-centres in India are just as informed as the call-centres round the corner in the UK, and the staff are better-trained and more helpful. Spoilt for choice, with burgeoning global supplies of educated labour and dependable infrastructure, so-called "*flying geese*" industries move from one country to another in constant search of cheaper labour. In such a competitive marketplace, how can a country first attract and then retain industries to meet the rising aspirations of its labour force?

Will NICs overtake MEDCs?

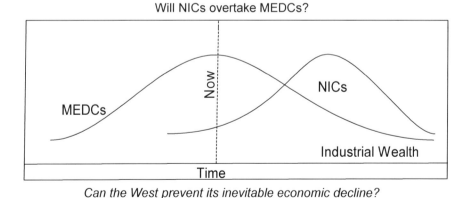

Can the West prevent its inevitable economic decline?

As we reject the early industrialists' ruthless exploitation of their workers and their environment, so we have also lost their hungry ambition and energetic optimism, and as a result there are others who are trying to loosen our grip from the higher rungs of the global economic ladder and take our hard-won position there. Just as it is necessary to revitalise our national economy so it is essential to revitalise our workforce. Yet most workers and their employment contracts are stuck in the historical pattern where a worker learns a trade and practises it in the same way until he retires. Managers face an uphill struggle to push through changes in the face of Trades Union resistance and legislation which protect the status quo rather than the employee's longer term job prospects. Compare this with the flexibility of the Far Eastern economies. Could the UK adapt that quickly? Does our governance and culture encourage or discourage this labour-force flexibility which is going to be crucial to our survival as an economic force in the 21st century? The emergence of the "BRICs" (Brazil, Russia, India and China) added over two and a half billion potential customers[32] to the global economy, opening up new markets for the rich nations, but also introducing stiff competition into the labour market.

How does a nation create jobs in a global economy?

Case study: Ireland: a (brief) success story

Ireland was, for over a decade before the recession, a global economic success story, doubling its economy, rivalling China and creating a new breed of Irish self-made millionaires. The economy went through a transformation from a failing economy with high taxation and net emigration to a thriving economy with low taxation. Up until the major financial problems with its banking system from 2008 its income per capita placed it amongst the top countries of the OECD. The Irish success had been achieved by an educated, flexible, English-speaking workforce and low corporate taxation, coupled with a convenient location as a first stopping-point across the Atlantic and a gateway to Europe, particularly since it was one of the original twelve nations who adopted the Euro in 2002. From 1989 onwards the economy was boosted with Foreign Direct Investment as a result of its investor-friendly regime, and as late as September 2008 Martin Sorrell continued this trend by announcing that as a result of recent UK tax changes he intended to move his business to a base in the Republic of Ireland. From 2004, following a familiar pattern, a huge wave of 170,000 Eastern European workers arrived in Ireland, where the total population is only just over four million, attracted by its booming economy. Then came the Credit Crunch, the Polish workers in Ireland began to lose their jobs and started returning home, and the computer giant, Dell, transferred its production to Poland, where wages were only a quarter of those in Ireland. With its exchange rate fixed through its membership of the euro, a general drop in wages would have been the only way to restore the international competitiveness of the Irish workforce.

The Irish government had followed all the classic capitalist advice and its main crime, it seems, was over-confidence – though with the global recession, commentators' vocabulary turned moralistic, and 'over-confidence' might now be condemned as 'greed'. Its major mistake was to boost this financial fillip with debt, and to ignore the upwardly spiralling property prices, a sure sign (with hindsight) that the economy was over-heating and that measures needed to be taken to cool it down. Like the rest of the world, only more so, Ireland rode the wave and crashed when it hit the shore – but this does not mean to say that the overall strategy was wrong, perhaps simply that warning signs were ignored and the good luck pushed too far.

Across the world, every nation is seeking a Unique Selling Proposition (USP) to market its national brand. Some of the tactics adopted are listed below:

Generally acknowledged investor/trading partner acquisition & retention tactics (not all advisable)

- ➢ Become a world leader in manufacturing/R&D (Germany)
- ➢ Better quality (Japan)
- ➢ Be smarter, keener and cheaper (Indian call-centres)
- ➢ Minimise risk to partner (subsidies, training – German engineering)
- ➢ Undercut your rivals on price (Bangladeshi sweat-shops, subsistence wages)
- ➢ Specialise (Guernsey tax haven)

- ➤ Encourage Foreign Direct Investment and thereby acquire new technology (China)
- ➤ Make it risky to use another supplier (H&S Regulations in the EU; litigation in the US)
- ➤ Insist on technical standards only met in your own country
- ➤ Use contacts (China as a Most Favoured Nation to the US)
- ➤ Form a Union (EU for trade; US textiles workers for protectionism)
- ➤ Demand minimum income through positive discrimination (EU Farmers/Fair Trade suppliers)
- ➤ Knife your rivals (Germany, with its light bulb manufacturer Osram, complained about China "dumping" low energy light bulbs)
- ➤ Support business not environment (Brazilian logging)
- ➤ Support of your suppliers in the political arena (French support for Iran)
- ➤ Trade arms for essential raw materials (China in Sudan)
- ➤ Bully suppliers/competitors/customers (Russian gas and oil)
- ➤ Deal with crooks (unpopular regimes, rogue states - China supplies narcotics precursor chemicals to Colombia)
- ➤ Become a crook (Columbian drugs; Chinese pharmaceuticals counterfeiters; Nigerian fraud; towns in Peru which thrive on the three 'C's: counterfeiting, contraband and cocaine)

As for companies, so, too, for nations, size creates economies of scale as well as influence in the market place. The US benefits from a large unified market of over three hundred million affluent consumers with a common currency and more or less the same laws. Alongside moves towards more regional government within its borders, the UK has also, though not without misgivings, joined a larger trading group, the EU, which has now further expanded its borders to include Eastern Europe, and unified its currency in sixteen of its twenty-seven member nations. It is no coincidence that "Euroland", nicknamed after its common currency, the euro, has about the same number of inhabitants as the USA, whilst the enlarged EU already contains over five hundred million people. If the possibility is considered that

China could reach a stage when it finds its internal market of well over a billion consumers, supplied with raw materials by a few strategic partners, sufficient for its trading needs, then one clear motivator for European integration is similarly to invest in developing an alternative market – its own internal source of demand.

There is not a clear-cut divide between rich and poor nations, however. In every More Economically Developed Country there is a Less Economically Developed Country struggling to get out. There are pockets of poverty in every major economy, existing cheek-by-jowl with the super-rich, often in the next street. In the West we're talking *relative poverty* – you simply cannot survive in the UK for less than one dollar a day, the official definition of poverty below which millions of people still exist in LEDCs across the world, from Bangladesh to rural China. Nevertheless, MEDCs are not universally affluent and are only a run of hyperinflation or a shift in world demand away from a downward GDP curve. At the opposite end of the scale there are also affluent pockets in poor countries– whether through inheritance, education, personal drive, military coercion, corruption or other dubious morals, every impoverished nation has its privileged ruling class.

But not all poor countries are catching up with the rich nations: some countries are getting poorer. In addition to natural disasters such as disease, most recently AIDS in Africa, there are also avoidable man-made factors which prevent growth, such as warfare, or the corruption analysed by Tim Harford in his book "The Undercover Economist".

Do any nations successfully protect industries and jobs?

Protectionism is universally condemned by economists and also by politicians, who, despite their protestations, secretly know that their electorate will approve if they manage to make a show of defending their nation's rights in the face of international demands. The US regularly protests against perceived European cheating through protectionism and subsidies in the Capitalist game. Yet it protects its textile workers against cheaper foreign imports. And what do we see in the US airline industry? No internal route rights across America are granted to foreign airlines. And in US shipping? The 'Jones Act' forbids 'foreign' ships (bear in mind that's *us*) from docking at two consecutive US ports – in other words, only American ships can offer cruises up the American coastline. And only in the face of indignant (and somewhat hypocritical) protests from the rest of the world were US government incentives to its car industry in the face of recession not explicitly closed to international beneficiaries. So "free trade" is never that simple, even for its most ardent and outspoken advocates.

What inducements can legally be given to manufacturers or other companies proposing to set up in a country? Of course, what is legal depends on your country's political and trade affiliations and your traditional ways of doing business. In the West, any company directors acting in a cartel are likely to be sent to prison, whereas the West is perfectly happy to deal with the official cartel of the oil-producing countries, OPEC.

In Europe, subsidies, special tax regimes, infrastructure targeted to benefit specific employers are all frowned upon or even legislated against, but all are practised to incentivise investment. Nicolas Sarkozy is not shy of asserting the French right to subsidise its own champion industries. In some parts of Italy and France tour guides and ski instructors must by law be Nationals – and that does not mean EU nationals. British guides have been arrested for contravening this blatant contravention of the letter and spirit of EU law. German Unions *do* protect jobs through the system of Workers' Councils, which are in a position to veto job losses at the expense of employees in other companies or indeed other countries, as illustrated by the merger between two major UK tour operators with German parents, where an announcement was explicitly made by the German parent that no job losses would occur in Germany, and any savings through rationalisation would be made from amongst the *UK* employees.

Such distortions would be scorned by any modern macro-economist as inefficient, yet they appear to work for those who practise them. Protecting strategic manufacturing such as the automotive industry has enabled German workers to supply a premium product – their car plants spin off high value-added R&D. These options are explored in *Chapter Six.*

<u>*Constant Immigration gets the jobs done more cheaply*</u>

Protectionism is one way to support an uncompetitive workforce. Another way is to open the workshop doors wide to cheaper foreign workers. When a civilisation espouses democratic ideals of social equality within its indigenous population, another solution emerges to support its affluent lifestyle, namely to allow or coerce the immigration of an underpaid workforce from elsewhere.

The much-eulogised Greek "democracy" was underpinned with slavery; the American Declaration of rights: "Life, Liberty and the pursuit of Happiness" side-stepped the issue of the black slavery which supported the wealth of the newly emerging nation, whilst in more recent times America admitted over seventeen million immigrants in the twenty-five years from 1971 to 1995; Germany flourished with "Gastarbeiter" from Turkey in the 1960s-1970s, as did Holland; England has always benefited from waves of immigrants – Florentine, Huguenot, Irish, Jewish, Afro-Caribbean, Asian and Eastern European. Most worked for less pay than the indigenous population, or just worked harder, and some brought specialist skills, and all suffered resentment from those sectors of the indigenous population who felt their livelihoods threatened. Karl Marx is hard to refute in his conclusion that in an industrialising society progress is typically made at the expense of an exploited group of workers, and nowadays these can be indigenous working classes, immigrants or even outsourced from the other side of the world.

Just like our Western governments, Chinese politicians, too, are struggling to know how to improve life for all their citizens when global economics is changing the parameters at break-neck speed. In the early 1980's Deng Xiaoping announced that in order to improve life for all the people it would be necessary to let some of the people "get rich first", as described in Duncan Hewitt's excellent book of the same title[33]. A wide gulf has now emerged between rural peasants living on less than one dollar a day and the Chinese jet-set of rich property developers.

Immigration is also boosting the UK birth rate. The birth rate in most developed nations is falling below the magic "replacement rate" of just over two children per woman. This situation is known as the "demographic-economic paradox", because early economic thinkers such as Thomas Malthus had assumed that as the world became more affluent and healthy we would face intolerable overpopulation because we would produce more and more babies, but in fact, the opposite has occurred, and as nations get wealthier, with very few exceptions, their fertility rate falls.

Whilst for the world as a whole leading economists are still warning of the dangers of growing populations, in the industrialised countries, which are already top-heavy with older people living longer, too few babies coming into the population will only compound the problem, with even fewer young workers to support the old. In the UK the birth-rate was above the replacement rate during the 1960s 'baby boom', peaking at just under three in 1964, but had declined to a low of 1.63 by 2001. Each year since then it has increased, but this increase is mainly due to births to mothers who were not themselves born in UK. In 1997 these accounted for about one in eight births, but ten years later they had risen to just under a quarter of all babies born in the UK[34]. The government will be hoping that in twenty years' time these second generation immigrants feel sufficiently warmly towards the UK to stay here and pay the UK's pension bills!

Immigration figures have come under a lot of scrutiny, and the main source of statistics, the International Passenger Survey, has been shown to underestimate the figures by a wide margin. Nevertheless they show that from 1971 to 2000 the UK population grew by about five million, with less than half this growth due to "natural change", that is, more births than deaths, and over half from immigration. Another source of figures are the "NINos" – the new National Insurance Numbers issued[35]. (This will show numbers of immigrants working officially in the UK, though of course there will still be a large black market of illegal workers, officially denied but clearly observable in the London tourist industry and even directly targeted in a government advertising campaign in 2009.) In the year 2006/7 there were 713,000 new official numbers issued, up 8% on the previous year. Half of these were to "Accession Nationals"[36] from the countries that joined the EU in 2004, and in turn nearly half of these were from Poland. Of the rest, 145,000 were from Asia and the Middle East[37].

If an immigrant workforce remains underprivileged and underpaid, then it will help to keep down the price of goods, but its members will be alienated by the second generation. Alternatively, if each wave of immigrants becomes established as part of the permanent population, the next generation expects the same pay and working conditions as everyone else. Neither outcome provides a long-term economic model. In the first case there evolves an alienated group of second generation immigrants stuck in a ghetto of language, education, lifestyle and aspiration barriers, whereas in the second, a new influx of immigrant workers is required, for whom more accommodation must be built and public services provided, to replace the previous generation who have now moved up the social, economic and workplace ladder.

So a new wave of immigration is always required to fill the gap, or at some point unskilled jobs are not filled and inflationary wage hikes are the only way to get the menial work done. Using this labour model, the UK economy, like the Roman Empire, would be predicated upon continual expansion to sustain its citizens' standard of living. The Migration Advisory Council has made the controversial recommendation that migrant workers are allowed to stay only four years to prevent this very situation[38]. Spain and other European nations are debating the same issues. Italy, with the greatest problem of falling birth rates combined with lengthening old age, is also considering how to tackle them.

A report on Immigration by the House of Lords Economic Affairs Committee[39] found "no net benefit" from immigration and proposed the restriction of immigration into the UK by skilled workers from outside the EU (apart from where there is a skills shortage such as, apparently, 'ballet dancing'). Countries such as Australia already tightly control immigration, as does America, with its prized "green card" work permit. As Ulrich Beck cynically writes "At the border posts 'desirable flexibility' thus turns into 'undesirable migration',"[40] noting that worker mobility *within* a country is encouraged, but the same migration *across* borders is often treated as a problem.

But can our economy survive without some form, albeit voluntary and even enthusiastic, of exploited proletariat at the bottom of the pile? Or conversely, have new entrants from Eastern Europe excluded members of the indigenous population who would have been content to fill the lowest-paid vacancies? The BBC documentary programme 'Panorama' found some evidence for this as its reporter followed the fortunes of four poorly-qualified school-leavers seeking employment and being passed over, quite logically, in favour of better-qualified Polish applicants.

Yet whether or not the economy is being underpinned by an exploited proletariat, either indigenous or migrant, at home, there is no doubt that we are all exploiting a proletariat abroad. We still buy goods manufactured with child labour abroad; we have strict laws on pollution in our own country, so we export our pollution to countries without such restrictions. Acid rain and CO_2 pollution do not recognise international boundaries, so ultimately we are both polluting our own environment and increasing our trade deficit. The logical but politically explosive conclusion is that either we should manage without goods produced by exploitation or pollution, or tax them to include the cost of paying a living wage or of cleaning up the environment, or else we might as well resume exploiting our own workforce and polluting our own environment - at least that way we would sort out our trade balance.

Too picky to pick
Yet already labour costs are evening out across the European Union. The Eastern European migrant workforce, estimated to have been arriving in the UK at around half a million economic migrants per annum, is already in short supply in some of the jobs traditionally taken by migrant workers. Fruit-picking is too lowly-paid to attract sufficient labourers, who are looking for more long-term employment in the towns, and as a result farmers are claiming that up to

twenty percent of the fruit may be left to rot on the trees. Other workers who abandoned their trade in Poland to earn more doing unskilled work in the UK are now returning home to their old jobs as wages in Eastern Europe start to rise towards the European average.

So the supply of cheap internationally mobile European labour has itself moved along the Product Life Cycle curve from New Entrant to Growth and onto Maturity in the course of less than ten years. What should we do to save our fruit trees? Close our markets to foreign fruit imports during our short fruit-growing season, thus artificially raising the price of fruit in the UK? Legislate for all fruit to be labelled with its carbon footprint, thus giving home-grown fruit a green boost? Or be positive and arrange for all community service to incorporate compulsory, healthy fruit-picking in the summer?

In India, too, wages are rising. An occasional ironical twist to the global re-pricing story is now being dubbed 'reverse outsourcing'. Some work that had been outsourced to Bangalore is being repatriated to California because salaries have risen so much in popular out-sourcing destinations in India.

Do we Work in a "Knowledge economy"?

Over the last couple of decades there have been some dramatic changes to the kind of jobs which make up the UK economy. According to the official UK Standard Occupational Classification there has been getting on for a doubling of jobs in personal service occupations, as shown in column 6 of the chart below – particularly in hairdressing, which has increased by over 300% in 10 years. Similarly customer service, ("*Major Group 7*"), has increased by nearly a third. Finally, we have all noticed the lack of plumbers, and this is evident in the 25% reduction in the Skilled Trades Occupations (*Group 5*). [41]

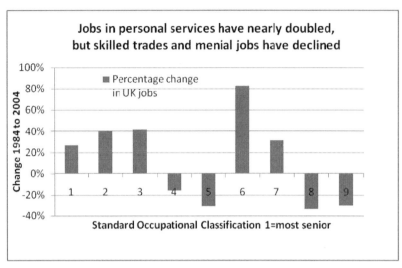

Source: Pauline Anderson, University of Strathclyde, adapted from Wilson et al., 2006

Standard Occupational classification groups (ONS 2000):

Group 1: Managers and Senior Officials

Group 2: Professional Occupations

Group 3: Associate Professional and Technical Occupations

Group 4: Administrative and Secretarial Occupations

Group 5: Skilled Trades Occupations

Group 6: Personal Service Occupations

Group 7: Sales and Customer Service Occupations

Group 8: Process, Plant and Machine Operatives

Group 9: Elementary Occupations

Yet the growth in some occupations and shrinkage in others seem to be a reflection not so much of customer demand, as of customer–oblivious supply. The lack of plumbers and over-supply of salespeople and hairdressers appears instead to reflect our bourgeois aspirations to wear office suits rather than boiler suits, and our attraction to the relative glamour of a career in hairdressing compared with plumbing. Similarly, whilst new graduates' interest in "green" technology is genuine, their willingness and ability do a technical job which makes green dreams a reality is not. If the mismatch between supply and demand is because of lack of graduate careers information, the task is easier than if it is due to the opposite: the unprecedented accessibility

Career Crunch!

of up-to-date information – about engineers' salaries, unfavourably compared with those of bankers and lawyers, reflecting, but perhaps also contributing to, the steady decline of engineering in the UK.

There is a widely-supported theory that in the West we are in an "hourglass economy" where jobs are becoming polarised between highly skilled and unskilled, or 'lovely' and 'lousy' jobs.[42]

The Hourglass Economy

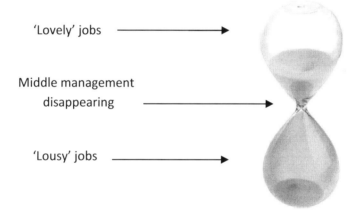

'Lovely' jobs ⟶

Middle management disappearing ⟶

'Lousy' jobs ⟶

At the top, we optimistically characterise the new breed of employees as "knowledge workers", in specialised and demanding, usually highly IT-literate 'iMacJobs', and the hourglass theory suggests that these jobs are supported by an increasing number of unskilled manual labour, or dead-end service industry "McJobs", such as serving, cleaning or driving, at the bottom. The idea that more bottom-end jobs are being created as others disappear in manufacturing is supported by a survey carried out by the Office of National Statistics: they show that the total number of manual workers has remained stable at just over ten million, which represents one in three jobs, and when secretarial and clerical workers are included this figure rises to seventeen million, or well over half of all UK jobs.

The new world of work is often referred to as the Information Age. Peter Drucker, the management guru, defined knowledge workers[43], who use their training and intelligence to supervise and design production and services. In this new structure there is little hierarchy, because speed and flexibility are of the essence, and therefore there is a further reduction in the need for middle management. For the UK, The Work Foundation published a report on "knowledge workers"[44] in 2009 in which they estimated that there is a "30-30-40 workforce – 30 per cent in jobs with high knowledge content, 30 per cent in jobs with some knowledge content, and 40 per cent in jobs with less knowledge content". That desirable top group of knowledge workers is rather broadly defined, however, because only one person in ten in the workforce is in the highest group of sophisticated 'true' knowledge workers and only one in a hundred works in genuine Research & Development. Levels of knowledge are perhaps more evenly distributed across the population than the hourglass graphically implies, but we are still a long way from being a sophisticated nation of knowledge workers. The hourglass shape is striking but exaggerated, rather like the Victorian ladies' hourglass figures achieved with unnatural corsets, so I propose instead to illustrate the knowledge levels amongst British workers by remaining closer to the numbers and only slightly stretching the shape of a common British fruit:

Is the British knowledge economy going pear-shaped?

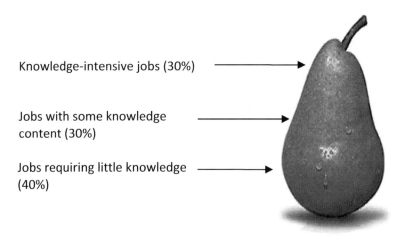

Knowledge-intensive jobs (30%)

Jobs with some knowledge content (30%)

Jobs requiring little knowledge (40%)

Career Crunch!

Hourglass or pear, one point shows up clearly: the bottom is still very big. Perhaps it needs to be and always will be? There will always be basic jobs to do that have to be done *in situ*, and not on the other side of the world, such as cleaning and driving. What mix is the optimum for the knowledge economy, and how should this be achieved? Would a bit of clear-headed planning as to what proportion of the population will in future require a university education be prudent, or does this all smack of Aldous Huxley's *"Brave New World"* where citizens were callously bred into pre-determined intelligence categories with '*Alphas*' destined for the cerebral jobs and '*Epsilons*' restricted to menial tasks? To increase the workforce in the most knowledge-intensive jobs will, after all, not only require appropriately-qualified staff but also appropriate employers who are willing and able to pay salaries high enough to attract in top students.

Can the next generation compete in a world where even sophisticated skills in business, from IT to call-centre management are being outsourced to locations such as India where employees deliver a high quality service at a fraction of the price? Academic theory informed the government policy of encouraging half the population to go to university in order to keep our economy one step ahead of the hungry emerging competition – but how realistic is this? In theory, our open free market economy benefits us all by providing cheaper goods and migrant unskilled labour, freeing us up to do research and innovation. Yet how many of us are profitably engaged in genuine original R&D or innovation? Possibly one per cent, as quoted above. In fact the OECD reckons that on average just over seven per thousand of its workers are involved in R&D[45], with Germany very close to that average, whilst the UK, despite its Information Age ambitions, trails at just under six! The UK's labour market-place is not providing the incentives in the form of hard cash salary levels to produce scientists and innovative engineers in sufficient numbers to underpin the UK's theoretical strengths – we are trading on an outdated image of technological and innovative superiority which only applies to a tiny minority of people and companies.

Career Crunch!

Germany has also identified a shortage of students taking up the sciences, whereas existing salary levels in India and China are high enough to stimulate a plentiful supply of engineers and scientists, so that manufacturing has migrated to these countries, and will be followed by R & D. India has the lowest number of researchers per thousand employees, at only 0.3, but given its huge population its absolute numbers of researchers are not very different from the UK. The United States and Japan are much higher, at around ten researchers per thousand employees. Unless the entire UK economy can be supported by an elite employed in finance and insurance, sectors which, along with Law, are still paying high salaries by any global standards, and, as a direct result, still enjoyed an over-supply of top quality applicants, then government intervention may be the only solution to provide work for the majority of UK citizens.

Salaries

Salaries for men seem to conform to the hourglass theory of a polarisation of job levels, but women do not follow the same pattern at all. Maybe women tend to follow a different pattern, with a career break and a willingness to temper ambition with family-friendly flexibility? In keeping with the general belief that knowledge work is the way of the future, workers in the most knowledge-intensive jobs are high earners – according to The Work Foundation "Eighty per cent of [these] workers were above the median 2007 wage measured by the Labour Force Survey."[46] Here there was little difference in the allocation of these top jobs to men or to women, which implies that they are held by ambitious high-fliers who have not compromised their career prospects by being anything other than dedicated to their work along the way. However, when it came to the middle band of jobs which require only some knowledge, comprising mainly female workers in care and welfare, selling and serving, only a third earned above national average[47] salaries, although about two-thirds of the small number of male employees in care and welfare had relatively higher earnings. This means that the female employees are underpaid, since those salary levels are on average lower than for the lowest group of jobs which require little knowledge, such as assistants, clerks and maintenance and logistics operators. So salaries vary according to how "nice" your job is: for a job you feel good about, the salary is correspondingly lower – helping others is a reward in itself.

Salaries also vary according to your age, and whether you are a man or a woman. But how clear-cut is this? How much does whether you are a man or a woman affect your salary? If you look at the striking pair of graphs below, from the Institute for Fiscal Studies[48] you can see clearly that the highest salaries are earned by educated male managers in the private sector, but that in this cut-throat environment salaries peak just after the age of forty. What happens then? They must be leaving their highly-paid positions and accepting posts that are lower-paid, perhaps as self-employed consultants or as interim or part-time employees.

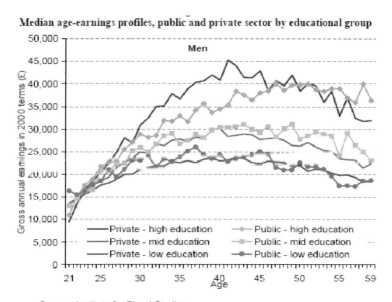

Median age-earnings profiles, public and private sector by educational group

Source: Institute for Fiscal Studies

Meanwhile, on average, female employees do not ever reach the salary peaks of their male colleagues, but their pay is more even throughout their lives. The graph of women's salaries shows two clear patterns: in the private sector, salaries are at their highest just after the extremely youthful age of thirty, which surely cannot be unrelated to biological clocks, and then generally decline, (with lesser peaks at around forty and fifty), but in the public sector salaries continue to rise, up to and even beyond the age of fifty-five! It certainly seems that what women lose on the swings they are starting to gain on the roundabouts.

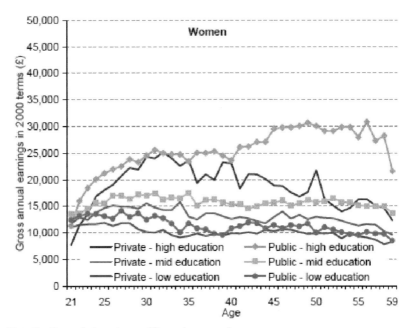

Note: Profiles exclude sector specific earnings growth.
Source: Authors' calculations using data from the LFS (1994 to 2006).

What this means for older workers' jobs and all our pensions

We are living on borrowed time, ecologically, and borrowed wealth, economically. Add to our mounting debt the possibility that the BRICs may eventually stop wanting to buy any produce from the West in return for the goods they sell to us. At the moment, when we sell sterling bonds and effectively use them to run a trade deficit with our trading partners, then someone is lending us our own currency to buy the goods, and that means we are paying them with currency that we already owe to someone else! We are

Career Crunch!

like a retailer trying to pay his creditors in vouchers that can only be spent in his shop – the problem being that there is nothing in there that the shoppers want to buy! There is a historical precedent for this: the Opium Wars. From their name, these sound like a moral crusade – perhaps the British were fighting *against* the opium trade? No. Britain was fighting to force the Chinese Emperor to *allow* the opium trade because it was the only commodity the British Empire had to offer that at least *some* of the Chinese actually wanted to buy! Britain wanted Chinese goods such as silk, tea and vases, so we went on the offensive, not with visits from senior politicians and minor royals, but with warships, and forced China to accept our opium from India in exchange. In the 'good old days' Britain wasn't averse to using a number of the 'dubious' strategies for increasing trade. Nowadays, however, when China supplies precursor chemicals for narcotics to Columbia, we are outraged and cry 'foul!'

So if the situation develops as it looks set to do, there will be no early retirement on generous pensions for the older worker and no hoping the state will look after you in your old age – global economic tides may leave you high and dry. The era of *gain* from *past* and *future pain* is over, our inherited pre-eminence in world trade is eroding and we are no longer comfortable with putting our future in hock. The higher your standard of living already is, the harder it is to improve it, without tangible incentives like those of the early settlers or today's economic migrants, to encourage the population to make the extra effort necessary to maintain our world-leading position.

But how can we be motivated to strive as hard as ever, just to stay still? How does an affluent economy become motivated, rather than depressed, by a gradual perception that its standard of living is unsustainable and that the next generation will have to strive more and even so drop in global status?

So, in the immediate future, what are our career and pension prospects? *Chapter Three* examines the implications of the change in our allotted lifespan.

Career Crunch!

Chapter Three

Time-left-to-go: *a new perspective on present careers*

Ancient Babylonian literature[49] tells of a Golden Age when the gods lived among men, there were no terrible diseases, and people lived long, civilised lives, aspiring to great deeds to earn them immortality. Then came the terrible flood, described in the "Gilgamesh Epic", perhaps the same flood as in the Bible, and the good times of disease-free longevity were over. The hero, Gilgamesh, attains a great age himself, but seeks immortality in vain. With similar optimism, the early part of the Old Testament of the Bible portrays extreme old age as a blessing for the ancient patriarchs: *"Then Abraham gave up the ghost, and died in a good old age, an old man, and full of years" (Genesis 25, verses 7, 8).* Adam reached the age of 930 years despite his eviction from the Garden of Eden; Noah survived the biblical Great Flood and lived to 950 years; Abraham attained the "good old age" of 175 years, and Isaac 180. However, this longevity does not continue: Psalm 90 puts a more familiar limit on the human lifespan, and expresses an uncannily contemporary pessimism about living beyond our allotted seventy years: *"The days of our years are threescore years and ten; and if by reason of strength they be fourscore years, yet is their strength labour and sorrow; for it is soon cut off, and we fly away." (Psalms 90, verse 10)*

Today, despite our personal aspiration to live to a 'good old age', society is greeting the new prospect of healthy longevity with dismay. Many mortals still seek eternal life for *themselves* – the US has a flourishing cryonics industry where customers pay up to $200,000 for their bodies to be deep frozen immediately upon their legal death in the hope that they may be saved by future technology (apparently "head-only" preservation is cheaper but the leading providers do not offer this option). We are, however, quite philosophical

Career Crunch!

about the human condition as it affects *other people*: we have got used to the idea that *other* people should live for only threescore years and ten, and have set up our social systems accordingly. Short-termist corporate culture is sometimes linked to the Western drift away from organised religion - the idea that with no everlasting life to strive for, people are only concerned with the here and now. Yet spiritual reward used to require little more than a personal life of virtue – not saving the rest of the planet, to boot. In the twenty-first century, greater self-determination means greater guilt, as we face the consequences of our own actions *plus* those of our entire generation *and* all of our ancestors. The current middle-aged generation has assumed longer-term responsibilities than ever before, without even a decent pension as consolation!

Most of us are going to get a lot more life than we were hoping for. Few of us have as yet adjusted to this. We may wistfully imagine longer days of retirement to learn to play the piano or any of those other "*Desert Island Discs*" fantasies, but the reality could be a lot harsher. The tropical heat oppressing our retirement will be a shortage of hard cash, the result of inadequate savings both privately and by the state. "Life expectancy" is turning out to be a lot more than any of us expected, in many different ways. We have in our possession a longer life span than ever before. In the mythological tradition of gifts to mankind, our new longer lives could be a blessing, or a curse. If we do not change our expectations rapidly, to adapt to our new human condition, then the global economy will sink under the burden of a top-heavy age profile. The warning signs are there, the economist Cassandras broadcasting their unwelcome message with their hair streaming wildly in the storm of demographic projections. Will we go the same way as Troy, our Trojan horse the extended old age we did not know how to handle?

To make the most of our extended active existence we shall need to break the mould of employer expectations, which are setting artificial limits to employee life-spans, and break down employees' own self-imposed barriers to their ambition and development. For many of us, steadily following a traditional career path, our life patterns have yet to take the first fundamental step away

Career Crunch!

from our primitive ancestors – we are born, we lead our lives according to instincts, parental aspirations and social expectations; we amass experience; we then produce offspring, and work to feed and teach them, before we are gradually deserted by our forces and faculties, and we retire to a quiet place to die. Where is the time to begin again after a false start? Where is the in-built retraining as opportunities increase, or as old, dirty or dangerous industries are superseded? When is the time to stop and take stock, choose a more conducive career or location, make an alternative life-style choice? Why are we all short of time? To prevent our ageing population from suffering forty years of pensions penury, we must acknowledge our new-found longevity. Most people will one day be dead and forgotten, but as any actor will tell you, it is worse to be forgotten and *not* dead. This is the fate not only of many elderly people, but also of many middle-aged managers, redundant solely due to their *date of birth,* applying for jobs but never receiving replies, rejected but never interviewed, capable but not given the chance to prove it.

Society as a whole, and corporate culture in particular, have yet to recognise that a longer life in good health offers previously unimagined opportunities. With a more flexibly structured workplace, relinquishing your current role without a guaranteed return, or even taking a complete career break of up to ten years, should not harm your ultimate prospects, if your career is expected to last fifty years or more. Internal peer group rivalry need not be 'to the death' if careers cease to be vertical races up-or-out, but instead an ever-broadening and deepening acquisition of both the skills to play a useful role in organisations, and the knowledge, experience and confidence to highlight where new opportunities lie. The 'feminised' career model should thrive: for women concerned by the ticking of the biological clock and even more scared that it will stop ticking completely, there should be no need to make the wrenching choice between a family and a career. The dedicated new father may not need to miss out on his child's first steps, or even his own first marriage, whilst he slashes out his career path through the inhospitable corporate jungle. In a more flexible world, maternity and paternity leave should cease to be the bane of a lean organisational existence. But getting to this ideal new work style will take a lot of re-thinking.

Career Crunch!

Shorter careers are distorting our lifestyles and work patterns

Yet, although there is much talk about the "feminisation" of the career model, this complete change does not apply to all careers, but only to the emergence of a new, *alternative*, feminised career, which allows for breaks for families and sabbaticals, and does not currently sit well with the dominant macho 'up-or-out' workplace culture. Women who wish to take a break have had to adopt a different attitude to salary and seniority. To get the megabucks and the top job still today almost invariably demands a total, unstinting dedication to your career. As a result, ambitious women are still delaying starting a family, in order to push up the career path *first,* so they don't miss out on a key career move, and have banked the option to come back later, at a managerial level, if they do decide to take time off. These high-flying employees display an *even more* aggressive commitment to the job. High fliers in the legal profession can disappear for three weeks on a major case – sleeping in the office (in special "pods" for the regular overnighters – they are rumoured even to have double pods for couples). Many are the tales of BlackBerrys crushed underfoot or thrown in the swimming pool by the frustrated partner of an ambitious thrusting employee defending his/her position in the company even whilst on holiday. The dawning realisation that many careers are currently lasting only around twenty-five years has, if anything, intensified the early pressure to do it all, in order to have it all. If you are to be perceived to be past your best by the age of forty-five, you cannot afford to take off extended maternity or paternity leave in your thirties and risk missing out on that key career move.

The graph of salaries at the end of *Chapter Two* shows the clear divergence between the salaries of women and men, and this reflects for the most part their view of working life. Whilst the salaries of men with a higher education rise sharply to a peak at around age forty, then fall equally sharply, illustrating precisely the pattern examined in this book, the salaries of educated women rise to a less elevated plateau but remain at this level for much longer. This implies that there are different career patterns and pay structures for men and women, and taking into account many women's preference for flexibility around the family, including career breaks and part-time working, and the female predominance in the caring professions, it is exactly what you might expect. With a more flexible employment structure, women or men should be able to leave a job to provide family care, or realise a dream, and still find suitable employment on their return – without needing to have their old position ring-fenced and set in inflexible concrete. Already in some organisations men are 'going part-time' – the Inland Revenue may not have the caring sharing image with the general public targeted by its PR men, but as an employer, it has offered flexible hours to both men and women for several years.

Up-and-out-and-roundabout Careers

In the place of central career-planning is centralised career-jamming, with the old rigid hierarchy still in place, but even tighter-packed, because reducing the levels of management has concentrated even more control at the top. Employers and employees alike will benefit from a culture change to recognise, and indeed legalise, the new roundabout career path, which is not always on an upward trajectory. We need to readjust our thinking to take a step sideways or backwards in order to go forwards. Recruiters need to review critically their readiness to take on younger management level recruits mainly for their perceived upwards career potential rather than their ability to do the job in question. Perhaps, contrary to familiar diatribes, recruitment policy is too *long-termist* - vacancies would be filled more efficiently if candidates were recruited to do a specific job, perhaps on a three year contract. This arrangement is becoming more common in the public sector, particularly when a position cannot be adequately compensated by existing pay structures and skills levels or for some other reason requires candidates from the commercial sector. It confers less job security than a permanent position, but more permanency than continual short-term assignments, and allows sufficient time for the incumbent to develop the role, without the risk of complacency creeping in. Knowing the staff are on fixed term contracts which can therefore be allowed to run to a natural end should also preclude the increasing tendency for incoming new directors to boot out the incumbent management without regard to their abilities and fill the top positions with their

Career Crunch!

'own men'. The old large company career model of moving round different roles, gaining and recirculating knowledge and skills, and gradually progressing up the salary scales, is being adapted for the 21st century by some specialists, but this time the movement is between different companies, accepting varying levels of pay and seniority with each new position.

Secondly, each individual employee may be obliged to take the opportunity to review his or her criteria for career success, which will no longer be based exclusively on the hierarchical positioning of their final role. Attitudinal change also needs to address the uncomprehending despair of the redundant employee, or the resentful anger of a former boss now effectively demoted - constructive dismissal is a costly HR crime regularly perpetrated by ill-advised or impatient managers, yet why? An employee is valued, but there are more appropriate people to do his role – then why not be legally entitled to keep him on, at a different level in the line of command, and with a salary commensurate with his new role – either higher, lower or the same, but not fixed immutably by the recent 'up-or-out' model? Instead of this compromise, managers are thrown out, possibly with their career over forever. Shifting them sideways, onto a different track, or possibly into a more interesting role, will enable the company to retain good staff - but only if the manager knows he will retain his colleagues' respect, previously afforded to him simply by virtue of his position in the hierarchy.

It is about time a new set of values emerged. Employment law, designed for now-outdated employment patterns, is the major barrier here – the rigid legal protection of an employee's status has become the reason why there is little choice but to make him redundant - or the reason why in future, his job will not be created. In practice, to prevent unscrupulous managers from abusing the system and saving themselves redundancy pay-outs by offering potential rivals such inappropriate jobs that they are forced to seek alternative employment elsewhere, one-off compensation will normally still need to be paid for a demotion or lower salary. But this compensation should be considered as transition subsidy, not a consolation prize for a failed or stalled career.

Career Crunch!

Structuring out middle-management and rearranging top management

This complete rearrangement of the traditional top-down hierarchy can already be seen around the middle levels of many public sector organisations, such as education and healthcare organisations. These are often populated by over-qualified and underpaid female returners, who are pleased to be able to structure around their family commitments a return to meaningful employment outside the home, with congenial, educated colleagues. No longer conforming to the old employment model of one educated manager, sitting above a wide pyramid base of lowly staff performing menial administrative tasks and requiring his direction, these employees are graduates, qualified accountants, even MBAs, their time leveraged with up-to-date computer skills. Such high quality, low-paid staff do not require close management supervision, and this reinforces the view that to employ a manager purely to supervise and direct other staff is wasteful, as a result of which the manager is given additional tasks, or made redundant, and empowerment and responsibility are increasingly delegated downwards.

The traditional tenet that only senior management can understand both the context of complex decisions and their ramifications has been undermined by the series of scandals in high finance. The cases of Societe Generale, where a rogue trader ran rings round management, and previously a similar case at Barings, demonstrated that the management simply did not know what was going on – they had long since passed the "doing" stage, and had not kept up a hands-on knowledge of the highly-specialised new technology. Those traditionalist institutions had failed to empower their hands-on staff, the only people who fully knew and understood what was going on, to query and contradict the edicts of senior management. In the entire US sub-prime market lending business there were no doubt many experienced members of staff shaking their heads and predicting it would all end in tears – unless such scepticism had already seen them dismissed as too old and unadventurous for modern markets, and ripe for early retirement or redundancy. In the UK, the Board of Northern Rock were pursuing higher returns without fundamentally questioning their provenance. Likewise, the top of the hierarchy at Lehman Brothers chose to ignore the realities of the market-place, and it was their staff, customers and trading partners who suffered the consequences. Generic Directors understand the stock market, the accounting rules and the legal duties incumbent upon a major corporation, but they do not have current practical knowledge the business. A fast-track up-or-out career structure only exacerbates this problem. Decision-making power has shifted towards the outward- and legally-orientated Main Board of specialist advisers, and away from the Operating Board of industry specialists, who are still in touch with the day-to-day business of the company. These are specific reasons for the declining reputation of managers, and these often combine with some of the age-related prejudices listed below:

Prejudices against older employees

"Before I was born" syndrome: If you are over forty, do you not realise that to younger people you come into the same category as Big Bang, the dinosaurs, the Romans and Henry VIII, namely: *'Existed before I was born'?* In fact, there is very little to distinguish you from the above, except the phrase "...and still exists now", with the implicitly attached question – *"why?"*

"Boring": Socially older employees are boring – constantly referring to music, entertainers, TV programmes and even politicians you've never heard of and insisting on giving the history of any company you deal with.

"We had it tough" syndrome: Why do the children of self-made millionaires often squander their inheritance? Partly because they can never do as well as the older generation, no matter how highly they perform. This applies across the whole of the younger generation, who are constantly reminded that they did not have to live through a war, nor mass unemployment and its accompanying deprivations, and whose main problems all appear to be self-inflicted – drugs, anorexia, obesity... They are left with a superfluity of material possessions and a resentful feeling of guilt.

"Time-left-to-go" mentality: Older employees haven't long to go before they retire so it's not worth trying to change anything about them.

"Declining in mind and body": Older employees are likely to be off sick more often and their brains won't be as sharp as they used to be.

Blocking: Old people block your career and your attempts to develop the business. They sit in the top jobs doing what they always did without regard to how the world has moved on. They also block all new suggestions with the same retort: "*We tried that twenty years ago and it didn't work then, so it won't work now.*" They are cosy in a world they know and have come to dominate, and defensive about new technology they don't understand, and don't want change at any cost.

Inflexible: Older recruits are less likely to be flexible about location. They may still have children taking important exams, or they may be starting to care for elderly relatives who are even less easy to trail around the world. With their spouses, who may be in senior positions of work themselves, they have a settled pattern of life which they are unhappy to disrupt.

Complacent: They abuse the system, thinking that after twenty years in the organisation they are owed a living. They take no account of the wolves circling outside – they are cosy inside, with a salary and pension related to years of service and similarly-accumulated redundancy pay-offs, should the company wish to rationalise out their job.

Legacy-driven: Some older employees have plenty of energy, but focus it on leaving a legacy. When this legacy is provided as a tax-deductible cost out of the profits of a public company, has a ruthless cost/benefit analysis been carried out? Grand Head Offices or generous charitable sponsorship have sometimes proved to be the signal that a company is on the way down, either because the management are focusing on their own prestige rather than on the bottom line, or because this is a last ditch attempt to raise the profile and standing of a failing company.

State of the world: How good can the older generation be at management when they have presided over the almost terminal pollution of the environment?

Socialising: Even socially, the stature of the older generation is diminished. Ever since the Charleston, dancing has been the athletic preserve of the young. Dancing is certainly no longer an elegant pastime shared by all age-groups; the loud music defeats conversation, the traditional fall-back of the old; disco dancing itself falls into the same category as drunkenness and romance – sweet that the old people still try to join in, but really it isn't for them.

Fighting back: The one card older employees have to play here is a negative one: the cost of their redundancy pay accumulated over many years of service, and, for members of a heavily-unionised workforce, especially in the public sector, usually substantially above the statutory minimum. This is one reason why older staff may survive longer in the public sector, yet this only adds to their unpopularity.

Some advantages of older employees

Yet older employees also have recognised strengths. Older workers can provide continuity, experience of economic cycles and a longer term perspective.

Trustworthy Experience: In the Public Sector, employees still generally serve a long apprenticeship before reaching the top jobs - there are few Head Teachers of large secondary schools under forty, and as discussed in *Chapter One*, most Prime Ministers are at least in their late forties to early fifties before they attain office.

Salesmen/Advisors: The older salesman is often more credible: he has survived, so customers are more inclined to trust his sales presentation. He is no longer thrusting ahead in his career, eager for the next bonus cheque or to step onto the next rung of the ladder. Older financial advisors likewise have been selling the product for years and are fluent in the jargon. Despite their cynicism and distrust of authority, the young, with their short memories, will be unaware of the false promises and weasel words exposed by market downturns, and have confidence, when making significant financial decisions, in the claims of seasoned professional patter.

Businessmen: An older businessman has experienced economic cycles and different management regimes. How many young managers remember the problems caused by 20% inflation and interest rates over 17%? Only those shopping in the mid 1970's i.e. those aged forty-five-plus now. Before the Credit Crunch began in 2007, few people aged under fifty were aware of the negative equity trap in the early 1990's – until the recent problems in the global housing market, the advice was still: *"Invest in property – it always goes up over time. Safe as houses."*

Judges/ Nurses/Doctors: We have more confidence in a Judge who has seen the world and many strange things in it, tempering her justice with pragmatic mercy. The older doctor has been round the block a few times, and seen it all before. He may be less sympathetic, or even appear bored with your affliction, but that in itself is reassuring – you have a common ailment and not a social leprosy, and you will recover. How did you react the last time a professional said to you with sympathetic enthusiasm: "Oh dear, that looks really *painful*."

Travel Agents/ Shop Assistants: If they are old enough to have had their own families they understand why it is important to you that you can buy your favourite brand of nappies in your Spanish coastal resort, and may hesitate to fob you off with vague reassurances. If they are older they may even have mature tastes – there is a possibility that they themselves genuinely enjoyed the peace of the watercolour painting course in the Tuscan hills. Older shop assistants' advice is practical: they recommend garments on the basis of how well they wash, and children's school uniform sizes on the basis of how much the kids are likely to grow in the next year (or two).

Saving us all money on Pensions: Workers who retire on a Pension paid by the State are now living directly off you and me, as a quid pro quo for the work they did in the past from which we are all benefiting. But this is a gentleman's agreement between the generations, an honour debt. Forget: "I've saved all my life for my pension": what does that mean in reality? Perhaps you have a stash of gold and art works and tins of beans and soup under your bed that you are slowly using up (and, if you are old enough, bags of sugar left over from the 1970s sugar shortage). If not, then what you saved and paid into National Insurance for all those years is in fact no more tangible than a *promise to pay* by the government, i.e. the taxpayers, i.e. the rest of us.

You may have indeed contributed to the country's wealth, both with your labour and by investing your savings, but the fact is that if the financial system collapsed tomorrow, what would you live off? You do not have any bargaining power to get someone to give you food and fuel, other than the moral argument that you worked for it and saved for it and were promised it and now you jolly well deserve it – with the exception (assuming the electoral system survives the hypothetical collapse of the financial system) of your increasingly significant trump card, the pensioner vote. As these older, fit and willing people are holding a "*promise to pay the bearer*" note that says that the state will look after them, then once we retire them off, the working population are effectively supporting someone else to go on painting courses in Tuscany whilst they slog away running their services: emptying their bins, providing them with heat and light and running the hospitals.

If employees are retired off early on a company pension, then not only do they miss out by being forced to manage on an unexpectedly reduced income, but the other members of the scheme are obliged to subsidise their early retirement, however much the actuaries may argue that they have factored this choice into the figures. Therefore it is madness to retire off healthy, willing workers just because they insist on boring you with reminiscences about Star Trek in its original TV format, or what it was like before we had mobile phones. It may be that current Western governments really care less than they claim about ageism as a *principle*: it is the unimaginable cost of pensions they care about, and in this case the pragmatism of their legislation is laudable.

Career Crunch!

Time-left-to-go: The population is keeping healthier for longer, with centenarians increasing in numbers from a rarity in the 1950s to well over ten thousand today, therefore at the age of forty-five the majority of the population will have at least another twenty-five employable years ahead of them, and on this basis are well worth investing in.

More contented: According to research published by Warwick University[50] throughout the world people experience a U-shaped dip from a high in happiness at age twenty to a low ("mid-life crisis") at forty-four up again to a high at seventy!

Does Price equal Value? We must, however, recognise the other side of the pensioner's coin, namely that work done by unpaid workers (housewives and others) is under-valued by economists, and therefore by governments, and by society as a whole, because a price is not put on it. Childcare is the clearest example – if a significant proportion of mothers with young children receive free childcare from an older relative, then their employers benefit from a more plentiful and cheaper labour force than they would otherwise, because these mothers are able to re-enter/remain in the workforce, without needing to demand a large premium for the extortionate cost of childcare. As a consequence, salary costs to the employer are reduced (and as a by product salaries become uncompetitive for parents who still have to pay for a couple of kids in a nursery), without putting a value on the benefit . A further contribution from family-provided childcare is yet more intangible and unquantifiable: you know your child is safely brought up at home and can have his quota of chickenpox and tonsillitis without your feeling guilty.

This kind of voluntary economic activity only really began to be acknowledged once the term *social economy* was coined by French social scientists in the 1980s to distinguish this third sector of activity from the private and public sectors. So to provide a balanced view, the economic contribution made by unpaid pensioners, valued at four billion pounds per annum in a report by Age Concern, should also be factored into any true measure of economic output, before all sprightly OAPs are rounded up and press-ganged into paid employment. This point was made by the Grandparents' Association in a campaign in spring 2009 for tax credits and even grandparental leave from work to care for a new grandchild.

Well-meaning legislation can be a help and a hindrance

In the UK, the country's first ever Ageism Legislation, passed in October 2006, gives employees the right to request to stay on beyond their company's normal retirement age, yet the ironic twist is that Unions joined forces with company bosses (in the form of the Confederation of British Industry) in opposing the complete abolition of the default retirement age, ostensibly fearing exploitation of workers who wished to retire at sixty-five and whose pension would no longer be designed for them to do so. Employment Law makes it increasingly difficult to sack incompetent staff without drawn-out unpleasantness, therefore risk-averse management will be reluctant to employ a member of any group more likely to become unemployable and thus cause problems - the text-book method would be by performance management, a drawn-out and painful process for all concerned and not often undertaken because of this.

As a result of such concerns, and more for expediency than practicality, employees can now *request* to stay on beyond this retirement age, but do not have the automatic *right* to do so. Furthermore, there is still inconsistency in the interpretation and application of the legislation. As the cases quoted in Chapter Five illustrate, anything that seems to imply that age is a factor in selection at work can be used to convict the employer of ageism. Yet Rolls-Royce tried to take ageist factors *out* of redundancy procedures, only to be told that this was against the law too! The only common theme is that in the Rolls-Royce case the ageism worked in favour of the older employees, by awarding them a point per year of employment. The judge said his ruling acknowledged the "loyalty and experience of the older workforce", but also gave Rolls-Royce permission to appeal his ruling, thus implicitly admitting that the whole situation is a shambles.

Another blow was dealt to all older workers Europe-wide, when, on March 5th 2009, the European Court of Justice rejected a case brought by Age Concern to outlaw the compulsory retirement age. So despite all the evidence to the contrary, the European courts still do not acknowledge either the change in human lifespan, or the acute and imminent pensions crisis. In the context of the near-collapse of the financial system, and in particular the French reduction in the working week, it appears that the immediate across-the-board jobs crisis took precedence. Yet we have a desperate need for older workers to keep earning money for their retirement and there is strong evidence that sixty-five is too young to be too old to work. Sadly, although forty years of work certainly deserves a reward, the financial reality is that a long retirement of penury is all that the latter end of the baby boom generation can hope for, if present trends continue.

There is perhaps one hopeful sign: a cross-committee of MPs has concluded that spies should be exempt from any retirement age in order to be able to make use of experience dating back to the Cold War. So just when his charms seemed to be getting rather dated, James Bond is trend-setting yet again.

Case studies

As early as 1989, the DIY chain B&Q removed their fixed retirement age, and in 1990 they opened their Macclesfield store staffed entirely by over-fifties. (This positive discrimination would not now be possible under 2006 Ageism Legislation!) According to their *website*[51], in 2010 their oldest employee was 95! Meanwhile, the Co-op Group scrapped its retirement age in 2006, and by 2007, of the Group's 65,000 employees, 825 were aged over sixty-five. Nationwide Building Society is also a pioneer in the retention and recruitment of older workers. It offers flexible retirement up to age seventy-five and its website states that[52] over 12% of its workforce is aged 50 or over.

So there any evidence of prejudice in companies against the older worker? Some research by the firm "20 plus 30 Consulting" is very revealing. It investigated the proportion of employees over the age of fifty-five in a number of leading organisations:

Deutsche Bank	1%
Microsoft	1%
The Carphone Warehouse	1%
Barclays	3%
Vodafone	3%
Mothercare	5%
BBC	5%
Nationwide	6%

Source: 20plus30 Consulting 2007 (Dick Stroud)[53]

Doing a rough mental arithmetic check on the numbers: If you simplify working life to 16-65, or nearly fifty years for men and 16-60 or nearly forty-five years for women, and say there are equal proportions of male/female employees, then you would expect on average about one in six employees, or *16%* to be over fifty-five (before age-related illness is taken into account). Compare this with the *1% to 6%* in the survey, and you get a feel for the magnitude of the problem.

Nuclear technology needs older trained engineers

With the rapid rise in oil prices in 2008 the oil and nuclear power industries became once more attractive, but in both these industries the older workers have largely been retired off and the new generation has not been trained to replace them in industries which were declining in the UK. Since 1980, when there were about nine thousand technologists working in nuclear research in the UK, this number has declined to only one thousand today[54]. According to Peter Bleasdale, Managing Director of Nexia Solutions, the company which has developed the National Nuclear Laboratory (NNL): "Nuclear skills were driven down because there was no interest in new build. You couldn't enthuse graduates to come into the industry because it was stagnating."[55] This de-skilling fits the general pattern described in this chapter. Now that there is a need for skilled energy workers, older workers are due to be brought in to cover the gap whilst younger future workers are trained up. Over the next ten years the nuclear sector will need to recruit between six and nine thousand graduates and over three thousand skilled tradespeople. The nuclear power industry is certainly looking to the older workers to boost its inadequate workforce, according to John Earp, formerly president of the British Nuclear Energy Society[56], who expects nuclear engineers to be brought out of retirement to help with the planning, training and development of a new "nuclear generation". The Institute of Mechanical Engineers has issued a press release confirming that at the moment the average age of a professional engineer is fifty-eight[57]!

'Too old' should be an objective statement

With cases like those quoted above of successful companies who are pushing the boundaries on retirement age, surely a new set of criteria, rather than an arbitrary calendar date, should be introduced to determine whether an employee can continue to carry out their job effectively? Increasing longevity will not only increase the length of time some employees are fit and able to continue to work, but, more confusingly, it will increase the *range* of ages at which an employee is no longer able to carry out their work – from those incapacitated by illness only a short way into their career, to those who carry on for decades after they would have been expected to retire – David Attenborough must be a convincing example of this. Compulsory retirement age could be replaced by a series of objective tests including a cluster of sight, hearing, physical stability and steadiness of hand, memory and brain speed, which could become increasingly tailored to different types of employment as they establish their usefulness – this sort of re-testing is already used (possibly too sparingly) for the driving test, and would have to come with all the usual safeguards, such as an appeals procedure. It would also be preferable for these standardised tests to become the norm for all employees - it should not be necessary to be able to prove that the employee *needs* to take the test before they take it, or the result will be that the *pre-testing* selection criteria will be endlessly debated. For the sake of convenience the default retirement age, contradictory as this sounds, might need to be chosen as the age at which tests become compulsory. Employers could retain the option to overrule negative test results.

Training and Intelligence: Are older workers less intelligent than younger ones?

There is a recent study[58] which debunks the idea that as we lose brain cells in the normal ageing process we somehow lose our intelligence as well. Research into the intelligence scores of US ex-servicemen tested when they were recruited at about age twenty, and again about twenty years later for the project, discovered that their arithmetic had not deteriorated at all, whilst their verbal ability had actually increased! This improvement in verbal ability was attributed to practice, an unusual concession to the self-evident truth that, to a greater or lesser degree, "intelligence", however many weird and wonderful definitions people come up with define it, can be learned.

When employees remain longer in the workplace they will provide the extra manpower to train and develop a labour force of knowledge workers, but this task will take more than merely time and money. Extra university places are already on offer and teenagers are encouraged to stay on at school. Do they all have the potential to benefit from a university style education? It might not appear so from the type of courses in demand – despite the growth in university places, the demand for the hard "STEM" subjects including bio-chemistry and engineering is declining. Are the "hard" subjects too intellectually demanding for the innate abilities of the majority, or do motivation and incentives play the determining role? In other words: what are the key characteristics of knowledge workers? Intelligence, hard work, motivation, adaptability? All teenagers master the use of mobile phones and

WAP technology, uploading photos and creating their own websites - this is only considered difficult by older people who lack motivation having got by perfectly well in the past without it. So quick brains might be less necessary to work effectively with the latest technology than the motivation to do so.

The worldwide GMAT entrance examination for Business Schools, and the British "11+" entrance exams for some secondary schools, are admissions hurdles that attempt to measure pure innate intelligence, or aptitude, in order to match pupils with an appropriate style and pace of learning, and as an indicator of their ultimate potential. Yet even this supposedly innate intelligence can be trained, as the many practice papers, revision courses and advertisements for private tutors testify. A second point often made is that intelligence tests are nearly always culturally biased. Consider this example from a 1960's grammar school "11+" entrance exam preparation book[59]:

"Tea is always: 1. hot 2. brown 3. with milk."

In an international consumer culture, where Japanese green tea and variously-coloured herbal teas are not uncommon, this question is puzzling, but in the 1960's, when even the examiners had often never left England, this question presented no difficultioo to a normally intelligent British child. Until you travel or have a broad education or a different cultural heritage, you can easily answer the question. Once you know a bit more, or rather, a bit different, the question becomes impossible. Does it matter? We set the tests and get a cluster of intelligent-like reactions which are a mixture of motivation, upbringing, training, powers of retention and mental agility, and this gives us a fairly good approximation. After all, the environment in which they will be learning and working will also be full of cultural bias, so might it not be counter-productive to correct for it in our test?

And how is this relevant to older workers? Well, one convincing theory is that older people also score lower in tests which contain more recent concepts, or jargon, which are less familiar to them, so just as social background, or race, can distort a respondent's scores, and bias the test, so can age. Needless to say, older employees who have not kept up with new jargon *will* be slower to grasp new ideas at work, too, so their lower test performance might well reflect their current performance in the workplace – however it would not be an indicator of potential, and would not show what a bit of training and perhaps a wake-up call to make the effort to keep up-to-date could achieve.

Whatever definition you choose, "Intelligence" is a cluster of features including:

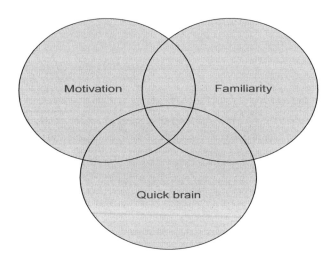

So "intelligence", or at least a good approximation to it, can be *learned*. Familiarity is a great intelligence booster. If you've come across a concept before, you are much quicker on the uptake. Consider the graduate in business studies on the graduate trainee scheme of a major tour operator. He caught on to the new concepts so much quicker than the other graduates in Classics, English etc. Not surprising - he hit the ground running - and to his credit, he kept running! Older employees, with their greater familiarity with economic cycles and experience of working with people, often appear more intelligent, or at least, wiser, in their general management and business understanding, though, for the same reason, if they have not familiarised themselves with the latest technology or jargon, then they may appear near senility when dealing with new concepts. Of course, intelligence has acquired multiple meanings in addition to 'quick on the uptake and able to master complex ideas', discussed above. It can also be used to mean 'intuitively understands' as in 'emotional intelligence'; 'musical intelligence' etc. Finally it can be confused with 'the way we learn' as in 'visual' or 'physical'. When we think of secret agents, 'intelligence' means information accessible by subterfuge, but in the context of computers 'Artificial Intelligence (AI)' is where logical computers abandon the area of competence where they have a clear competitive advantage, and instead attempt to imitate the less linear workings of the human mind. Whatever it is, we need to nurture it in all employees if we are to remain at the forefront of innovation and global advanced industries, and there is now good reason to think that it is at least equally present in older and younger minds.

Down-up retraining

The worst scenario is that individuals, companies, industries and whole nations get into a rut. They feel bored, secure, fat and happy or, alternatively, chronically insecure, obese and unhappy, and they can't see any way to change that situation that won't make life more uncomfortable at least in the short run – and who wants to do that unless there is a real incentive? This kind of employee is the obvious candidate for redundancy and yet is also the most indignant when they are exited. They can't see why the boss isn't happy with them – they were doing *exactly* what they always had done! But that is the problem. Contracts should include a commitment on both sides to ensure employees' skills and detailed knowledge of how the business functions day-to-day are kept up to date.

Companies and organisations benefit from enabling all staff to keep up-to-date, not only with major technical developments, but also with how the company operates. Staff newsletters, corporate mission statements, staff Awaydays are all commonplace, but a more skills-based approach would pay dividends. This need not be through expensive external training courses. Far better for employees to devise their own presentations on their areas of work and their own questions on new developments they have observed in their own or other areas of related work. Preparing and facilitating these meetings will be a learning curve that any ambitious employee should be keen to ascend, so again they need not introduce more expensive overheads for the company. Awaydays should not consist of travelling to the countryside and tying each other to rafts or trees – let the management accountants organise the next fun Awayday – you'll be taking over the old meeting room with a packet of Rich Tea biscuits and a flip chart and bringing your own chairs. But it might actually be useful.

The Chartered Institute of Personnel and Development is in the prime position to take the lead on cost-effective retraining programmes, recommending and showcasing Best Practice for continuous cost-effective up-down and down-up staff retraining and updating. Detailed template agendas for staff retraining days can easily be made available to organisations and companies on the Internet. Again this will cost very little to provide, and in addition to being less expensive is also quicker to update than a printed manual.

Managers need to keep up an active skills exchange with their reports in order to keep up to date with industry and functional developments. For managers who can see that they do not have the skills of their juniors the solution is simple: they need to spend at least two to three days of every year on the front-line doing their juniors' jobs as "Work Experience" on the shop floor. Whereas a subordinate will be reluctant to share their job expertise with their peer group rivals, they will not be able to build so many barriers to informing the boss how they do their work if he comes to do the job himself. The excuse from the managers will always be that they don't have time, but this is where leadership needs to come from the blue chip organisations, the Chartered Institute of Personnel and Development and even government guidelines to convince top management of the validity of the exercise, not just for the personal benefit of the managers themselves but also for the company as a whole: managers usually have to push through new procedures or a change of structure despite the moans from front-line staff that it can't be done, and practical knowledge of how things are currently done and an insight into the difficulties to be overcome would enable managers to pre-empt objections and continuously develop the company to keep pace with market conditions. There is no reason why these same training modules cannot be available to young and old. The *learndirect* website[60] is directed at people aged fifty plus and in 2007 it was contacted by 35,000 over-fifties willing to start new career.

(Re)Training for a Knowledge economy

The future of the UK workforce is often said to be as "knowledge workers", but a university education may not be the most appropriate for even the most complex and highly paid knowledge work. This point is borne out by a quotation from the report by The Work Foundation: "about 44 per cent of graduates in low knowledge content jobs reported that their job duties corresponded well with their current skills." The conclusion must be that they may have had high levels of academic knowledge (*or not*), but that they did not have the specific skills to move up to a higher level job in the organisation where they were working.

So there is not just the problem of achieving an agreed standard but even more difficult, in ascertaining what that standard is for different types of work. Even if our future economic success depends on knowledge workers, what do these workers need to know? Is it as simple as the World Bank's distinction between 'information' and 'knowledge' in its Knowledge Economy Index (KEI)? If basic information can be acquired from basic schooling, but the ability to manipulate that knowledge only comes from higher education, it seems a simple equation: higher education creates more knowledge workers. The OECD implicitly uses this formula in its composite indicator of knowledge investment, where it includes spending on higher education as a share of GDP. And it makes general sense that the more an entire population pursues academic studies, the more sophisticated they will become at abstract tasks.

Yet for the older worker such simple definitions do not apply. As The Work Foundation ascertained: "About 20 per cent of people engaged in jobs with high knowledge content – our core group of knowledge workers – were not graduates[61]." The successful entrepreneur who left school as soon as he could, to set up his own business, can hardly be accused of not being able to manipulate information – academic knowledge he may not have, but he's certainly got nous. To succeed in business he must have sharp acumen as well as common sense, yet he will not have a qualification to prove it – until he makes his millions, and then generally he uses his luxurious house, car and private jet to speak for him. How can the older worker with no formal qualifications demonstrate these qualities, particularly if he has just lost the one proof of his ability – his well-paid job? His reputation in his industry is all that remains, so if he is to find a new position it must be within his own sector, even if this is shrinking. Furthermore, the ability to manipulate generally available information is only part of the story. Equally important in many jobs is the inside knowledge gained through experience, which again is hard to prove other than when probed by an expert interviewer, and impossible to acquire as an outsider trying to get into a new industry.

These two types of knowledge have been differentiated as 'tacit' and 'codified' knowledge[62], and only the knowledge that has been 'codified', that is, set out in a manual or a text-book, or on the internet, can be prepared and learnt up by anyone trying to penetrate a new sector or company. This distinction is crucial if you are trying to work out why you are not being offered a job interview, or always in the end being passed over in favour of an industry- or company-insider. It may seem unfair, but they have spent many months, if not years, acquiring 'tacit' knowledge that is not available to you until you do the job – they can hit the ground running, whilst you may have the potential to go further, but you haven't yet even tried out the course.

So what kinds of skills and qualifications can be taught to employees, old or young? The German academic, Ulrich Beck, is cynical: "Cheer up, your skills and knowledge are obsolete, and no one can say what you must learn in order to be needed in the future." That training is crucial to the future of all UK

Career Crunch!

employees is agreed, but exactly what to teach them is less clear. The Work Foundation found a major mismatch between the work people were employed to do and the skills they had.[63] There are certain skills that are common to a number of potential areas of employment:

1. *Basic Skills for all employees*

- ✓ Literacy
- ✓ Numeracy
- ✓ Computer skills
- ✓ Presentation skills
- ✓ Interpersonal Skills

White-collar workers may need more general skills than blue-collar/ manual labourers, though as The Work Foundation report on Manufacturing reveals, increasingly a high level of education is required for industry as processes become more complex and the basic repetitive tasks are taken over by machinery: "When jobs are classified by knowledge content, high tech manufacturing has as many knowledge intensive jobs, proportionately, as high tech services."[64] Statistically, one of the few occupations for which illiteracy remains almost *de rigueur* is 'prison inmate'.

2. *Knowledge of Professional Theory ('Codified knowledge', or 'information')*

From Childcare to Accountancy, from Car Mechanic to Lawyer, passing exams to gain vocational qualifications is becoming essential. At graduate level, the intelligent amateur is no longer the most desirable candidate for most companies. With the disappearance of life-time career loyalty, fewer companies are prepared to invest in training up raw graduates with degrees in academic subjects. They want new recruits to "hit the ground running", even straight from university, with a good basic understanding of Marketing/Mechanics/Strategy/Finance.

- ✓ What is the function and purpose of the "naughty chair"?
- ✓ How do disc brakes work?

Career Crunch!

- ✓ Does anyone know what the tax rules really are?
- ✓ Is the Law an ass?
- ✓ Name all the body parts and all their possible malfunctions.
- ✓ What does 'BOGOF' mean in Marketing?
- ✓ How do you design a simple footbridge across the Thames?

3. *Practical Professional Skills ('Knowledge' i.e. how to use the information)*

Practical Skills have to be learnt initially, but then "practice makes perfect". A brick-layer becomes expert at doing exactly that. A lawyer needs the practical skill to draw up a will that says what you stipulated (as opposed to the *exact opposite*, as happened to me); an accountant should just fill in the form the way the tax man likes it, rather than embroiling you in a long debate over what the rules *might* mean. The doctor who thinks it might be *interesting* to operate on your left ventricle is to be avoided at all costs – skills should be drilled till you can carry them out almost without thinking. Doctors should be able to discuss the pros and cons of different expensive cameras with a prospective father at the same time as delivering his baby by Caesarean section - I know: thanks to the wonders of modern medicine I heard the whole conversation.

- ✓ How do you keep your wig on in court?
- ✓ What's the most popular story to tell to children being anaesthetised?
- ✓ How much chocolate can you give pupils before it ceases to work as an incentive?

4. *Sector Expertise ('Tacit knowledge' – mainly passed on by word of mouth)*

The hardest knowledge to acquire is the elusive sector expertise, specialist detail not systematically set out in books, nor taught in any courses, because it is constantly changing. This is one of the potential attractions to employers of mature candidates, but also why they prefer someone who is not only capable of doing the job they need to fill, but has already done it, or is preferably doing it for a competitor at the moment, so his expertise is both current and endorsed by his employer.

- ✓ What's the going rate for Wills/ international company audits this year?
- ✓ What time of year are the London Hotels busiest?
- ✓ Where's the cheapest place to source cotton cloth this year? How long before the media expose the sweat-shops there?
- ✓ Which are the countries where alcohol is legal but cartels aren't, and where is it the other way round?
- ✓ What new ideas are getting the industry leaders excited?

Where can these different skills be learnt? Can they be taught formally?

Basic General Skills	✓ At School or
	✓ In Private Home Study
Professional Theory	✓ Day release Course or
	✓ In-house Training or
	✓ Evening Study
Practical professional skills	x Through working
Sector expertise	x Through working

Basic skills are taught at school and professional theory at college, but practical professional skills are learnt on the job, and some qualifications such as BTECs and NVQs are based mainly on these vocational skills. Sector expertise is the most elusive knowledge of all. It can be learnt on the job, from trade magazines, from colleagues down the pub after work, or from customers/suppliers. As The Work Foundation research revealed, knowledge is overwhelmingly shared and captured face-to-face, by talking informally to colleagues (90%), asking a supervisor/manager (60%), socialising/conversing with others (44%); alternatively employees turn to the internet (60%). Compare this with the more formal methods of publishing written material

(15%), attending induction meetings (18%), attending an external training session (26%), or even the essential reading of professional journals/trade magazines (26%). This explains why jobs are shut to would-be applicants who cannot access the "tacit" knowledge that the recruiting managers are looking for. Mastery of the general skills is offered by all sorts of genuine expert coaches and charlatans alike, advertising in newspapers and on the internet or by word of mouth. Who doesn't know a "resting" actor who can teach you voice control and public speaking to improve your presentation skills, or a former army officer who can teach you leadership?

The conclusion is stark: all jobseekers require the basic skills, and, increasingly, formal vocational qualifications, but even if they study, gain experience and get qualified, they are still not ready to do any job until an employer gives them the opportunity to learn as they do it. As a result, law placements are few and far between, and competition is fierce to get an internship in any large or well-known organisation: without this extra notch on your CV you are as good as useless.

Of course, there *are* senior managers with no formal vocational qualifications. They have usually worked their way up within one sector and gained practical skills and sector expertise through observation and implementation rather than study, but their ability to convince future employers of their worth if they lose their present job, where their practical ability is known and valued, relies on a sector-wide reputation. To any potential employer in a different sector, they effectively have nothing to offer, without a qualification and without the backup of their sector-specialist reputation. The Credit Crunch revealed that many top bankers did not have any banking qualifications, and when things went wrong, the lack of formal study seemed proof of their unpreparedness for the complexity of the tasks of which they were nominally in charge. Across most industries, the majority of the older management layers developed their understanding of business concepts, their practical abilities and their advanced skills on-the-job. The main proof to an employer that they can do a job, is that they are still doing it.

Career Crunch!

Some qualifications seem to be more attractive to employers than others. The Child Care and Education CACHE Diploma (formerly NNEB) for nannies is sought-after because it is a rigorously taught course which ticks two different important boxes: how you should *in theory* look after children and how to deal with real children *in practice*, because to pass the course you must also complete rigorous practical experience and assessment. Similarly, trainee accountants have to supplement their full week at work with evening study; doctors complete a three-year undergraduate degree followed by several more years in work experience, often followed by specialised training on the job; teachers in state schools have to pass both written exams and practical observations; the Driving Test now has a theory paper and a practical test.

To provide reassurance to employers and to stand out in a crowded market, a vocational qualification is the least you need to offer, unless you have a reputation stretching back over many years, or your services are extremely cheap and flexible. The MBA (Master of Business Administration), a demanding and respected course (though increasingly variable in its content as more and more institutions offer it), is not the automatic passport to high-flying success that it was when the courses were first developed. The same applies to other optional professional qualifications such as book-keeping, IT or marketing courses. Whilst these courses are invaluable as basic training, they do not guarantee to employers that the candidate can do the particular job for which they are recruiting, so, if they have the option, they make the safe, albeit potentially suboptimal choice, of the candidate already doing the same job for a competitor.

Then there are senior managers who seem to have it all. Pre-requisites for the top jobs are a high level of competence in the basic skills and in professional theory and practice, plus:

✓ Political Astuteness
✓ Thought Leadership (Latest Management Theories; Strategy)
   and more recently:

✓ Major Project Leadership (Increasingly senior managers are losing their jobs over IT, Construction or other big-spend high-profile Projects that have gone wrong: CEOs, Marketers as well as IT/operations specialists)

A sure-fire career route?

According to a report in April 2008[65] by the specialist recruitment consultancy, Robert Half, nearly one in three of the CEOs of 200 leading companies (the FTSE 100 and S&P's Global 100) had a background in finance, with the UK proportion nearly 40%. By the following year, in response to the Credit Crunch, over three quarters of newly-appointed FTSE 100 CEOs had a strong financial background.[66] Meanwhile, the world-renowned management consultancy firm, McKinsey & Company, states on its website that over 150 of its former employees are now CEOs of companies with a turnover of $1 billion or more[67]. Why are high-flying accountants and management consultants currently in demand in business? How are they disproportionately getting the top jobs over the heads of comparably well-qualified Chartered Engineers in engineering companies, marketers in FMCG companies, and IT and industry specialists across the board?

The reason is that their training and experience enables them to tick so many desirable boxes, not only in their own area but also across the range of necessary advanced skills. Like the financiers, they come with the guarantee of a rigorous training in tricky areas of corporate management. A key current external factor is supply and demand: surprisingly few candidates have demonstrable experience in the varied Board-level leadership roles, particularly financial and strategic, that suddenly become key skills when you are running a major corporation. Of course, an accountant or management consultant may turn out to be an incompetent CEO or MD because they may lack any number of less easily measured abilities, such as trades unions negotiation skills or even business flair, but the fact is that on paper they are a safe bet when you need to ensure that your company will survive the next economic downturn by having its finances in order and a clear, ruthless strategy in place. If you compare your own skills and experience to the ideal job specifications for the job you are doing now, and the one you hope to do next, what type of training do you need?

Personal Development Plan

In contrast to the good old days of genuine company career planning, the Personal Development Plan is now a form-filling exercise usually drawn up by employees for themselves, in a rush late on the day before annual appraisals are due to take place, and then agreed with the line manager and the HR Department, indicating the level of training and practical experience they need to acquire to progress (or *remain*) within the company. Ambitious employees will no doubt develop their own separate plan, which may or may not share with the HR Department. Ideally someone, usually HR, also sets out objectives for the company workforce overall, and plans for how the employees are going to acquire the genuinely necessary skills from amongst the entire flip-chart of skills the management have insisted are essential for the company to hit next year's targets. Skills get outdated, and new skills are constantly needed, so this process of personal development is "lifelong learning".

The professional bodies have taken this on board in the form of Continuous Professional Development (CPD), which is in theory the way to avoid getting left behind. Retraining is high on the UK government agenda: it has already asked Universities to create up to 10,000 extra places, funded partly by the taxpayer and partly by employers, for older workers possibly on evening, weekend or part-time courses. This is a cunning plan to address two problems simultaneously: firstly, the expansion of places for the teenage population which will peak in 2010 but then drop by 12% over the next decade – the fees from mature students can supplement the declining funding from school-leavers; secondly, the employability of the older workforce will be extended, thus saving public funds as they continue to create rather than only consume wealth.

Career Crunch!

The solution to updating all your skills: the One-Day Training Course

In-house, day-release and evening training courses are all on offer to employees in various companies, but are they genuinely useful? For instance: the much-vaunted One-Day Training Course. Why do one-day executive courses on "Analysing Reports & Accounts for Non-accountants" almost invariably start with:

"A market stall-holder buys some apples to sell. The entry in his accounts will look like this:"

We don't care, and we'll never get through to 'Potential misinterpretations arising from differing accounting policies in the oil industry' by tea-time if you start in this pedestrian way. The problem is that this kind of course, in order to be credible, is usually run by a qualified accountant, who thinks of it as an inadequate crash-course for inferior beings who secretly wish they were proper accountants, rather than an introduction to one of many necessary business skills.

Instead, a more interesting course-leader starts with: "Here are the accounts of Easyjet/Virgin etc. published last week. What can you tell me about their profits? What can't you tell? What have you heard on the News about the financial environment this company is working in?" This approach will stimulate much more engagement and participation from the class, who will look for what they can get out of the accounts based on their general knowledge and then be more open to investigating the underlying principles. Of course, this way the participants will end the day still not knowing what entry the stall-holder's book-keeper put into his T-accounts for the purchase of those apples, but you may have enabled some participants to pick up a set of accounts and make an initial stab at analysing them, and dare to query any analysis done for them. Not bad for one day's work!

Ambitious new recruits to management consulting are keen to ditch all their preconceptions in order to learn from scratch the rigorous methodology of "The McKinsey way" of analysing business, and a couple of years later they have been trained into sophisticated clones, all working to a high, consistent standard, presenting fluently at Board Level, smooth and interpersonally skilled to the highest level. The majority of experienced adults, however, are resistant to re-learning skills and facts which seem inconsistent with either their experience of the world or their previous training. In that sense only they are harder to teach. An older experienced teacher, who can credibly explain the business theory to a more sceptical audience grounded in hard-nosed practical realities, is more likely to gain their respect

Where can you get training?
There are millions of pounds of funding and thousands of colleges providing hundreds of courses. The government is so desperate to train people that they have resorted to stating their intention to incarcerate young people in schools until they either learn something or reach the age of eighteen. If you want training, just stand in the middle of any town and shout: "I need skills training!" and a civil servant will run out and usher you onto a computer terminal. There are subsidies and bursaries and apprenticeships and company sponsorships for skills ranging from basic English Language to Law, with numerous courses on "Using eBay"! There are day-release, full-time study, residential courses, evening courses, one-day courses, home study for a term or as many years as it takes, or on the job training and assessment. There are schools, colleges, universities, institutions, private educational establishments and company training schemes in every town. *The Appendix lists a few of the hundreds of Institutions and useful websites.*

For most employees there is no longer a clear career path on which they can plan to progress through five or six relevant positions from trainee through to a secure position as an experienced middle-manager, and possibly up to director. Old skills are being superseded ever more rapidly and new skills are mainly offered to the young who are seen as a better long-term investment, despite an increasing likelihood of their changing companies every few years. However, training will increasingly be the personal responsibility of each individual, as will career planning and pensions provision. Each of us has to plan for a long life which will not develop as expected - after all, even the venerable Adam didn't exactly have a smooth career – he didn't escape being thrown out of his cosy sinecure through no fault of his own, and left to make his own way in the harsh world outside the Garden of Eden. No doubt this change in his circumstances necessitated the acquisition of some new skills and a willingness to reinvent himself as a worker and start over again from scratch. But by all accounts he certainly made the best of the situation.

So what is stopping us from celebrating our new-found longevity? The actuaries know the precise figures, but all of us have the gut feeling that something fundamental doesn't add up. What are these numbers that everyone is so worried about? *Chapter Four* delves deeper into 'We-Pay-As-They-Go' Pensions apartheid and Baby Boomer Bulges.

Chapter Four

Ten thousand UK centenarians: *long life is expensive*

There are now well over *10,000 centenarians*[68] in the UK – and counting! By 2020 this number is set to double, and by 2056 it is predicted to be nearly 300,000![69] This graph shows the exponential increase in centenarians in England and Wales over the one hundred years since 1911:

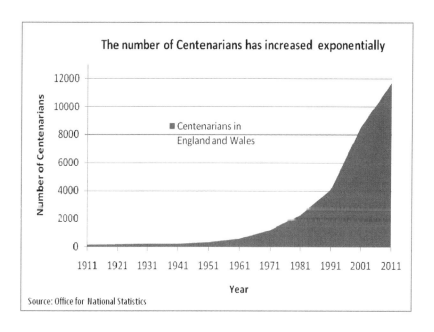

Meanwhile, in keeping with its much larger population, the USA has five times as many centenarians as the UK, with the total already above 50,000 and rising – by the year 2050 there will be over 600,000 US residents aged one hundred years and over!

Life expectancy has increased astonishingly across the advanced economies. In the UK in 1900 a boy was expected to live to forty-five, and a girl to forty-nine, whereas on the same conservative basis a baby boy born today is expected to live to seventy-eight (eighty-two for women)! Over the last century, dramatic improvements in life expectancy were initially due to improvements in peri-natal care: in 1901 infant mortality still accounted for as many as twenty-five per cent of all deaths. Nowadays, infant mortality accounts for less than one per cent of deaths overall, and infant deaths are down to fewer than five per 1,000 live births, an incredible drop from a rate of over one hundred and fifty at the beginning of the 20th Century[70].

A hundred years ago, more than half of all people died before their forty-fifth birthday, but now this age group only accounts for a tiny four percent of deaths[71]; and whereas in 1901 only about one in eight Britons reached age seventy-five or over, now about two-thirds of the total population reach this ripe old age[72]. This means that more recent increases in life expectancy are due to increases in life span for those who have already reached adulthood: in other words, older people are living on much longer. The more conservative life expectancy numbers are based on what the statisticians call "period life expectancy", and this uses historic figures, whereas the more dramatic "cohort life expectancy" figures are based on updated or projected figures, and these predict *even longer* lifespans for wealthy nations. As a result, the statisticians are expecting people to live longer than *they themselves* expect to live! Managing expectations is a key task for leaders of industry or society, and in this case encouraging people to be more optimistic about their life expectancy could be crucial to the stability of future society.

What does this mean for State pensions?
When state pensions were first introduced into the UK in 1908, they were more a charity than a due: they were non-contributory and means-tested and only available to the over-seventies, at a time when life-expectancy at birth for men was forty-nine (fifty-three for women). So pensions were set to pay out twenty-one years *after* the average man was expected to have died – the equivalent of at least age ninety-nine today!

Career Crunch!

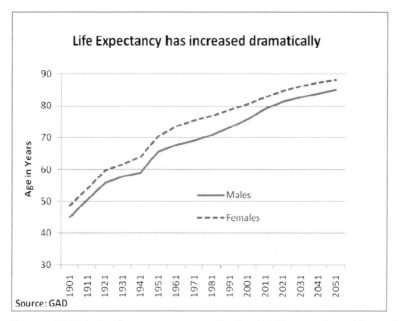

Source: ONS (using the more conservative 'period life expectancy' figures)

Even in 1946, when the National Insurance Act introduced compulsory contributory state pensions for everyone, life expectancy for a man was sixty-four, and two years later, when the State Pension Age was set at sixty-five for men, it had already inched up to sixty-six. So this time the pension age was set one year before the average man was expected to die, the equivalent of age seventy-seven today! Women were puzzlingly set to receive a pension at the lower age of sixty, even though their life expectancy in 1948 was already seventy.[73] So whilst a male pensioner was expected to die soon after he started drawing his pension, a female pensioner even back then could expect to draw her pension for ten years after she retired!

A sixty-five-year-old male retiring now on a state pension in Britain can expect to keep drawing that pension for at least eighteen years,[74] and a woman retiring now at the current State Pension Age (SPA) of sixty will on average draw her state pension for at least twenty-five years – so even when the pension ages are all equalised at sixty-five she will still draw her pension for twenty years! The predictions for new-born babies improve (or from the funding perspective, *deteriorate*) into the future: using the more optimistic

Career Crunch!

projections boys *born* in 2008 are predicted to live up to age eighty-eight[75] and girls to ninety-two years! The State Pension Age has been slightly increased by the UK government, but it is too little, too late. For women born from 1955 onwards it has now been increased to the same age as men[76], and into the future, between 2024 and 2046 it will increase gradually to age sixty-eight for everyone, but this still means that the new baby boys (and girls) are set to draw their pensions for at least twenty (and twenty-four) years on average!

As a result, funding for pensions is near crisis–point, particularly in the public sector: this alone is a liability for the country of over a trillion pounds (£1,000 billion) according to a leading firm of consultants, Towers Watson Wyatt. They issued a press release in March 2010 claiming that the UK government has underestimated the liability of unfunded public sector pensions, which they say is almost double the already huge official £770 billion (half our annual GDP) and really stands at £1.2 trillion, or not far off the entire UK annual output[77]! The huge deficit for the private pensions in all FTSE 350 companies[78] would be wiped out if it were assessed on the same lenient basis! Teachers, the NHS, civil servants, the Armed Forces and the police all have *unfunded* pension schemes. This means that whilst these employees *do* make a contribution to their pensions out of their salaries, the major part of the fund needed to pay out their guaranteed final salary pensions simply does not exist, because instead of insisting that the employer puts it aside ready, as companies are obliged to do, the government is paying *present* pensions out of *present* taxation and leaving *future* pensions to *future* taxes.

This system, known as 'Pay-As-You-Go' pensions funding, really turns out to be "We–Pay-As-They-Go". This was a perfectly reasonable approach when the system was first started with only a few pensioners, but it never received the radical overhaul necessary to address the massive increase in the number of pensioners, and this is now half a century overdue. Even the official figures published by the UK Government in the form of the Public Expenditure Statistical Analysis has projected a series of increases in the necessary funding including £27 *billion* in 2010/11 alone - and much worse is yet to come.

Final-salary pensions discourage mobility and flexibility in the workforce, and, with increasing longevity, are financially unsustainable. What employee with any gumption is going to agree to take a lower-paid job to gain experience if this affects not only her present income, but significantly diminishes her long-term pension income? What trades union is ever going to agree to the raising of its members' pension age? What benefit is there for its members? The Pensions Policy Institute (PPI) has stated that public-sector pension benefits are worth between five and twenty percent on top of salary. And the situation has been getting worse - between 1998 and 2005 numbers of public sector employees rose to over twenty percent of the workforce[79] - in other words, over one in five employees are working for the government on generous guaranteed pensions, to be paid for by the next generation. Whereas public sector workers used to be less well paid, this too has changed: the average full-time wage in the public sector in November 2009 was £459 a week, a rise of 4% over the preceding three months[80] - higher than the £447 earned in the private sector, which had dropped slightly. Almost all public sector employees (about 90%) belong to 'defined benefit' pension schemes, compared with less than one in eight private sector workers (12%),

Public sector employment is rising across Europe as well as in Britain, and strong unions in these massive organisations ensure that their members are very expensive to make redundant. Employment laws are even less flexible in mainland Europe, where wages and employees are described as "sticky" - across Europe, unemployment had remained high since the jobless recovery after the bursting of the dot-com bubble at the turn of the millennium, and this unresponsiveness to market growth is described by the term "Eurosclerosis". The reasons for that "jobless recovery" were complex, including increased productivity and computerisation, but one further attraction of employing more machines instead of people is that employment laws do not apply to them, and they don't require crippling redundancy pay-offs or pensions.

Career Crunch!

Pensions did rise up the public agenda in 2009 with the shocking revelation that the failed banker Sir Fred Goodwin had taken early retirement at the age of fifty, with a pension pot variously valued at around £16 million which would pay out upwards of £693,000 a year for the rest of his life. So some private sector workers, it turned out, were doing rather well on such previously unpublicised benefits. Indeed, the population seems even more financially divided in old age than during their working life, with the State pension set at £4,716 but (because not everyone has built up full benefits) only paying out £3,500 on average; private pensions averaging £5,000 compared with public sector pensions at £7,000, and then, far, far away at the other end of the scale, Gordon Brown with an accumulated pension already standing at £87,000 and numerous top executives receiving annual pensions of £200,000 and more – eight times the average national wage every year of their retirement.

Beware: "Pensions Crunch" in the making!

In the midst of a global financial meltdown caused by the breaking of the link between lender and borrower, another clever financial innovation is emerging. At a time when a vast global insurer has had to be bailed out by the US government because it is "too big to fail" (AIG), and debatably took on excessive poorly understood financial risk including on derivatives such as swaps, pensions schemes are being invited to insure unanticipated longevity – "longevity risk" - with counter-parties offering insurance. So, when the longevity that we are all expecting is not adequately factored in by the pension schemes, they will turn to the insurers. Who in turn, if the current situation were to repeat itself, will not have made adequate allowance for it either. But the problem will be too serious to let it take its course, so governments will have to bail out impoverished pensioners, and if the 2009 crisis is anything to go by, any more prudent private pensions investments will suffer as their funds are weighed down by the unanticipated longevity burden. Pension schemes are starting to take up these 'longevity swaps', which mirror the structure of an interest rate or inflation swap. In 2009 the major industrial company Babcock International had one of the first pension schemes to enter the market. So far the reaction reported from the Pensions Regulator is that he is urging schemes to use realistic assumptions. Given recent events, how likely does it seem that the financiers are going to err on the side of caution? In a few years' time, when swaps and options will have lost their current stigma and been reinstated into the derivatives catalogue, how many of the new generation will remember their disastrous failure across the world? And that point could signal the world's readiness to re-enter the whole downward vortex, as the pension funds collapse, dragged down by underestimated longevity and the swaps that were meant to underwrite it, compounding the suffering for the hundreds of centenarians who have lived too long.

Now that sixty is the new forty, pensions across the board need to be adjusted to reflect this. Giant private companies are facing up to the problem by closing their pension schemes to new members. In 2009 Barclays[81] announced plans to close its final salary pension scheme to nearly 18,000 existing members, having closed it to new members back in 1997. Only a few other firms have taken this step, such as Rentokil and WH Smith, and those companies, had to face angry members. BP had just announced that it planned to close its final salary pension scheme to new members, making it one of the last FTSE 100 companies to do so. Such moves are immensely unpopular, especially with the Trades Unions, and Lloyds Bank trades unions demanded a guarantee that their final salary scheme would be kept open.

According to the Office for National Statistics, there are more lower-paid workers in the *private* sector than in the state sector, and these people particularly, on low pay and with negligible benefits, will constitute an underclass of impoverished pensioners, to say nothing of a drain on public resources, as any pension funds they may have become terminally exhausted before they do. The figures make it clear that no sector of the population can reasonably be guaranteed a pension from the State, unless that pension is fully and demonstrably funded in advance - and yet this is still the contractual right of public sector employees; no privileged section of the population can reasonably continue to be promised retirement as early as age sixty – yet, in October 2005, this pledge was renewed to millions of public sector employees by the UK government in the face of threatened strikes.

Funds for pensions also need to be completely sealed off for that purpose only so that they can be easily monitored and preserved. The official term for this is apparently "hypothecated" – doesn't it sound so much less worrying to say "*our pension funds are not hypothecated*" than "*they can be borrowed for other uses*" or even "*they are no longer there at all*". A state pension has been promised to every single qualifying OAP, and this is in theory funded (along with Unemployment Benefit) by National Insurance Contributions, which provide nearly £100 billion, or getting on for a fifth of UK government revenues in 2010-2011. Yet although the National Insurance Fund is in theory hypothecated, so that its revenues can only be spent for its stated purpose, in practice the government borrows these revenues for investments, for example in the NHS. This practice is in danger of turning NI Contributions into another "stealth tax", not sufficiently rigorously ring-fenced, a further element of the pensions time-bomb.

Yet bad news as the 'pensions apartheid' between the public and private sectors may be for the UK as a whole, it appears to be relatively good news for some older workers, because the public sector workforce is older than in the private sector. Nearly three-quarters (72%) of public sector workers are aged thirty-five and over, and this is ten percentage points higher than private sector workers (at 62%). They are also more likely to stay longer with their employers: in 2004, 57% of public sector workers had been with their current employer for five years or more, much higher than private sector workers at 45%. They are also more likely to be women and to work part-time than private sector workers: 65% of public sector workers are women, and just under a third work part-time, whilst women form only just over 40% of the private sector workforce, where less than a quarter work part-time[82]. Is this part-time model the employment pattern for the future, or just the most convenient option for older female workers, who often carry out caring roles for relatives at the same time?

Meanwhile the looming problem of an ageing population is being partially obscured by the reassuringly corpulent size of the generation now in the middle of their working lives - the same generation that will in twenty years' time swell that elderly group to unmanageable proportions. The '60s generation of Baby Boomers is enormous compared with the generation above it, and all those Baby Boomers are currently sharing out the burden of supporting the first generation of long-lived pensioners. When the Baby Boomer generation retires, the reverse situation will apply – a huge generation of long-living pensioners will be supported by a much smaller younger generation from the years of low fertility since the '70s. There have been baby booms before – so what is different about this one? Last century, the UK population experienced a total of three baby booms: a sharp peak in births after the end of each World War, and a much more extended bulge from the early 1960s to the beginning of the 1970s, and these are the key features of our present demographic pattern, as graphically illustrated below:

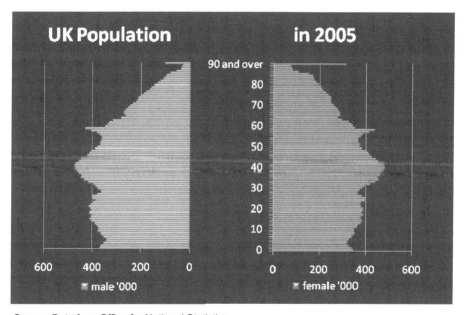

Source: Data from Office for National Statistics

The fascinating chart above also uses figures from the Office for National Statistics whose website displays an exciting interactive graph showing how the pattern of bumps and dips in population age groups varies over time. The static version above shows the numbers of males and females in the UK population by each year of age, as of the year 2005. There's a sharp peak

Career Crunch!

amongst today's sixty-plus-year-olds[83], born after the soldiers returned from the Second World War, and a large bulge of baby-boomers centring on our present forty-plus-year-olds born in the Swinging Sixties. (Ignore the huge peak in the '90 and over' age group, except to note that there are far more women in this group than men – the reason why that peak is so high is that, at the moment, all the oldies are still lumped together – up till now they have been too few to worry about.)

This graph could also double up as a psychometric test to see which readers are naturally analytical and who are naturally dreamers – do you see a series of fascinating statistics - or the profiles of two big-nosed men in hats?

Two old men in hats - with the ageing population and a predicted gradual increase in the longevity of men in line to catch up with women, is this a sign of the future? Although baby peaks occurred after both World Wars, many still died as infants and in the 'flu epidemic that followed the Great War. The Boomers born in 1947, post World War Two, are mainly still alive today, but their births constituted a sharp peak, as you can see from the diagram above: it is the peak of each man's hat that curves steeply back downwards again, in contrast with the 1960's Baby Boom, which is a wide bulge of the old men's bulbous noses, much fatter and curving down much less steeply - the mini skirt, free love and flower power appear to have had a lot to answer for.

This pattern of births has shaped our society into the twenty-first century. The chart below tracks the twin peaks of the Baby Boomer Bulge and the Post Second World War Peak as they move through time across the chart from front to back. The ridge at the front is 1971, where the baby boomers are still young children and the post-war peakers have just entered the workforce. The population pattern moves back and to the right towards the projection for the year 2011, when the post-war peakers have mainly retired, and the '60s baby boomers are in their mid-late forties and aspiring to more senior roles.

Twin Peaks progress through Time

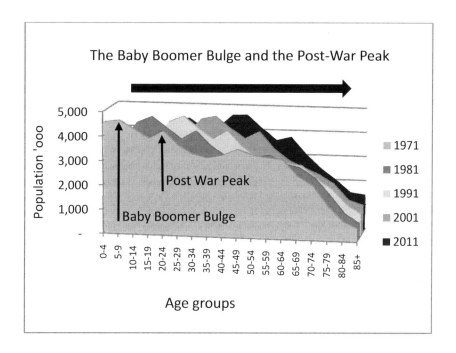

The Baby Boomer Bulge and the Post-War Peak

Source: Data from Office for National Statistics

Yet the Baby Boomer Bulge is now exactly the opposite shape to that which would be required to fill our hour glass economy – a glut of middle-aged would-be managers is oversupplying industry, just at the time when technology has enabled it to reduce its girth of management roles. Oversupply allows recruiters to become very choosy, and this includes indulging their ageist preferences. Therefore the main driver for early redundancies and the proliferation of self-employed consultants and interim managers is directly attributable to a little ageist prejudice and a lot of demographics. Look hard enough, and most abstract ideas and views generally derive from, or defer to, practical reality. Older employees tend to be more expensive, so since there are more of them than are required, you can pick and choose whom you employ.

Nevertheless, the problem is not the number born, but the fact that people are not dying off as they used to. The Baby Boomers are not only still here - they expect to remain here for a very long time:

Death is dying

Rate per million population

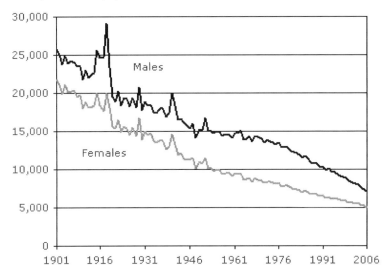

Source: ONS death rates for England and Wales

As you can see in the above graph, apart from peaks during the two World Wars, the death rate fell dramatically over the last hundred years, from nearly 26,000 men per million of the population in 1901, to a mere 7,000 by the year 2006, and for women from 22,000 down to only 5,000! This has further contributed to the ageing of the population. Combine the falling death rate above, with the arrival of a new generation of OAPs, sixty-five years after the Baby Boom, and you get the chart below. It shows how dramatically pensioners grow as a proportion of the UK working population, taking off sharply as the Baby Boomers retire around the year 2030, to form a group almost half the size of the entire working population. The statisticians call this the OAP dependency ratio, and it is predicted to increase dramatically by the year 2051, when today's babies will be reaching middle age.

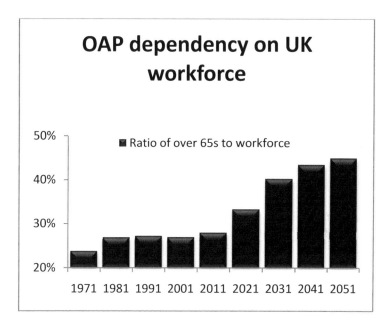

Source: ONS population data

Even taking into account the higher future retirement age of sixty-eight, which is being introduced gradually between 2024 and 2046, the graph barely changes. As a result, the burden of retired people on the working population is even higher and growing, with the ratio of pensioners to workers already nearly one in three today. Of course some pensioners will have their own sources of income – but do not be too reassured by this. Don't forget that a large proportion of the six million public sector workers think they have a pension fund set aside, but in fact the bulk of the pension they have been guaranteed by the government has to be funded out of future taxes, which we hope will be paid by today's babies. And even for those people who have savings in pension funds, the workforce still need to create enough wealth to ensure that those funds retain their value in real terms.

Throughout the OECD, populations are ageing. Japan and Italy already have a big problem, whereas the high birth rates in Mexico, Iceland and Turkey will mitigate their problem in the short term. The UK is in the middle, at about the OECD average. The number of Japan's earners is shrinking both in absolute numbers and as a proportion of the total population, so that in 1950 there were twelve Japanese of working age per person aged sixty-five and over, by the year 2000 this number had reduced to only four, and it is predicted to be as low as 1.7 by the year 2050. The total Japanese population, currently 127 million, is also set to decrease to around 100 million by 2050, whilst fertility rates have dropped to 1.3 babies per woman[84]. The Japanese are so conscientiously saving for their old age that high savings have reduced interest rates to zero per cent at times, and the funds have been invested in so much infrastructure that Japan has an excess of highways, conference facilities and expensive bridges leading literally nowhere.

The problem is exacerbated in France, with one of the lowest state retirement ages in Europe, and special union-negotiated early retirement rights at the giant state gas and electricity companies, as well as at the railway company SNCF, where workers retire at fifty-five and train drivers at fifty. This explains the otherwise mystifying remarks made by France's President, Nicolas Sarkozy, during his presidential campaign, deriding the idea of retiring at fifty, and also explains why, when he took office, he immediately made daring moves to introduce the same retirement age for all employees, despite the failure of a previous attempt to reform the French pensions system which had provoked a government collapse in 1997. He didn't go out of his way to offend the unions for political posturing – he had good macro-economic reasons for doing so. The same applies to his making moves to deny pre-retirement-age British nationals in France the right to free medical care – though it probably did no harm to his domestic popularity ratings anyway - the logic appears to be that so many Britons are fulfilling the "Year in Provence" early retirement dream, that he is seeking ways to avoid the danger that France could go the way of Spain, with the burden on its healthcare exacerbated by the influx of large numbers of British early retirees.

Career Crunch!

OECD Population projections for major global economies

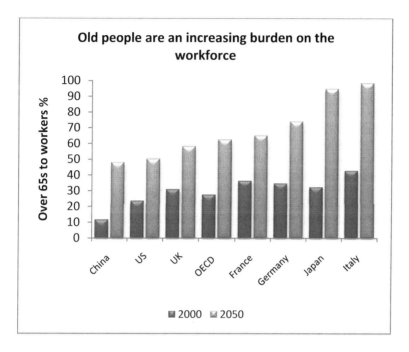

Data sourced from the OECD[85]

China will experience the most extreme change because of its one-child policy: its new pensions situation is in the ratio 1:2:4 representing one child, supporting two parents and *four grandparents* (just stop and think about that!) By 2024 people aged over forty will make up 58% of the Chinese population, with three-quarters of all households childless.

Re-balancing the demographics – will someone please have some babies to pay our pensions?

Even though birth rates in the UK are declining, the population has increased from fifty-five million in 1971 to over sixty million today, due to a combination of the longer-living pensioners and immigration. The elderly are forming a growing proportion of the overall population. And, with UK fertility rates falling, from the peak in 1964 of nearly three children per woman, to only 1.8 children

Career Crunch!

in 2005, we are not producing enough of the next generation to support them and ourselves. This second component of the so-called 'demographic time bomb', at the opposite end of the age spectrum to the problem of an ageing population, is a threat across Europe. In 2007, the fertility rate across the EU was on average only 1.5 babies per woman, with Italy surprisingly low for a traditionally child-friendly nation at 1.3, and Germany little better at 1.4. France, with its looming pensioner crisis, has, as we are finding time and again, taken pre-emptive State action, and offered incentives to mothers to produce more children, and these are literally bearing fruit. Its fertility rate has risen to two, almost the magic 'replacement rate', thanks to cash payments, tax reductions for each extra child and subsidised nannies. Britain's rate has now risen slightly to 1.9[86], but this rise is entirely thanks to immigrant mothers, particularly since the beginning of this century, and still remains below the replacement rate:

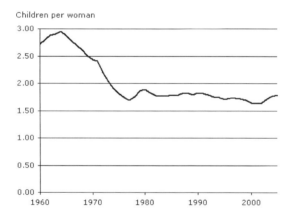

Total Fertility Rate, UK   Source: ONS

One solution is an influx of young workers to fill the gap and even out the ratios. The policies of different governments now reveal their logic. Whilst the French are paying mothers to produce babies, similar macro-economic reasons have prompted the UK to welcome immigration, and the demographic change it has brought about is clearly shown in the following graphs using data from the ONS website. The rate of *net* immigration into the UK rose dramatically during the boom years and continues at around 200,000 people per annum, even after subtracting the migrant workers who started returning home to Eastern Europe in response to the Credit Crunch, and the British residents emigrating either to find work or to spend their retirement in the sun.

Net Immigration to the UK

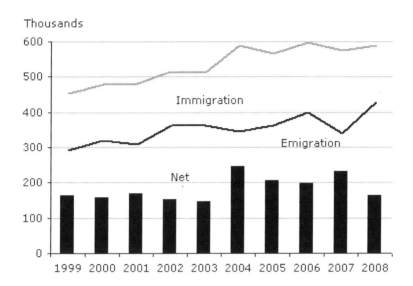

Source: Office for National Statistics[87]

This demographic solution is presumably why in 2004 the UK was one of the few existing member states (along with Ireland and Sweden) to allow the new members such as Poland, the Czech Republic and Lithuania virtually unrestricted access to the UK labour market. (Germany and Austria held out the longest before allowing free access - the EU had in fact agreed an optional delay up to May 2011 before these new citizens had the automatic right to enter EU labour markets). As a result, nearly a million people moved in or out of the UK in 2004, with a net inflow of people well above 200,000[88].

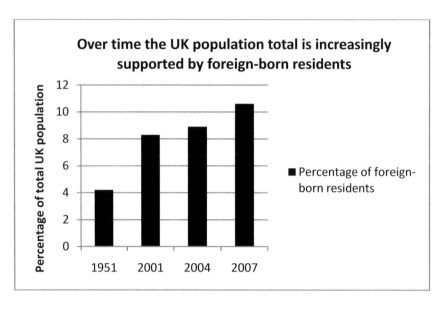

Source: Office for National Statistics

The source of immigration has changed over time. Ireland, India and Pakistan remain in the top five countries of birth of residents born outside the UK (plus movement to and from German military bases), but the Accession of new countries to the European Union in May 2004 brought an increasing number of workers from Eastern Europe, particularly Poland, until the Credit Crunch began to reverse this trend.

The benefits of immigration were recognised by the US over most of its history, and whilst here in the UK we boost our younger generation through immigration from Eastern Europe and the Commonwealth, so the US, which now tightly restricts immigration through its Green Card system, benefits from the high birth-rate of its growing Catholic-Latino ethnic group, who now make up one third of its young people. This group is set to make a major contribution to evening out the US workforce demographics, and may eventually overtake the present white majority to form the largest single group in the United States. Meanwhile, in Japan this solution will not be used to solve the country's demographic imbalance (discussed earlier in this chapter) since it accepts almost no immigrants at all.

Career Crunch!

In addition to bringing younger people into the UK from abroad, the other obvious course is to encourage older workers to stay in the workplace - a major impetus to government projects such as the website *learndirect* and initiatives by government bodies such as NESTA, and of course the 2006 Ageism legislation. Now it becomes clear why governments often drive through legislation that the voters didn't even know they needed. Far from ideology, it appears that it is the study of economics that inspires many politicians and their advisors. So, it seems that as a predictor of government policies, the latest socio-economic reports are far more useful than any political manifesto.

Older workers – a spent force or a growing asset?

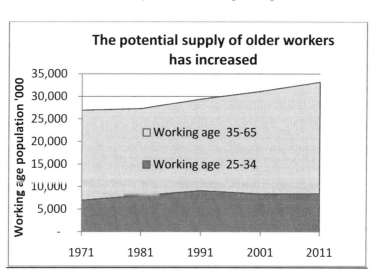

Source: ONS population data

The increase in the numbers of older workers is partly explained by the rising population in general and ageing baby-boomers in particular: there just are more people of that age around. Better healthcare (the ONS reveals that most people who retire early feel they have been forced into retirement by poor health) should enable people to work longer, which will please the actuaries, but also to *die later* – a real downer for the pension providers. Economic imperative is another reason why there are more older workers: they have to take what work they can get to earn hard cash, because their pensions are not worth what they had anticipated since the spate of pensions scandals, tax changes and the credit crunch, and their mortgages will not be fully paid off by their endowment policies for similar reasons[89]. Women are increasingly remaining in the workplace or returning to work once their families are growing up.

What is the reality behind this graph?

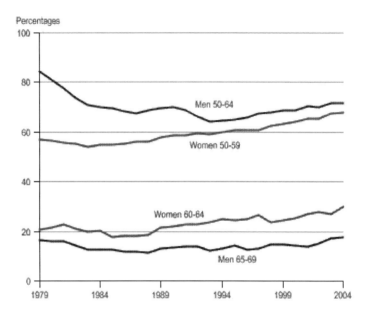

Employment in older people: by sex and age, 1979 to 2004, Great Britain
Source: Office for National statistics

As you can see from the graph, the percentage of older people in employment in Great Britain aged between fifty and state pension age *increased* in recent years.[90] (Looking at the lower pair of lines, the trend is also for workers to continue beyond the state pension age.) But this is only part of the story, because the growth is only reversing a major previously downward trend, and has still not reached the level of employment back in 1979. According to a report for the Centre for Analysis of Social Exclusion[91], the number of jobs for men aged over 50 declined by 600,000 between 1979 and 1999, and in contrast to the *one*-fifth of men without work over the age of fifty in 1979, there were *two*-fifths by 1999. Meanwhile older women's employment increased steadily from the 1980s, particularly in part-time work, but less dramatically than general female participation in the workforce.

The graph does not show whether older employees are working in the same positions as they were when they were younger, or in equally senior positions – far from an upward progression, they may have had to take a cut in pay or status if their main job became redundant. This is borne out by figures from the Annual Survey of Hours and Earnings in the UK, showing that men in work over the age of fifty had an hourly wage of £10.95 per hour, compared with men in their forties who earned £12.77 per hour.[92] The rise may represent employees who are being kept on longer at their work, running their self-employed businesses for longer, or being retired off from their first job and taking on interim/temporary or part-time work, often consulting into their seventies.

And then, what does being "*employed*" actually mean? To be precise, the definition of "*employed*" is working *one hour* in the reference week when the survey was conducted - not at all the full working week the graph implies! This leads to all sorts of confusion, not least that a 17-year-old in full-time school can also be "employed" if she has a small part-time job, or even "unemployed" if she can't get one! Here's the official definition verbatim:

"People aged 16 or over are classed as employed by the Labour Force Survey (LFS) if they have   done at least one hour of work in the reference week." (Source: Office for National Statistics)

The category "Employed" also includes *unpaid* workers in family businesses owned by themselves or a relative! I must be missing something here, but whilst I can see that these employees are indeed busy working, I've always tended to think of 'employees' and 'remuneration' as the kind of pair you might link together in one of those psychometric tests. So don't rush off and pop the corks yet: "*rising employment amongst the over 50s*" turns out to mean that if

Career Crunch!

in 2004 you were over fifty and were thrown out of your comfortably paid job, you had about a 8% higher chance of finding at least one hour's work a week (albeit maybe as an unpaid family worker) than you did in 1993. Whoopee!

The way people are employed is also a technicality which makes the figures more difficult to get at. Whilst short-term consultants are often 'self-employed' for tax purposes, in order to pay lower National Insurance Contributions (if they can justify this status by working for more than one firm at a time), 'temps' are usually employed by their agencies, such as Manpower, (which in the 1990s was reported by Time magazine as the largest employer in the United States), as are some longer-term interim managers, although these are, for technical reasons, also often employed by their own companies, classed as 'micro-companies', or 'enterprises with no employees' (i.e. employing themselves). At least this way they're unlikely to get fired.

As a result, when asked in a survey to classify their employment status, they might respond "temporary worker" but they might equally well categorise themselves as either 'unemployed' (when they are between jobs), or as a permanent 'employee' of their own (micro-) company specially set up for the purpose (despite the inconvenience and irritation) and so may not feature in the 'temp' classification at all. The number of people working in micro-companies (1-4 employees), *did* increase significantly in the mid 1990s. Overall, there has been a small increase in people who are either self-employed or working in micro-companies, and this is probably because older workers are managing to find some work as consultants or interim managers.

Some researchers[93] call temporary or part-time jobs for older workers, "bridge jobs", because they can offer a more flexible emotional and life-style bridge between full-time work and retirement, but equally they may simply be a bridge across the gulf of unpaid bills which pile up on the mat of the redundant permanent manager. Whatever their purpose, the researchers found that it is only the more educated professionals with a good network of contacts who are able to get these 'bridge' jobs, as would indeed be the case for interim managers and consultants. The pattern is confirmed when we learn that these workers have often "chosen" to take voluntary early retirement from professional or managerial positions. Until recently more people were retiring at a younger age, particularly between 1979 and 1999[94]. This pattern was evident not only in the UK but also in the US.[95]

At a time when employees still felt they could rely on their pension providers, and a large young workforce was entering the market from the late 1970s, early retirement seemed a good solution to free up jobs for younger people, here in the UK and eventually on the other side of the globe in China. Manufacturing decline displaced another group of older workers. Some workers are taking retirement from one company - not always at their own initiative - and, where they can, going to work for another, so whereas twenty years ago they might have felt able to retire early and relax, they now have to take on some other kind of work. According to the Employers' Forum on Age, the UK's average retirement age is 63.8 years but the Department for Work and Pensions found about one in ten people over pension age still working in 2006.[96]

Working beyond the State Pension Age is more common in small companies[97] and generally older workers are more common amongst the self-employed. Why do self-employed workers stay on longer? One reason might be that their National Insurance Contributions do not cover Unemployment, so they cannot afford to stop seeking work, or that they haven't saved enough pension to retire. It might be that self-employed men are more committed to their work or that they enjoy their work because they are in charge so they want to stay on longer. Or perhaps, because no one can turn round to them and say they are too old, they stay on as long as they are economically useful. (Though perhaps the younger generation, if they hope to inherit the business, or if their promotion prospects are based on "dead men's shoes", might disagree). On the bright side, there is more for older people to spend their money on – with better health, longer life expectancy and more holidays designed for the over-fifties, there is also more incentive to take a job or stay in a job to pay for the extra fun.

Old entrepreneurs

The US economy has the same problem of an ageing population, and its people are trying the same solutions. As a result of consolidation, small firms are being bought up, leaving fewer openings for small start-ups, in the UK as well as in America, but whilst overall self-employment in the US fell over the last decade, the exception is amongst older entrepreneurs, perhaps driven by necessity. The trend challenges conventional wisdom that entrepreneurs are mostly young and bucks the trend: in the US overall, as in the UK, self-employment fell over the last decade. This move to start again at a time when workers had been getting used to thinking about retirement is further discussed in *Chapter Six*.

Can someone be neither employed nor self-employed, nor unemployed?

In total there are about eight million 'economically inactive' people of working age, and of these in 2006 there were 2.7 million people aged between fifty and the state pension age who were not in work but able to work, of whom up to one million wished to work.

Other misleading statistics about people seeking work

Official UK statistics are carefully compiled, but they are only as good as the responses that their official surveys request and receive, and as the conclusions that variously-motivated analysts choose to draw from them, so not only can they themselves be inaccurate but then they can be used (or abused) misleadingly. It's a familiar phrase on the radio: "the number of people out of work *and claiming benefit*". The figure being quoted here for "Unemployment" is only about half what it should be – that is, too low by up to a million jobless souls. It isn't a secret, if you know where to look. The Office for National Statistics states clearly on its website:

"Unemployment is different from the claimant count, which measures only those unemployed people who are claiming unemployment-related benefits (Jobseeker's Allowance and National Insurance Credits). The claimant count is normally the lower measure because some unemployed people are not entitled to claim unemployment-related benefits, or choose not to do so."

Career Crunch!

Unemployment figures are still sometimes presented using the lower "Claimant Count" figures based on workers claiming Jobseeker's Allowance (numbering 1.6 million in December 2009), instead of the official unemployment figures based on the quarterly International Labour Force Survey (2.5 million Sept-Nov 2009). This latter measure is carried out every quarter, and divides people of working age into three major groups: those in "employment" (about 29 million); those "unemployed" (actively seeking work and available for work); and those who are "economically inactive" (about 8 million), including people not seeking work because they are at home with children, because they are students, or because they are too unwell to work and are claiming Incapacity Benefit. The most blatant use of the lower jobless figures was in the 2010 Budget speech when the Chancellor, Alistair Darling, shamelessly quoted the Claimant Count, thereby neatly forgetting nearly half the unemployed people in the UK!

Many redundant older managers are not included in the "Claimant Count" because it is not worth their while to sign on. For a start, the hurdles to claiming benefit are more onerous than in the past, when the first thing any redundant employee was advised to do was to "go and sign on". They have to go back regularly to the Job Centre to "sign on" to be quizzed about their job search, and this is disruptive if they are attending a large number of interviews around the country. If they are managers, they are hoping to get another job soon that pays £40 - £60,000 plus, so to go through what many see as a humiliating process does not seem worth it to get £60 a week, or £1,500 for six months, a sum that they hope to earn in a week or two when they get a new job. Initially, new signers who have been made redundant do not even receive any Job Seeker's Allowance for time for which they have been paid in lieu of notice, which may be a couple of weeks or a few months.

It is also usually officially assumed that more senior employees have received six months' money as a pay-off, so they will not receive their benefits before that period has elapsed, and yet they still have to make their way to the Unemployment Office and sign on every two weeks. Even then they are only eligible for six months' money, after which time they will only get Job Seeker's

Allowance if they have almost no income or savings – and this does not apply to most middle-to-senior managers.

Also, after six months, if you are over fifty or under twenty-five, you currently get the "New Deal", presented by government as a great deal, but more like a raw deal if you are in the midst of long drawn-out interview procedures for senior management positions, as it obliges you to attend special courses to be told by an earnest clerk how to write a CV and apply for jobs. Furthermore, the way National Insurance Contributions (NICs) work is that employers and employees have to pay towards pensions and unemployment benefit, whereas the self-employed pay a slightly lower rate of NICs but get no contributions-based unemployment cover. (They could get income-based cover but this is means-tested.) After about six months of job-seeking many managers have registered to work as self-employed consultants to tide them over until they get a permanent position, and this will over time make them ineligible for the Job Seeker's Allowance (JSA) even if their consulting work dries up.

As a result there are disproportionally few professionals and managers on the Unemployment register, even those who have been jobseeking for a year or more. Since it is not worth their while 'signing on', they do not do so, and conveniently they therefore do not feature in the "Claimant Count" statistics at all: they simply disappear. Professional statisticians are fully aware of these discrepancies in the Unemployment numbers, so it isn't a problem. Unless you happen to be everybody else.

Professor Steven Fothergill of Sheffield Hallam University and his co-authors have produced research into why the overall figures for UK employment appeared, before the Credit Crunch, to be increasing. According to his study, "The Real Level of Unemployment"[98], it did not come from unemployed people getting jobs: it came from a combination of women returners, people staying on longer and not taking early retirement, and from massive immigration, mainly from Eastern Europe, particularly Poland. Meanwhile, he argued that even the higher and more representative unemployment figures from the Labour Force Survey are too low, because they do not include any of the people on Incapacity Benefit, which is more generous, is not means-tested, and once established has not hitherto continued to be reassessed. On the basis of these figures he identified a total of 1.7 million *hidden* jobless within the 2.7 million total on Incapacity Benefit, which he argued should go *on top of* the official figure of just under one million for the official "Claimant count" at that time. In a newly harsh economic environment Professor Fothergill's revelations have prodded governmental interest and new targets to reduce the total number of people claiming these benefits.

Other official government statistics that are misleading, if you don't look at what they're *really* measuring, are the numbers for UK Public Sector Employees, as mentioned above. Did it really sound convincing when we were told that these numbers had been going *down*? Well, that is what the government had been saying; that is what the economists were saying; that is what the journalists were saying – because that is what the numbers appeared to say. But what were they *really* measuring and where did they start measuring? In fact, numbers went down to 1998 and have been rising more or less ever since, the rise only mitigated by an innovation called *Public-Private Partnerships*. Yes, over 150,000 workers[99] who used to work in the "public sector" now work in "Public-private partnerships" staffed by private sector companies such as SERCO and CAPITA. They do the same job, for example working at "leisure centres" which used to be the municipal baths, but they don't work for the government any more.

The motivation for this arrangement is not clear, but its effect might have been to bring more funding into public amenities although, one way or another, existing pensions arrangements have generally been negotiated to remain the ultimate responsibility of the government. It certainly reduced the official number of public sector employees, and even convinced some eminent economists that a number of new jobs were being created by the private sector, when in fact they were the same public sector jobs under a new employer. The official figures have not been re-worked and re-stated to take this into account, because this would apparently be even more confusing. So if you don't know what's behind the numbers, and don't have time to make the huge effort necessary to find out, then *caveat emptor.*

Money is the root of all......... passionate statistical analysis!

Passions are not often aroused by pure statistics and a row about immigration was no exception – the root cause was not accuracy or pedantry, but money. Not necessarily the root of all evil, but certainly the root cause of local Councils' sudden passionate interest in the immigration statistics. The problem was that their grants from the government assumed a certain headcount which they claimed was being massively underestimated by the government, using ONS data, and giving far too low a figure for Eastern European immigrants. Because of the largely underestimated influx of Polish and other workers to the area, there are therefore far more children in the schools in Slough, more people registered with its doctors and more houses needed, than the government made allowance for when it calculated Slough's grant.

Councils closely examined the official figures and how they were collected and protested vociferously, armed with new statistical insights. The ONS understated the figures for the UK's increasing Eastern European workforce because it used an airport survey in which immigrants to the UK were asked how long they intend to stay. Fearful of legal restrictions and unsure of the implications of their answers, many immigrants said "less than one year". Perhaps at that stage they did only intend to stay for a few months to make some money. But as in many centres of economic immigration throughout the world, the short-term migrants adapt and stay on, and play havoc with the carefully compiled official data, which does not record them as longer-term immigrants.

Then in early 2009 a major row erupted yet again between the egregiously inoffensive and apolitical ONS and the UK Labour government, just for issuing statistics about the proportion of UK residents who were born abroad, statistics that were sitting there on its website, accessible to every member of the public. This data was due to be issued soon afterwards in a regular release, but drawing attention to them at a politically sensitive i.e. *relevant* moment was apparently not a statistician's helpful duty, but an act of wilful political subversion. This is presumably because of the sensitive and controversial nature of immigration data. It is presumably also because, even though the data were already there for all to see, no-one had actually bothered to look for quite a while, whereas in reaction to the ONS release highlighting the figures, the tabloids carried indignant headlines the next day. The Immigration Minister[100] went so far as to accuse the ONS of "sinister" behaviour – that issuing regularly collected, openly displayed, accurate statistics can be dubbed "sinister" by a government of any country is the truly sinister aspect to the story.

If your own experience suggests that the official statistics are wrong, then there's a fair chance that you are right and the statistics are misleading. Our own Office for National Statistics does a heroic job of compiling data from a wide variety of disparate sources: surveys with inconsistent aims and methodologies; scrappy forms filled in by lowly employees with no resources from their companies except the instructions "just don't rock the boat", and whose line managers see the exercise as nothing but a cost, even if their top bosses publicly support it. Nevertheless, ONS staff remain diligent, well-informed and proudly impartial in their provision of the most accurate data possible in the most trying of circumstances. It must be heart-breaking for them when eminent economists, journalists and successive governments themselves, use or abuse this very carefully defined data with cavalier superficiality. Support them in their quest for truth and follow the maxim: Better humiliated than manipulated – challenge the data!

Chapter Five

Short-Term Fixes: *What can I do now?*

Since the Credit Crunch, the problem of redundancy has become acute across the age spectrum and workers of all ages are asking the same questions and pursuing the same solutions. Whilst there are hundreds of articles, leaflets, books and internet sites on this subject, there still remain a number of less candidly-discussed aspects of mid-career job-seeking. The following irreverent but pragmatic exposition of these is designed to inspire, goad, caution or console a redundant middle manager in his quest for his next job.

Many adults, particularly men, still consider themselves to be defined by their work. As a result, the loss of their job initially causes anger, but after a year this subsides into depression, and the belief that they will never find another job. This is a self-fulfilling prophecy to be avoided at all costs by instituting a regime of job-applications and training, and setting up a new regular routine to avoid morale-sapping daily re-examination and recrimination.

Career Crunch!

There are plenty of steps to keep the redundant older worker fully occupied and even stressed, if a workplace-like existence is desired. The following are some less frequently-mentioned examples:

Love your present employer

Ironically, the first thing to do when you are being made redundant is to take an enormous interest in your soon-to-be-ex-employer. *Why?* Because no matter how much you avoided talking shop when you were employed, you will have to spend a lot of time talking about your company, your role, and the broader business you were in, once you are looking for a new job. You will have to know your company's turnover, profitability, staff levels, global markets, customer profiles, and all the same facts for each of the company's major competitors, to a level of detail that your own role never demanded when you were actually doing it. In fact, if you are living in fear of, or even happily contemplating, the prospect of redundancy at the moment, this tactic may have an unexpected spin-off: your new apparent interest in your employer and insight into its problems may just swing the pendulum from redundancy to promotion.

Don't jump at voluntary redundancy

Next, stop and think before you apply for voluntary redundancy. A pay-off of one year's money may seem like a fortune now, and the lump sum on offer may sound even higher if a pension uplift is included, but remember how long it can take to get another job. Your increased pension is prudent, but can only be enjoyed later on; and one year's money may be used up before your next pay cheque comes in. If you are able to line up another potential employer, then a redundancy pay-off could indeed be manna from Heaven. If you have been planning a business venture and just needed a lump sum to start it off, it could also be a godsend. However, if you have worked for the same company for twenty years and don't have a clear business proposition, a business plan and in-depth knowledge of the sector you wish to enter, as well as the explicit support of your spouse/partner, running your own company may be more of a challenge than you think. Resist the academic text books advising you airily to "become an entrepreneur": your career, your house and your marriage and are all at stake if it doesn't work out.

Up-and-out-and-roundabout Careers – Sideways, downwards and upwards
The traditional paternalistic boss never cedes authority until he or she relinquishes the top job, either willingly or under duress. Unlike a rotating Presidency or Chair, it is rare to find a rotating Chief Executive. A rigid hierarchical legacy from a former era combines with rapid promotion for rising stars to create a log-jam just under the top management level. Any departures, voluntary or otherwise, from either of these levels, are likely to be greeted with private enthusiasm from surviving colleagues, as they leave more room for everyone else. Only a complete culture change, which acknowledges that a career, like life, may at times seem more like a game of snakes and ladders than a Pilgrim's Progress, will enable a company to offer suitable alternative positions to good staff by moving them into different roles, and will allow management, duly compensated for any reduction in income, to remain in the company but move both up and down levels within it.

Identify Transferable skills
As with researching your current employer, in preparation for your exit, identifying your transferable skills just might help you to identify areas where you could apply them within your *current* place of work. Skills can be divided into two groups:

1.   Broad general abilities such as: people management, organisation; project management. Employers may insist that these elusive skills are essential, but then prefer to take them as read.

2.   Specific skills such as: management accountancy; website design; H&S; legal; making people redundant without triggering tribunals.

Then you need to convince your targeted employer that your skills are what he needs. You will be more attractive in most functional roles if you have kept your practical skills up to date, and you will certainly need to demonstrate that you are au fait with all recent market developments, at least through reading the trade press, attending trade fairs etc.

Develop a Personal Brand; Plan your own up-and-out-and-roundabout career
Develop your Personal Brand throughout your life, build your CV, keep it up to date and front of mind so you can sell yourself at all opportunities. Who are you? What can you do? What are you aiming for? You need to have a career strategy, not just to get to the top, but as a medium term survival plan. You would ideally present a solid career with posts of responsibility, achievements and a reasonable tenure but not too long - say three years. Tell the story of your career history as an exciting, well-planned progression – stick to the facts, but also remember that your interviewer is judging your career with the benefit of hindsight, so why shouldn't you?

Your Job – what is it? What will it be in the future?
The long-term unemployed are now often well-educated white-collar workers in addition to unskilled workers. But perhaps in the constantly-changing workplace their sophisticated but generic education amounts to little more than a lack of specialised skills. This is the pattern of the future.

So what does your job consist of? It is obvious what a teacher or a builder is meant to do, and where they should be all day, but what do people who sit at computers *all day* actually *do*? Do they need to be doing it at all? In which case, would they be missed? Does your job consist of doing the same thing over and over, or is it composed of many varied tasks? Do you use specialist skills all the time, and how long do these take to acquire? Are they being superseded by new methods or technology? If so, can you acquire these? Can you apply your existing skills to other areas? Introducing techniques such as call-centre management from your sector into other sectors could pay huge dividends. Can you suggest changes to "the way we've always done it" that add value to your employer, give you a new role and above all position you firmly as an 'innovative thinker'. Why are most office jobs still 9-5? It's obvious why a teacher has to be in school at a set time. It's equally obvious why we'd prefer call-centres *not* to work 9-5, just when we are stuck in the office, with everyone listening in to the sad history of our broken toilet seat, or the reasons why our account went overdrawn. Similarly, High Street shops are very relaxed places in the week, but frantic at weekends. If your job is getting stuck in a rut, re-write your own job specification and suggest it to your boss. It might be a risky strategy, but if you've noticed aspects of your job that are not really necessary any longer, it won't be long before someone else does, and catches you napping (and napping in the office *really* shows your age).

If you are ambitious there are two main ways of getting to the top: always looking to the next job and how it can be reached from the one you're doing now, or alternatively, focusing on becoming an expert specialist - you cannot do both without a lucky break. The days are numbered for the paternalistic style of companies of the likes of Shell, BP or IBM, with their managed international career paths and family feel. Any career planning has to be done by the individual for himself and herself, often by changing companies, sectors or countries. You need to prove you are flexible, international and broadly experienced, as well as highly motivated to learn new skills and operate in new environments. Always keep an eye out for anything new. Haven't used the latest version of Microsoft's operating system Windows Vista yet? So how are you going to look when you try it for the first time in front of a group of colleagues and you don't know what the big bright button on the bottom left of the screen is for? It's no good muttering "*It's just the same old system with a few extra bells and whistles – I know where I am with the old one, why did they have to change it?*" because that only sounds even more out-of-touch. You need to keep an eye on any developing areas within your business or substituting for it and train yourself up in the new skills that you see are starting to be called for. Adopt an 'up-and-out-and-roundabout' strategy – don't stay with your industry or product life cycle as it declines – target a job in a growing market, on a new life cycle, and work at your skills until you are in a position to move on into it.

You also need three good references: keep good referees close and unreliable former colleagues closer - unofficial references are often taken up by phone and remain strictly 'off the record'.

Job-hunting

So, you are ready to work, but out of a job. When you wake up in the morning, there is nothing to do and nowhere to go. Wrong. Job-hunting is a full-time job itself, and one to which you need to be dedicated as a part of normal working life. Your unrealistic optimism is your single most important qualification. Without fail you must expect to get the next job, be outraged if you don't, expect to get the job after that, consider it the company's loss if you don't and so on, every working day for a year or more if necessary. You are good - at least as good as the irritating interviewer - though once you have emphasised all your unparalleled virtues the interviewer usually prefers you to exhibit a veneer of modesty.

Living off your redundancy cheque can have an unreal feel to it. Everyone else goes out to regular work with its irritations and oppression, and you make job applications from home and go out to interviews here and there. If you can set the worry to one side, it is quite pleasant. Any people you don't like don't reappear too often; you don't need to get up too early unless you have an interview first thing. Your feelings may vary between good days, when you console yourself that you have only temporarily left the fast lane, and bad days when you resent that you have been involuntarily shunted off onto the hard shoulder to see life speeding past you. At first it is agonising to question each day where to go and what to try next, but gradually you fall into a routine. As you receive rejections you go over all the disadvantages of the job you didn't get, until you are quite convinced that you are better off unemployed.

This is a dangerous state of mind. Do not sink into a slough of despond, but do not float on a cloud of self-delusion either. You cannot afford to be petrified by angst or soothed into acceptance: both are equally dangerous. Your nearest and dearest will not be as relaxed as you and for their sake as well as yours you need to plan your job-hunting in as much detail, both short- and medium-term, as you plan your work diary. You will get a clear over-view of your situation and possibilities if you draw up a Master Plan setting out your overall strategy, detailing the companies and people you intend to target, resources at your disposal (from your family computer to your mother's spare room as an office, with a spreadsheet valuing your savings and how quickly you are spending them) and a calendar including "time-out point". This is not a game to while away the time, but essential preparation for the oncoming battle. Being in a job may be like warfare, but fighting to get one is an initiation into the SAS.

There are two types of stimuli for your jobseeking activities, responsive and pro-active:

Responsive:
- answering job adverts in the newspaper, specialist press and online;
- being invited to head-hunter interviews;
- going to courses and contacts insisted upon by the Job Centre;
- meeting up with your mother's neighbour's partner who might have a job going.

Pro-active:
- networking with former colleagues to remind them you exist, alert them to your availability and find out what jobs may be about to become vacant;
- mailing head-hunters your CV;
- cold-calling industry insiders at your level and just above;
- registering your CV with online recruitment agencies.

To keep your spirits up you could make one aspirational job application for a position you don't expect to get per week - and tell everyone you've applied for it, discuss how life would be if you got it, accept their commiserations when you just miss getting it. They'll be relieved - they were getting quite jealous. After all, remember you just *might* get the job of your dreams out of this. Take your increasing pile of rejections as a sign of your diligence and motivation - though it is best not to use this as an illustration of your steadfastness in a real job interview.

Don't be embarrassed when you meet the same interviewer for the fifth time at the recruitment consultancy:

1. he may not remember who you are

2. he might think he successfully placed you last time and now you're moving on and up

3. it's a game you are both playing - the only difference is that he's getting paid for playing it

Positive - and free - advice

You can get free advice from *local job centres* – no longer the sad, dilapidated dives where even the careers advisors had jobs to which you did not aspire, but bright, open buildings with earnest, welcoming staff. No need to linger there though, just check the online terminals, grab the free leaflets and leave, and read them later over a reassuring mug of hot chocolate downtown. Likewise your local *library* - going in to your local library on a weekday does not mean that you are consigned to the ranks of the over-seventies Book Club in the comfy chairs in the corner. Just get the leaflets, use the computers and attend the IT courses.

Research your targeted employers on the internet and without charge at the British Library if you live in or near London, in the Business and Intellectual Property Centre. There you can read (slightly old) Mintel or Key Notes reports and access some online databases which otherwise charge a prohibitive fee. Also good are the City Business Library or Westminster Reference Library. But you need to look around as Mintel vary which libraries they agree to sell their reports to each year so that you can never predict where you will find the one you need. Business Enterprise Schemes will provide advice if you are interested in starting a small business. Read sensible and thorough self-help guides such as *"How to Find Work When*

You're Over 50"[101], but don't take them too seriously when they suggest that you could still get a job working in a children's play group - you could, but you aren't yet that desperate.

See Appendix for a list of information sources, contacts and websites

<u>CVs and Job interviews</u>

There are plenty of self-help books dedicated to the perfect CV, and numerous websites *(see Appendix)*. Everyone who interviews you will have their own preferences, and you could change your CV every day and never perfect it. Ask for advice by all means - just remember that each person's advice will contradict the last - in the rare instances when they all agree, *then* act upon it. Above all remember that for all the hours you spend pondering and perfecting it, it will scarcely be more than skimmed. This does not mean you can get away with gaps, unrealistic claims or internal contradictions - those are what the recruiter is focused upon - but make it clear and easy to understand - the recruiters really are oblivious to positive details - in a recruiters' market they are only sensitive to negative signs that screen you out. They too have a leaky washing machine and a messy personal relationship to deal with at home - you are not of intense interest to them, you are just a means for them to earn money, which should at least fix the washing machine, if not the relationship. As such you need to come across as competent, qualified and personable. Consider the recruiter's needs and don't get defensive about your redundancy, abusive about your former colleagues or negative about your achievements - you'll just be giving them more work, as they've wasted time interviewing a hopeless candidate with the wrong attitude whom they can't put forward to the new employer.

Know what points you want to make in an interview, and use every opportunity to make them. This does not include the polite pre-ambles about whether you had a good journey, though remember that the interview starts the moment the interviewer catches sight of you reading GQ Magazine/ the Financial Times in the waiting area, and from this point on your body language is already speaking for you (or against you). In the interview, whilst you need to be responsive to the interviewer, the fact that you observe from her desk that she is a family-loving Guardian reader doesn't mean she is unaware that that the recruiting manager is a hard-nosed, divorced Tory, so don't tailor your interview persona to the wrong recruiter. Stick to your prepared key examples and focus on making your six or seven key points about yourself and your career.

Prepare answers for all the "surprise" questions you will be asked and analyse what this reveals about you to the amateur psychologists who are interviewing you. ("*If you were an animal, what animal would you be? What would you take with you on a trip to the Moon? What annoys you most about your colleagues? Do you usually get on with the Human Resources Department?*"). Be aware of the implications of your answers: knitting may be your main hobby, but perhaps better to focus on the water-skiing you almost managed in Mauritius if the job spec demands a dynamic go-getter. Also, just because the potential employer makes a big deal of the happiness and personal fulfilment of its staff in its Reports and Accounts, does not mean that they will necessarily take you seriously as a hard-hitting highly-paid manager in a competitive industry if you give this as your reason for wishing to join the company. Focus on "*quality of my life*" in the interview rather than "*what I can offer to the company*" and you will be out of the door before you can complete the phrase "*life-work balance*".

What are recruitment consultants or HR interviewers actually looking for in the course of a first stage interview? Qualities pre-determined by someone else who isn't necessarily capable of defining what they really need, but will be irritated if the recruitment consultant takes the initiative and strays from the brief. How many driving macho managers will stipulate to Personnel that they want to recruit a pallid yes-man who will unquestioningly carry out their every order and be honoured to do so? Maybe Margaret Thatcher bucks the trend here, but more probably, over time, the colleagues and subordinates who survive just turn out to be a certain type. No. A traditional manager says he wants 'driving, dynamic go-getters' because that fits his own macho image. Even the less-self-deluding managers cannot generally define exactly what type of personality and experience should be stipulated by the job specification. How can anyone, in the abstract, rate the qualities of an applicant, in order of importance, and then interactively and iteratively filter them according to the weird and wonderful combinations of skills, experience and personality disorders that present themselves as potential candidates? The first-stage interviewers have to second-guess what the ultimate recruiting manager's subconscious 'gut feel' will be when he meets the candidates face to face.

Remember that CVs are usually filtered by what the applicant is doing now, and what their job titles has been for the last two years only. You may feel that just because you have done *more* things since you last did whatever the job requires doesn't mean you can't remember how you did it and couldn't do it again. Yet most interviewers assume that candidates can *only* do the things they've *just* done – most head-hunters or recruitment consultants would discount "riding a bicycle" if you hadn't done it in your *last* job. Certainly: "regularly rode bicycle to work in 2002" would be discounted – "Well, would you not agree that bicycles and road conditions may have changed quite a lot since then? What makes you confident you can still ride a bike?"

Psychometric Tests

Psychometric tests are used by the police, the Civil Service and over 95% of FTSE 100 companies, so you are likely to have to complete several in the course of your job search. These can be part intelligence tests, part personality tests. In the latter you are instructed to respond spontaneously - but can you always afford to? - they are structured on in-built prejudices and the latest fads of the psychology profession and of the creator of the particular test-sheet. You must play the game and answer all the questions or you will automatically categorise yourself into the 'uncooperative rebel' box, and in fact computer-based tests will often not allow you to progress unless you have literally checked every box. In the face of a series of offensively black and white questions which force you into unrealistic and over-simplified scenarios, you must decide to depict yourself either as a lonely analyst or as a gregarious half-wit: "Would you prefer to work alone analysing numbers or to go to a party?" Then you must admit to being either irascible or temperamental: "Are you irritable or moody?"

There are even controversial new tests that claim to be able to identify subconscious racism - another way for the recruiters to justify employing their own cronies rather than the person best qualified for the job. The candidate may, when the test requires them to categorise a face as either 'good' or 'bad', mark the blonde blue-eyed face as 'bad' because it looks just like their neighbour with whom they're currently in a border dispute over the height of their Leylandii hedge. But they will probably never be given the chance to answer the charge - it will just be mentioned in the briefing meeting: "We have identified some racist tendencies in this candidate - a possible aversion to blue eyes - and now that we have this evidence it might count against us in an employment tribunal if we ever had any problems." So the candidate who currently has a negative association with blue eyes is screened out. And is it a subconscious prejudice against blue eyes, or ginger hair, or fat people or thin people, or young people or old people, or is it only specific politically correct fashions that the tests are targeting? When the next wave of political correctness arrives, the psychometric tests will also change.

There is a shelf of books in the careers section of any large bookshop entitled: "How to pass Psychometric Tests". You might cynically imagine that these deal with "How to fool them into thinking you're a 'team player'" (whatever its merits - after all, so are rugby players, and quite friendly chaps off the pitch for the most part, but do you want all your staff to have cauliflower ears and broken noses?) But no. "How to pass" books actually tell you how to do the basic intelligence tests, taking them all in deadly earnest. If you have run multi-million pound businesses you may find this irritating, but console yourself that you will clearly be the best candidate they've ever had. Surely you can still find the next number in the series, work out which shape is the odd one out and see which little pony image has been rotated but not flipped - still, just buy a book to make sure you can, and vow to ban them when you are Chief Executive. 'Transferable skills' is the buzzword, but recruiters are sadly slow to adopt this approach. Tests used to be set for a shorthand-typist: could she take dictation and then type at the speed and with the accuracy her certificates claimed? Simple: 'go into that room and type this'. Nowadays it's more a question of: can you stomach yet another personality test?

Yet does this not run counter to the previous section describing how employees are only being valued for their demonstrable skills? The issue is that recruiters are so much more sophisticated nowadays that they don't test for the obvious. A typing test will not reveal whether you are a duplicitous mass-murderer, but neither do these black box personality tests, and what's more, since the managers do not understand how they work, they do not have the confidence to overrule or even question them. The results are also set in stone: you can say you had a bad day on your *typing*, could you please retake the test, but can you claim you had a bad day on your *personality* - though in truth, who doesn't? Most tests state that the results should be reviewed with the individual candidate, but only the most conscientious interviewers do this.

Differentiation:

From university applicants to graduates seeking their first jobs, students are desperate to differentiate themselves. Word in the morgue has it that prior to the Credit Crunch a number of (mainly male) undergraduate medics were actually planning to quit Medicine in favour of a career in the City and were only studying for a 'hard' degree in Medicine in order to differentiate themselves at the City Milk Round. One just hopes that they do not take out their frustration on their innocent patients now their dreams of a penthouse office in Docklands and nights in theatre-land are replaced forever with a wheezing surgery or the blood and guts of the operating theatre. Meanwhile Law graduates with First Class degrees are being turned away by the top City law firms as degree inflation churns out thousands of Law graduates, undifferentiated except that some ran the university debating society, some spent their summers teaching in Africa and some have relatives in Chambers – it's a difficult call - which are more likely to be an asset to your firm?

This situation is repeated when you have been made redundant. Unlike your youthful counterparts, you are by now 'warts 'n' all' and your rugged features, etched with years of experience, are more distinctive than the fresh-faced hopefuls. But you still need to show why you should be given the job when there are other well-qualified candidates. Instead of *no* distinguishing features you have a range of attributes and experience, but what you need is a meta-tag to say: "This is the combination you want". Just like the 25% of 2007 candidates with 'A' Grades at A Level, your business qualifications are well below your ability, even if you hold an MBA, LLB or ACA, as you have spent years since gaining your academic and professional qualifications sifting the knowledge wheat from the fad-blown chaff and found what stands the test of time when applied in the real world. You have all sorts of experience to which no CV or qualification can do justice – how can you demonstrate it? In an interview, one of the only convincing ways is to develop a series of brief anecdotes to illustrate different situations that you used your skills to handle, and hope that the interviewer is competent enough to give you the opportunity to tell them.

Reinventing Yourself

Ageist job advertisements are illegal and you could sue any companies that screen you out on age. Or you could spend that time getting a job. It isn't easy to change the world when you are just seeking a niche in it, so it might be more prudent to plan to change the world once you have achieved personal economic security. There is no need to give up your reforming zeal – but it would be more productive to start with yourself then move on to the rest of society. In the West you will not see job adverts such as the following:

"Currently looking for an attractive female professional preferably with at least 1 year of PA or secretarial experience."
"POSITION: Sourcing Coordinator - Plastics Division   PROFILE: AGE 25/35 YEARS and Not married"

Two job adverts posted on a Shanghai newspaper's website

Career Crunch!

but there is no point in applying to companies that clearly do not want someone like you, just to make a point. First get yourself in a position where any company would regret having rejected you out of hand.

Personal Re-branding

Personal appearance is the first indicator of attitude, character and aspirations when you walk into an interview. Superficial? After all, how you present yourself reveals how you see yourself and your relationship to others, and it is also how others will pre-judge you, rightly or wrongly. Have you updated your skills recently? Well if you haven't updated your haircut in twenty years, what do people imagine?

I'm new!

(OK, same old me, new spin - and it works!)

Dying your hair to hide the grey is the last resort of a person who has not come to terms with his age. Try it. Console yourself by vowing to expose these tactics in others once you yourself are established, and secretly start writing "The Art of War, Sun Tzu updated 2,500 years on". Ageism is illegal and you should never judge a book by its cover. It's the interviewers' fault if they are superficial, not yours. Men's suits all look alike, until you analyse the difference between a young man's and an old man's (starting with extreme examples where the differences are most marked, such as your father and your nephew) or between a rebellious youth statement and the well-cut lines of a tailored statement of early success. Work out the difference and dress accordingly. Just don't buy a red sports car or pursue younger models of any other sort. Some concessions to maturity are respected.

Signals that you are still employable

Perhaps it is the plethora of wildlife TV series, where animals grimace horribly, screech ear-piercingly or change colour dramatically as a substitute for or precursor to physical activity, either bellicose or amorous, that has encouraged Behaviourists to emphasise the significance of body language for business people. In the office there are certain characters who you know won't survive the next cull because they are simply out of tune with the company trends. Take the potted plant enthusiast who applies Feng Shui principles to achieve a harmonious office and waters his plants in times of commercial stress instead of going to the coffee machine to show solidarity with the bosses. Or the analyst who just can't help spelling out the writing on the wall, oblivious to the cool response that his message receives – the unpopular Cassandra of the take-over battle, proven right in the end, but for ever damned. The role of analysts ever was to support in numbers and colourful graphs the gut feel of the boss, and, young or old, an analyst must play the puppeteer, pulling the strings of his spreadsheet to bend the number puppets into acceptable displays. Then there's the life and soul of the office, who sends round a card for each person's birthday, bereavement or blessing – when accountants are in the ascendancy and are looking to cut, any signals of jollity are generally the first to be axed with stoic satisfaction.

In the public sector, outstanding achievement may not always be viewed as desirable. Beware of phrases like "cracking eggs" – coddling/slow boiling is preferred in large bureaucratic organisations. As for improving the numbers – it is *consistency,* not *accuracy,* that is required to chart trends or benchmark across sectors. What is the point of improving the numbers if it makes a nonsense of the resultant analysis? So listing your ground-breaking achievements may not gain nor retain you a place in a bureaucratic organisation – in fact it may well automatically mark you down on 'interpersonal skills'.

If your lack of perceived value is because your area of expertise has been elbowed out by a substitute, then turn the prejudice around - who better to understand the initial applications of a substitute than an expert in the old

Career Crunch!

product? New products are never used to their full potential at first - they are used as a better/cheaper version of the old product until other uses are discovered for them. So do not be deterred - you have not been supplanted by the new product - on the contrary, your usefulness has gained new applications.

Practise! Practise! Practise!

There is a fatalism about older people who have allowed technology to advance without them, which sighs that: "you can't teach an old dog new tricks". This is nonsense. What you can't do is pick up effortlessly a skill from which you have remained snootily aloof for several years, while everyone else devoted hours late at night to its mastery. Younger colleagues without your experience and reputation to rely on are still in the business of constant self-reinvention, and they take every opportunity to prove their adaptability and discover new ways to make themselves useful to the company. So just because you understand the *theory* of sending a text message doesn't mean you will be able to do it first time. If you haven't mastered the skill and end up fumbling in front of colleagues, they will quickly conclude you are ready for the scrap heap. Observe teenagers everywhere – they use every minute on the bus, at the station, and especially in their school lessons, to practise and master this essential life skill. Just because they wear scruffy hoodies and trousers which trail along the ground doesn't mean that anything they can do should be a doddle for you. They are specialists; you are a novice.

Likewise with all new technology - every day you are free, work on computer applications: updating your Facebook and Linked-In entries; creating spreadsheets and presentations. The ability to create and talk interestingly to PowerPoint presentations is an essential management skill, so choose topics (starting with "My career and aspirations", and moving on to your specialist sector e.g. "Threats and exciting Opportunities in the rodent disposal industry") and practise presenting them. Walk the walk and talk the talk - it's surprising how much more readily you will be accepted as a potential colleague.

Career Crunch!

Adopt this motto:

<u>*Other job-acquisition/retention tactics (some strictly inadvisable)*</u>

- Undercut your rivals on price (*see below*)
- Look smarter and keener
- Better quality (qualifications, experience, up-to-date skills)
- Specialise (become an expert)
- Use contacts (Apply to everyone you know and use relatives/old boy/ former colleague network)
- Form a Union
- Minimise risk to employer (*see below*)
- Make it risky to take another candidate (develop specialist knowledge or qualifications e.g. Chartered Director)
- Use the diversity policies in the public sector to your advantage
- Knife your colleagues to eliminate rivals (now known as "the Weakest Link" tactics)
- Buy the support of your suppliers (dinners, supplier events, networking)
- Deal with crooks
- Become a crook

These tactics are also used very effectively by companies and countries.

Career Crunch!

Re-price Pete

How to re-price your services temporarily without losing your quality price point:

    1. Interim work

    2. Special offer - for friends, long term potential etc

    3. Special deals - work 4 days and floating 5th day for other interviews

    4. Different job with clearly job-specific pay structure

    5. General pay-cut/Individual gesture

Interim work is increasingly a vital transition phase and there are several logical reasons why you should pursue it. Firstly, you are attractive because you are a *less risky* candidate - if you don't work out, you are only on a short-term contract so can be cheaply or even costlessly parted with. The other side of this coin is that because you do not represent a long-term commitment the company can afford to take *more of a risk* on you if your skills are not precisely what they were seeking, and you look interesting although less solid than the alternative. Finally, by definition the company is in a hurry, so their acceptability threshold may be lowered from nine or ten-out-of-ten to seven-out-of-ten, and with a limited number of suitable candidates immediately available you have fewer rivals. After securing one interim position you have greater credibility for the next, and the last position on your CV is a successfully-completed task with a clearly-defined end, not a permanent position with an untimely end. At some point you will need to start applying in earnest for permanent jobs again, (unless you choose to join the ranks of career interims), or convert an interim position into a permanent role, for which the agency should receive a generous fee.

In order to make yourself affordable you could position your interim/consulting fee as a '*special offer*' - taking into consideration the fact that 'the employer is a friend/ family' or that there is 'potential to convert the role into a permanent position'. You could alternatively negotiate *special deals* such as being paid on a weekly basis but with one day (or two half-days) free for interviewing for a permanent role. Temporarily taking a lower-paid job that is not comparable with your usual job need not unduly affect your earning capacity when you return to normal, though you will need to address the issue that your absence from your profession may mean that your skills and insider knowledge have become outdated.

Different pay structure

Pete's wife wishes to return to work – she has become a Mature Returner. She decides the City's too far to commute, as it would keep her an extra two hours every day away from the toddlers at home. However, as a management accountant she needs a large company to work in, so it's hard to set up locally. She trains as a teacher on a one year PGCE. Now she earns only £25,000 but everyone knows, as with voluntary work, that teaching is a vocation with a different pay structure from commerce. Compared with working in the private sector the salary is low, but the hours and location fit better around a family; it also has a huge strong highly-unionised workforce so she will not easily be thrown out, but neither will she be paid more for doing her job better, only by spending time and effort working up the scale to Head of Department, Deputy Head and so on. All she can negotiate is a slightly higher position on the scale for her business experience. So the pay is not comparable, and therefore will not unduly affect her salary expectations on her return to a commercial role if she wishes later. (Of course the fact that she will have been out of management accounting for some years *will* affect her attractiveness to an employer, but she'll cross that bridge when she comes to it). She's not worried, because her priority is getting some paid work to cover gaps when Pete is jobseeking, now that he is redundant for the second time, whilst not compromising her ability to be at home for the children's holidays.

Different contract – minimise risk to employer
You can adopt an innovative but increasingly common approach and minimise the risk to an employer of taking you on by offering to do a "trial period". Just make sure there really is a job there to be had if you pass muster. Imaginative contracts can pre-empt some age-related issues. Fixed-term contracts are now common in the public sector. These may lead to "churning" rather like mobile phone contracts that are constantly changed by the salesmen so they can earn more commission on selling a new contract, or investments that are bought and sold to earn new commissions for the financial advisor or to avoid accumulating capital-gains tax. The old ludicrously wasteful practice of 'bed-and breakfasting' shares to avoid accumulating capital gains tax is starting to be applied to employees in slightly different form, whereby employers oblige them to move around every two to three years and so avoid the accumulation of onerous employee benefits. These can be from redundancy and other pay-offs, or the need to go through a very unpleasant 'performance management' process over a period of six months to exit an underperforming employee, who hasn't done anything overtly sackable, mainly because she hasn't done anything much at all. These intended benefits are so problematic to companies, and so well-established and belligerently defended by the trades unions, that they militate against employing staff in general, but particularly against older people who are suspected of ceasing to give their all once they are approaching retirement, either because age slows them down or because there is a decreasing incentive of promotion as their 'time-left-to-go' diminishes.

General pay-cut

Finally in times of general economic downturn the entire staff of a company may, generally in the course of a consultation process, offer to take either reduced days/hours or even a general pay-cut. As economic conditions improve, this voluntary general pay reduction can legitimately be pointed to in the course of central pay negotiations. Similarly, even at a higher, more individual level a senior manager can offer to take a pay-cut, officially as a gesture of solidarity with staff, but with the ancillary benefit of preserving his own competitiveness and diverting any thoughts of the Peter Principle. By 2009 as the Credit Crunch intensified, more than one director who suspected his latest pay award had raised him above the industry average was adopting this approach, generally presented as a sign of his commitment to the ongoing profitability of the company.

A case study

A major airline recently considered plans to freeze salaries at a given level so that they pay the rate for the job and the salary progression over time is inflation-adjusted only until you change jobs. Bonuses would be awarded for good performance, but these would not be automatic. The company saves on two counts: it pays for the job done, not the expectations of the employee, and it also has more flexibility to reward good work rather than long tenure. The employees, disgruntled as they may be now, will gain in the long term as a group, because their jobs will be more secure and they will not be carrying less motivated time-serving colleagues. In future pay structures, experience may not be recognised, but at least it will not be penalised. This arrangement, shocking to corporate employees, is the norm for teachers, for instance, where jobs are graded according to union-defined standards and jealously guarded union-negotiated pay scales.

Things to *Beware*

Beware trick jobs and services:

£250,000 p.a. Consultancy earnings!

Sounds appealing? Read the small print and be cynical. You will be eligible to earn these fabulous sums once you have completed a "certification program" or some other over-priced training course leading to an unrecognised qualification. Be aspirational but not gullible.

£60,000 p.a. Executive coaching!

This can be a pyramid-selling scam. They make their money because you recruit other members who pay a fee to join a "marketing network" which they claim will provide clients for all of you. They may also sell you the extortionate training scheme leading to a meaningless 'accreditation certificate' or other services.

You do not need to pay extortionate *executive coaches* yourself. This is a booming industry. There was an entire shelf devoted to executive coaching in my local bookstore. How many coaches can one executive need? But of course it's a great job. Anyone can argue they have the skills to do it - resting actors can teach you voice projection, unemployed consultants can teach you to talk the jargon, tired accountants can teach you the basics of finance; military men can teach you the strategies of war. Everyone can teach you something useful.

Beware *"outplacement consultants"*. Some may be helpful, but never pay out a large lump sum (£11,000 is not unusual) for advice and introductions that gradually peter out as the months go by. It is worth considering using them if their services come free with your redundancy package - and are not deducted from it.

Buying a company

Beware glib suggestions such as "Why don't you buy a company? I can put you in touch with a good little business. All I charge is 6% - or I can do a completely different deal: 4% plus a 2% carry" (*actual words recently – these 2 deals are basically the same*). However persuasive he is, say no. A head-hunter might get a commission equivalent to 20% of your first year's salary from the company who recruit you, as her finder's fee. Depending on your salary this might be £20,000. A broker who is offering an introduction to a £2 million company, which then he expects you to buy with your friends' and relatives' savings plus a bank loan, will try to charge you 6% of the purchase price of £2 million i.e. £120,000 for doing basically the same job as the head-hunter plus giving obvious advice about writing business plans and making your case to the bank.

Being adaptable and entrepreneurial is not the same as being taken for a ride. If you are thinking of buying or setting up a company you need to know or learn quickly on the one hand how its market functions, what the key drivers of the business are etc, and on the other hand you need to do the rounds of potential funding providers and find out what they will offer and on what terms. A rough guide to their requirements is an extortionate rate of return, half the company and your life for the next five years with no guarantee that they will not throw you out under "Good leaver/Bad leaver' clauses in your contract. They do always earnestly stress that they are not mean or greedy – it's just that they need to justify their enormous salaries, and despite their expertise as investors a startling proportion of their portfolio gradually sinks into oblivion or even fails spectacularly, so any successful business such as yours will have to compensate for the rest.

Even when you 'go it alone', you are never in sole control of a company – in addition to the Bank Manager, whose funding may run dry if your business hits a downturn, a significant supplier or even your business partner can scupper your business by withdrawing suddenly, making you very vulnerable unless you have ready substitutes, whatever it says in those carefully-worded contracts you all signed.

Career Crunch!

Setting yourself up as an entrepreneur

Another similar suggestion: "You should set up your own business". How many career employees have the knowledge to set up a small business? The rules are all different: in a large company the HR department dealt with employment legislation, hiring, firing, training, whilst the accountants dealt with National Insurance, payroll etc.; even if you did deal with your large employer's NI calculations, the regulations relating to this and much other bureaucracy are different for a small business - even the tax rates are different. As an entrepreneur, you are the HR department, the Marketing Department, Operations, Accounts, H&S (your personal liability) and 'paterfamilias' to any staff members. An entrepreneur needs not only specific skills but a specific temperament - optimistic, somewhat ruthless, risk-taking and definitely cavalier compared with the close attention to detail required of an employee in a large firm whose main asset is its long-term brand and reputation. Felix Dennis's blunt and earthy book "How to Get Rich" covers the bumpy ground of setting up or buying companies more thoroughly than I can here.

Becoming a Consultant

A consultant also needs specific attributes: salesman; analyst; highly developed specialist - you must supply whatever is not easily available within the organisation. How many employees have such in-demand skills? This is the most common form of self-employment amongst older workers following redundancy, but getting regular work is not the independent existence consultants may wish to imply. As with interim work *(see below),* far from giving up the stresses of a permanent job, you are often doing two jobs at once, as you are pitching for new business whilst on your current assignment in order to avoid long gaps with no income.

The cachet of a Non-executive director

"Have you considered 'going plural' – taking on a few non-exec positions?" people ask casually. To be credible for these you should have already been a director, preferably of a large firm in a similar industry. And these posts are only a day or two every month so you then need to acquire a portfolio of them and even then you are still unlikely to be able to pay the mortgage.

To take up any of the above three options you need to think well ahead whilst still employed. Many employees will lack the appropriate experience, or more importantly, the contacts to get them, and there will still be a time lag before you start to bring in a useful income.

Beware: Secret Gatekeeper Veto

One chilling aspect of jobseeking is the gatekeeper veto of the recruitment agencies/head-hunters. They can block off access to a whole raft of employers - maybe a rival who never forgave you for getting promoted over her head now provides damaging references when contacted informally. Don't expect head-hunters to weed out genuine problems with employees - it's surprising how easily employees actually dismissed for misconduct get new jobs as long as they have some influential referees. (Government ministers regularly resign their post in a blaze of publicity, soon to pop up in a new one once the fuss has died down.) Head-hunters pride themselves on getting the true facts about employees by taking up informal off-the-record telephone references, but as with ageism and other prejudice, if you are not given the right to reply, how can they be sure of getting the true picture? If you suspect this is happening it might be worth getting a sympathetic professional to take up references on your behalf - but only as a last resort, as your referees can get impatient if they are taxed too often. But try to resist paranoia - it is not necessarily a lukewarm reference that cost you the job.

Beware eBay

This will drain your time even faster than the bargains will drain your bank account. Now is not the time to focus on setting up that vinyl collection you could never afford in your youth - you have full-time job-hunting to do. It goes without saying that the same applies to movies of all sorts and day-time TV. Be sceptical about some much-repeated fallacies:

Interim Employment Fallacies

Do not be fooled by arguments that working as an interim is advantageous to you because you have "increased flexibility for your free time". The opposite is often the case: if you do not accept that urgent commission just when they need it done, they will not offer you the next one. However inconvenient, you have to be grateful for work as it comes in. Firms would like a flexible workforce. Employees would like flexible hours. But each wants the flexibility to suit them. Firms are also reluctant to pay interim employees a premium when they do employ them to cover the times when they do not (hence the discrepancy between the individual's need for a regular stable income and the company's wish to flex outgoings). They will get away with paying you as little as they can, whether this is fair or not. It is a case of supply and demand, so the more over forty-fives who can remain in permanent employment, the better the rates will be for interims.

It is also inefficient to keep pitching your services to potential new employers every few months - like a building firm boss who now spends a third of each day quoting for new work when he really wants to supervise what his men are doing to his neighbour's new kitchen. Regular interim employees therefore use agents. But you still need to keep reminding them of your existence, and as they are all small you need to be registered with several agencies, thus multiplying your work-load. Actors employ agents - but they are viewed as an exception. They also have long periods "resting". The benefit of having an agent also depends on how good the agent is. In any case, interim agents are basically head-hunters – they fill assignments from thousands of CVs, they are not seeking work for you personally. The fundamental problem is that society is not yet set up for people to keep moving jobs. Homeowners need to make steady mortgage payments, or alternatively pay a premium to have flexibility in their payments to the building society, whilst they are paid only a modest premium to offer flexibility themselves. At the most basic level, they need to eat every week, not swing from feast to famine.

Transferable skills fallacies

Despite your enthusiastic identification of your transferable skills you may encounter a problem - they may not be all that transferable after all. The problem is Specialisation. The general transferable skills (man management etc) are taken as given if you have been a manager, even though this is not necessarily the case; what are sought after are specialist skills within a sector, and each sector has its own legislation and specialised relationships.

Portfolio career

A 'portfolio career' was anticipated by Charles Handy, with a former high flier spending some time at home, some on his job, some doing charity work and so on. But think about employing an accountant. This *could* be a portfolio accountant who does a bit of accounting and has other strings to her bow. But wouldn't you prefer an accountant who has numerous clients each with similar needs so it makes sense for her to read specialist articles in "Accountancy Age" and pick up the latest tips about recent legislation and tax man practices in your sector? After all, barbers used to double up as surgeons - would this be popular now?

Trading on old skills works if nothing moves on - in medieval society the technology stayed the same, surgery didn't advance for hundreds of years, neither did hairdressing, so you could afford to have a portfolio career. Medieval builders could trade off their skills acquired as apprentice, honed as journeyman and perfected in a masterpiece, and even when Gothic architecture began to make Romanesque look passé, there were enough half-built rounded arches to keep you in work. Nowadays there are stacks of new building regulations to observe before you even begin to talk about bricks and mortar (or solar panels and heat exchangers). In the office, typists and secretaries are out and the modern Executive Assistant has to demonstrate skills in Word and PowerPoint, communicating with BlackBerrys and iPhones. If you pursue a much-postulated 'portfolio career', you leave little time for retraining, as your time is divided between the different activities. This leads to inefficiency and sub-optimisation of skills and information levels. When you telephone a call-centre, it is pretty obvious who has just nipped in from their college lectures and been given a sheet of standard questions and answers, who also has a part-time job as a waitress, and who works five days a week and has stayed in the job longer than the average (and by 'average', twelve months would be long service for many call-centres).

Using your skills to set up on your own

Chartered Accountants can decide to downsize to working locally and do people's tax returns at their leisure; Management Accountants, by contrast need a large organisation to value their analytical contribution. Hairdressers can set up on their own account too, but school teachers need a school if they wish to work during core hours. So your ability to set up on your own depends partly on your professional skill. It also depends on the regulations applying to your industry.

Decision time.

You've followed every piece of advice you've been given by friends, relatives, self-help books, the Job Centre, chance acquaintances in the pub. Still no job. Your money has run out; your bank loan has run out; your wife has run out. You will have to compromise. This point will arrive sooner in China, where you are one of, depending which sources you trust, between 20 and 100 million unemployed - statistically, how many job interviews would you have to do as an unskilled worker before it became probable that you would get one job? Or again, as a blue-collar worker in the West - when your speciality in car manufacturing is redundant along with 5,000 other workers, how likely is it that an employer will pick you out? As a white-collar worker, where your skills are, at face value, transferable, there appear to be an infinite number of possible job openings, so when do you decide to call a halt? It can take a year or even two more to find a really good position in an overcrowded sector. Partly it is a numbers game, and you have to wait until your number's up. But what if your time is up before your number?

Finally, the really tough decision point has come. Eighteen months have passed and you have to take the next job that comes along. What are your new criteria?

Career Crunch!

± Are the location, salary and job acceptable?

± How good/bad do you feel about the job itself?

± Is training available?

± What is the future of the new sector/industry?

± Can you see any progression for yourself once you join?

± How secure will you be?

Helpful or impatient relatives will advise you to take a step down. This may be just as hard. The rung below is just as tough - remember how difficult the struggle was to get there. Taking a salary cut is more feasible.

Retraining after all?

So you may decide to retrain despite your reservations. You should already have spent your months of unemployment working up the basic requirements for any job:

✓ *suitable wardrobe* (not as easy as it once was - many firms favour a half-way house between formal suits and leisure clothes – Goldman Sachs in the City have recently been favouring very sharp suits but no tie, whilst some other firms like a tie but no jacket – the variations are almost endless, and that's just for the men; state comprehensive schools are not averse to a brightly-coloured baggy jumper in winter, whereas independent schools still look favourably on a ladies' suit at interviews;)

✓ *up-to-date current affairs* and business knowledge;

✓ *computer skills* in Word, Excel, PowerPoint;

✓ *fluent and entertaining presentation skills.*

You might identify or be directed towards an area with a skills shortage and decide to train yourself up to fill it. This is of course easier said than done. Temporary work in a sector in which you are interested may be an entry point. Or you could choose a complementary area with a skills shortage and offer your services in this capacity as an entry point, like the apocryphal would-be TV-presenter who begins at the BBC as a typist. Subsidised courses are offered by the government and numerous private firms in basic business skills such as book-keeping, though it would be better to find a firm to sponsor you in some way, even if it only a promise to interview you on completion of the course. Certain jobs are under-subscribed (Bus driver; Teacher), though you may see why, and they may entail a cut in salary or status, or require a vocational calling – an appetite for martyrdom is not unusual.

Retraining, even successfully, may still not provide a permanent solution, however. Let's say you do take a salary cut and retrain for a job where you identify a skills shortage. The industry consolidates and there are now only three major players in the country. One company has a blanket recruitment ban, one doesn't like you at the interview and you are still trying to get into the third, knowing that once all three doors are closed to you all you can do is keep trying them or emigrate.

Fearful of losing his personal price point, Over-Priced Pete does not think he can afford to take a low-paid position which offers retraining. Only graduates first entering the workforce can afford to take wages that are much lower than they realistically expect to earn later - accountants, lawyers and other graduate trainees on recognised company programmes - because they are on track with a promise, their potential is acknowledged so they can afford the relatively low starting salary. Half-way through a career this is not on offer – the only time an executive can afford to be seen temporarily doing a job which is priced beneath his level is on an official induction programme. With his demotion to trainee salary would go Pete's whole personal pricing strategy. Like his wife when she was holding out for a fully-fledged return to work at a professional salary - and therefore temporarily preferred to use her skills as a volunteer for no salary at all – Over-Priced Pete cannot afford to re-enter the workforce as a trainee, even if he found an employer willing to offer a trainee position to a mature worker. Even though he may have the potential and past experience to overtake his fellow trainees and present managers, he is too old for the for most company systems to allow him to do so.

Employees cannot afford to take retraining positions, and employers are not obliged to offer them. Even the 2006 Ageism legislation allows an exeat in the form of a dispensation releasing employers from offering training courses to older employees where the employer cannot recoup the outlay over the employee's future employment. And how many older trainees are there on graduate recruitment programmes? Ageism can always be dressed up in other terms. This issue was highlighted in a survey conducted by a student magazine in the mid-eighties, and little has changed since then, except that graduate recruitment schemes themselves have been progressively cut back.

But is this so unjustified? Even when he has learnt the basics of the new business, an industry-outsider will take years to familiarise himself with the mountains of legislation relating to the H&S, Accounting rules and business practices of the new industry. The reality is that each industry has its own industry-specific regulations, too many and varied to teach in a formal course. The more red tape, the less mobile the workforce between sectors - a clear choice for government between imposing restrictive regulation and allowing individual opportunity. Ironically, whilst Pete's twenty-five years of expertise acquired in his present industry do not command a job-security premium, his lack of expertise will count against him if he tries to move across to any other sector.

Furthermore, not only is there industry-specific legislation, there is also industry-specific knowledge as to how to get round it, what passes muster, and what is hauled over the coals. Then there are industry-specific relationships. These build up trust and credibility over time – you are known to be a "safe pair of hands" who will not rock the boat, and furthermore, who might be expected to value those colleagues with whom you have worked, and who expect to have to call on your support in the next cull.

In other words, by retraining on the outside, with no job guarantee at the end of it, you are pursuing not a prudent, but a highly risky strategy, using up resources of time and savings, retraining for a job which may not materialise. You could apply to a company as a trainee. But if there is a pool of skilled workers available, or if the company has internal candidates who will cost money to make redundant, or if you are too old to offer a good return on your training cost in your remaining years of employment, the company will not consider you. Companies such as B&Q, which have made a point of offering positions to older employees, are the exception to a harsh rule.

In conclusion, if your generic skills such as computing are not up to date, then retraining is essential. For all other retraining, the only sure way to get a job at the end is either to be sponsored by a company who undertakes to employ you at the end, or to join a company on the understanding that you will be trained internally or sent on day-release.

New job contract

Once you are offered a position, the challenge is to remain level-headed and negotiate while you have the chance. Pay, perks, pensions – all might be improved with negotiation, along with holidays and flexible working. You hope it won't be an issue too soon, but notice period on either side affects your security and your finances and also can affect your ability to get your next job, especially if non-compete clauses are included – try to negotiate out of these, as they make you much less attractive to a future employer, who always needed you yesterday, and while you sit on 'gardening leave' your skills go cold. It is worth trying to gauge where the recruiter has room for manoeuvre – any inside information you can glean makes your position stronger.

Hirer hypocrisy

Recruiters patronisingly dismiss candidates' concerns about status to persuade you to accept a job on either a lower salary than market rate or with the wrong job title. Don't be brow-beaten. The professionals are only too dismissive of the significance of job titles when a candidate for a job they have to fill hesitates over a title which sounds more like a political compromise created by committee than a remit to get on and do some work. However, when they are interviewing you for your *next* job, their key questions are about your job title, salary, budgets, number of reports and closeness to the board.

Career Crunch!

If they try to tell you that job satisfaction is more important than salary, this means that the job is underpaid; if they say that you need to be skilled in matrix management, that means that when your rival boss is seen to be more politically influential, nobody works for you at all; if they tell you that you will need to 'persuade and convince' colleagues, then you have no clear remit or lines of responsibility and will have to spend your life politicking to get anything done; if they say that 'Marketing Manager' is in fact the most senior marketer in the business and that the Sales & Marketing Director is your boss in name only, as he is really just chief salesman, this signals that Sales has all the budgets and that the company thrust will be towards short-term sales drives as opposed to building a long-term marketing brand. In these cases (which will apply to some degree in every job you interview for), if you are still interested in the role, insist on meeting the boss and also some future peers, to explore the role responsibilities and remit, and obtain the intangible information which may turn out to be even more significant to your daily job, about 'company culture' and 'working methods'.

Beware the 'future structure and budgets' trap. It is easy to put notional staff, budgets and reporting lines into a job description, but if you find that you haven't got the staff or at least the budget for the staff with authorisation to recruit when you start, you never will, as something of higher priority will intervene and they will be indefinitely deferred. The same applies to vague promises of succession to someone due to retire – if your anticipated future promotion isn't announced when you start then you can be sure that you are only one of several internal candidates. Even if it is announced, it won't definitely happen: some years ago a major UK airline publicly announced the appointment of a Corporate Strategy Director in waiting – but by the time his predecessor actually retired the balance of power had shifted internally and someone else was appointed instead.

Networking

Accepting a position comes at a cost: You are no longer available to that wide network of contacts you have spent the last year establishing, should a position with them arise. By the time you are next in need of a position, your leads will be cold and you will have to start from scratch. Or not quite. Because it is essential, distracting as it may seem when you are working flat out to impress your new employer, to keep up key contacts and your profile in your industry. A boss who steals all the limelight is not just stealing your glory - he is stealing your future earnings stream. In this new world of heightened personal responsibility you must already have a game-plan for your next move as you start your new position, and you need to ensure that you gain all the right skills, experience and qualifications, both at work and in the evenings and weekends, to pursue it. If you continue this pattern you will minimise the discontinuity that increasingly characterises the latter half of working life, and multiply your opportunities to define the rest of your career. A puppy might be for life, but a job isn't, so just as you set yourself up to keep that puppy constantly fed and exercised throughout its life, and not just when you first get it, so must you keep alive your own skills to last throughout that very long professional life-time that you can now expect.

Career Crunch!

Chapter Six

Longer term solutions:

What can business and government do?

Who will be the employers of the future, and what form will employment take? A "traditional" career has not always been the work pattern for the majority of the population: many of the great scientists of the Enlightenment were amateurs, unencumbered by the necessity of earning their daily bread, whilst at the other end of the social scale around two-thirds of the population in the 1800s were day-labourers with no regular source of income.

In 1930 the English economist, John Maynard Keynes, already busy advising international governments what to do about the Great Depression, envisioned a society at the end of the twentieth century where the pursuit of wealth would not be paramount, and workers would learn to appreciate their increased leisure time[102]. Three years later, a similar vision informed "Babar the King", the popular children's story by the French writer, Jean de Brunhoff. The elephant hero, Babar, founds an idyllic new city, Celesteville, where the elephants only need to work for half the day:

"*In Celesteville the elephants work all the morning; in the afternoon they do whatever they like. They play, go for walks, read and dream.*"[103]

This is more than fairy-tale utopianism - it reflected a response to the devastating unemployment rates at that time, when one worker in four was out of work. Unions and academics were calling for a general reduction in the hours each labourer worked, in order to share out the jobs so that all citizens could earn money to spend on the goods being produced in the factories. In 1933 one of Keynes' friends, the well-known philosopher Bertrand Russell, argued that the available work should be shared out between the workers working only half-days. A reduction in working hours was widely supported in America and other countries such as Italy, but it was opposed by the employers. In the twenty-first century there is also a movement to reduce the length of the working day, particularly in France. In many countries, however, the opposite has happened, with those relatively secure employees inside large organisations working even longer hours to keep their positions, a pattern already familiar to Japanese 'salarymen'.

Various theories have tried to explain our emerging employment patterns. They are all very well-known in academic circles, but that is where they have remained, because even today, people generally feel that a man, as the traditional breadwinner, needs a recognisable, full-time job. If a male friend or family member hasn't got a "proper job", this is still talked of in hushed tones, with fingers-crossed that things will work out for him eventually. In contrast, working part-time might suit his wife as she juggles work and home, and, finally, "temping" is reserved for those who just won't settle down and take life seriously (such as a 'resting' actor, or a would-be J K Rowling).

Yet work no longer fits into the "Tinker, tailor, soldier, sailor" categories for many people. As long ago as 1989 Charles Handy theorised that as people got older they would develop "portfolio careers", doing different activities on different days of the week, but this option has mainly been ruled out by increasing specialisation. The German academic, Ulrich Beck, concludes that: *"The 'job for life' has disappeared"*[104]. He has made great play of the disintegration of traditional full-time permanent jobs, a phenomenon which he describes as the "Brazilianization of work" to reflect the more fragmented nature of work in the emerging economies. Maddy Dychtwald and her husband, the well-known American gerontologist Ken Dychtwald, approach the issue of jobs from a demographic perspective, and predict that people will cycle in and out of their careers, alternating between periods of employment, breaks to look after the family or for sabbaticals, and re-training. Governments optimistically cling to the idea that re-training in computer skills will rapidly equip redundant sales managers to install nuclear power stations and run wind farms.

Career Crunch!

Ulrich Beck predicts a much more significant role for the caring sector, which would fit well with the needs of an ageing demographic, but perhaps less well with the preferences of thrusting male go-getters who see themselves as successful businessmen: whether exchanging exotic pole dancers for elderly ladies with Zimmer frames will fully engage this type of employee must remain questionable. Former Masters of the Universe may not be as effective when deprived of the motivators of profit, glamour and high profile, and care work is definitely not glamorous. It is directly personal and therefore labour- intensive, since by its nature it cannot easily be automated (though there have been attempts to do so: Thomas Midgley, a scientist who was already a leading light in unhelpful innovation as the creator of both lead in petrol *and* CFCs, also devised a machine to lift and turn him when he was confined to bed by polio in later life, but his contraption finally strangled him). And how well are we willing to pay our care workers? It appears that care workers in the UK are predominantly women, and that this significantly affects their pay. In countries like Denmark, care workers are better paid and more highly qualified and therefore do a better job – but at a cost that we in the UK are not prepared to pay. As its voter profile ages, government may make its policies more old-age friendly, but as its workforce ages, it may not be able to pay for them.

Parents have already seen the problem
The primary concerns for young people currently stepping up to the career ladder directly reflect the concerns of their parents, who are now middle-aged and at exactly that juncture in their careers where they are feeling vulnerable to redundancy and side-lining. Their overriding concern is for their children to be insured against their own employment worries, by ensuring that their child's chosen career will continue to exist for the next forty to fifty years, and that there will not be an oversupply of qualified labour driving down salaries or driving out older colleagues. "*People will always get ill, so they'll always need doctors*" is a typical logic – but then people will always need to eat, too, yet farmers' incomes have been dropping for many years. Even at the most academic universities, courses which clearly lead to a career are intensely

over-subscribed, as ambitious but pragmatic teenagers compete to secure their futures. At Cambridge University there are seven candidates for every place to study Economics, and more than five per place in Law or Medicine, whereas Classics is down to two applicants per place. Meanwhile, reading in the careers section of the Oxford University online prospectus that "Graduates in Economics and Management are amongst the most sought-after in the University" it is clear why there are seventeen applicants per place on this course. Teenagers who are less academic are urged by parents, teachers, the government and Alan Sugar to take up apprenticeships as hairdressers or mechanics.

In the professions, entry barriers and bottle-necks can limit the number of new entrants qualifying, but Medicine and Law have begun to lose control of personnel numbers through new developments such as the arrival of overseas doctors, and in the legal profession role distinctions are being eroded between barristers and solicitors. The accountancy profession still has some methods at its disposal to limit numbers, such as raising or lowering the bar of required pass marks to ensure that only a certain number of accountants qualify every year. In terms of older professionals, legal and accountancy practices have traditionally been run as partnerships, where no sensible employee would dare to suggest that a senior partner was getting a bit doddery. However this may change, as partnerships are going public and thus becoming accountable to external shareholders. Other partnerships are recruiting practice managers in order to increase their competitiveness, and with this brief in mind, the job security of the senior partners may come under increasing scrutiny. None of which is reassuring if it is your life-style, rather than your skills, which have kept up with your income.

"Flexemployment": the winding path to a new career

Whatever future pattern of work is envisaged, flexibility is always the buzzword, yet how flexible are most jobs or most employees?

Career Crunch!

×   Flexible workforce (hours, location; 'temps')

×   Flexible employers (permitting flexible hours, home working)

×   Flexible pay (unlike "Over-Priced Pete")

×   Retraining (makes employees more adaptable)

×   Reduced bureaucracy (min. wage vs. apprenticeships; easier to switch to and from self-employment)

×   Flexible employment law (easier hiring/firing)

None of these is fully in place in any economy at the moment. Labour force flexibility is desperately needed by the European economies in order to compete with China and India, and even the USA. European unemployment rates remained high in the relative economic boom throughout the decade up to 2005: in France with its vociferous trades unions at an average of 10.6%, and in Germany, with its strong worker councils, 9.3%, and was lower but still too high at 6% in the UK, and 5% in the USA, but only around 3% in India and China (though in those countries to be unemployed is to suffer much greater hardship so there is an even greater incentive to find some kind of work).

In contrast with the US, where over a quarter of working Americans were in non-standard jobs, according to a report in Bloomberg's Business Week magazine in 2010[105], recent legislation advocated by the EU and supported by trade unions to give equal rights to part-timers and temps will have the effect of reducing labour flexibility, serving the interests of permanent employees, as it makes employing flexible staff much less attractive. From an employee's perspective, fewer than half have any say in the hours they work, even if they are knowledge workers, who are by definition more in control of their own tasks. According to a report by The Work Foundation, "The reality is that less than fifty per cent of all workers and less than sixty per cent of knowledge workers said they have some flexibility in their work schedule, and only a very small minority said they can freely determine their own hours[106]." The report also ascertained that overall other flexible forms of work – self-employment, home-working, portfolio working, temporary work and job-shares have all either remained low or fallen over the past decade. In terms of job tenure, long-term jobs (over ten years) were held by only a fifth of the workers, and nearly one third of employees had been in their jobs between one and two years.

Nevertheless, amongst a sometimes reluctantly pioneering group of experienced managers, interim work is on the increase for very powerful economic reasons. Hitherto permanent employees, whose salaries have risen with inflation every year since they were hired, are now out of line with current market rates, and could be replaced more cheaply. This brings us back to the perceived Career Value Gap, introduced in *Chapter One*.

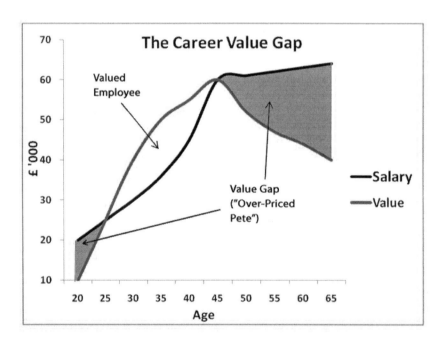

For his employer, the solution to the gap between an employee's perceived value and his salary is to make him redundant. For the employee, it is to try to increase his perceived value. He may work longer hours, gain an extra professional qualification, or make a bid to enlarge his empire, but if head-counts are on the agenda, his bosses may not be moved. A third way to close the gap would be for the employee to be offered the opportunity to take a lower salary, and indeed this has started to take place as a result of the credit crunch. However, other than in the depths of a recession, this rarely occurs, because any internal route is in danger of appearing to be "constructive dismissal", and without a framework to facilitate a salary decrease, the employee himself has had no incentive and no mechanism to address his inflated salary until, apparently out of the blue, he loses his permanent position.

After seeking another permanent job in vain, the only work he can find to tide him over is '*Flex*employment', as a consultant, an interim manager or a 'temp'. With a careful choice of interim role, however, his involuntary change to *Flex*employment can be turned into a positive development, as it enables the interim manager to move round different companies and sectors using his existing expertise. Whilst the illustration below shows the flexible employee earning *less* than previously, in fact interim managers can be paid significantly *more* than equivalent permanent employees because they offer advantages to the employer: flexible employees are only paid for the work they do; they do not need to be paid redundancy when they are no longer needed, and they are recruited for their proven skills against a tightly targeted specification, so they are more likely to succeed in the projects they are given to manage.

After a period of working flexibly, accepting sometimes higher, sometimes lower rates of pay than previously, and moving around companies and locations, interim managers who have chosen their assignments carefully have often built up sufficient expertise in a new sector, or in a newly-emerging or under-staffed function within their own sector, to be attractive as a permanent employee. They can then begin a new career stage, building up to their previous salary and even progressing beyond it in a completely new role, as illustrated below. These opportunities cannot be mapped out in advance, and will not be the standard career models envisaged by parents for their children, nor can subsequent careers be entered into in the same formal way as the first, because they will be in response to the market-place, rather than imposed upon it.

Career Crunch!

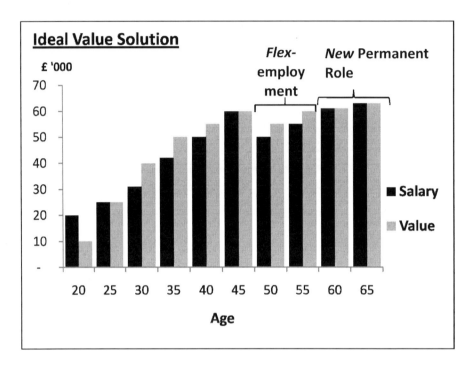

In the ideal Value Solution, the enterprising redundant manager has created his own new career path by emphasising his flexibility towards role, remuneration, location and availability, moving sideways and even downwards in the short term, in order to redirect his new longer term career across and upwards into an emerging role in a new sector or a new function.

The Price is right - but where is the job?

Yet it is very difficult for an individual, no matter how flexible, willing and entrepreneurial he is, to create paid employment out of nothing. If the job he does is no longer required, and all the other job vacancies are over-subscribed with experienced applicants, the situation can seem hopeless. He can target what he sees as a growing industry with good employment prospects, such as nuclear power in Britain in the nineteen-fifties, only to find it is then supported by governments in other countries, but not in his own, where it gradually all but dies out. Jobs do not exist in a vacuum, but in the global market-place. Some need to be carried out in a certain place and therefore cannot be directly substituted from abroad, but many of the localised services are provided for the people doing the international jobs, and these *can* be substituted. Whilst someone based in Singapore cannot directly take on the role of nanny to your children, a trader in Singapore can perhaps take on *your* job in global equity trading, so that you can no longer employ your nanny in the UK, no matter how qualified, experienced and hard-working she is, but conversely a position for a children's nanny has now been created in Singapore. So even localised jobs are lost when a country allows its industry to move abroad, and there is little that those workers can do about it.

Is there anything more that can be done to preserve or create jobs, especially for older workers? How far are we willing to go? Are we prepared to view world trade from a global point of view and accept that there will be winners and losers? If so we'd better wake up and smell the Fair Trade Coffee – and hope global warming will enable us to grow it too, in twenty years' time. Our ethical standards will no longer allow us to revive our fortunes the Elizabethan way, through the kind of privateering which is still pursued by our less fastidious rising competitors. It was a great business model – the Spanish did all the work: hacking their way through jungles, subjugating tens of thousands of natives and enslaving a sophisticated civilisation to bring gold to be melted down and loaded onto ships - only to see their booty purloined by the British on its way home. It's almost enough to engender a sneaking sympathy for the doomed Spanish Armada. Still, we weren't actually breaking any sort of GATT regulations at the time – in fact our privateers such as Sir Francis Drake became national heroes. The modern equivalent, pirating the products of years of R&D investment in designs and formulae and manufacturing them for a few pence, counterfeiting everything from fashion to pharmaceuticals, isn't the stuff of swashbuckling yarns in the same way, but is equally effective at transferring ill-gotten wealth to the pirates. Still, as the current perpetrators are mainly located in far-off countries which are not yet seen as rivals for economic power, there has been no Armada launched against them so far.

Career Crunch!

A more comparable model of the modern UK economy, though it still relied upon some dubious practices, was the Industrial Revolution, when Britain grew rich on the back of plentiful natural resources - coal, clay, iron, cheap child labour - and a well-developed infrastructure - state-of-the art waterways to transport our produce, and an excellent merchant fleet developed through the slave trade. Then, when we banned slavery 1807 did we say "Well, we grew rich from it, so it's your turn now"? No. We turned the same naval gunships that had been protecting our slave ships, onto any British ships that tried to continue trading, along with the slave ships of other nations, especially the French[107]. We had no moral qualms about this because: a) we were generally at war with them anyway; b) we could not allow the French to exploit our ethical sensitivities; and c) we had now seen the light that slavery was morally wrong, so it was our ethical duty to persuade everyone else of this too, and cannons are very persuasive.

Nowadays, any progress that can be made based on either the immoral means that we reject, or on the plentiful raw materials that we no longer have, is being pursued somewhere else in the world. We need to use both tangible and intangible means to create a supportive environment for new industries. It was no coincidence that the individuals who re-shaped the technology of the late twentieth century, and made themselves billionaires in the process, were based in the United States – they immediately benefited from a supportive entrepreneurial culture, available capital and a large, affluent domestic market with no trade barriers, into which to launch their products. China could soon have a sufficiently affluent internal market to service its own needs. Ricardo's benefits of trade may still apply, but China is as populous as Europe, the US and South America combined, all trading with each other. It requires raw materials but for this it has already set up close links with Africa. What have we to offer to the global marketplace that is unique? Not only individuals, but also business and government must provide a coordinated response to the new trade patterns which will soon fundamentally shift the balance of world economic, demographic and, consequentially, political power.

Career Crunch!

What business can do

1. Salaries and bonuses: Correctly-Priced Pete

A fundamental change in the way salaries rise over time with inflation would pre-empt the problem of Over-Priced Pete. Employees cannot afford to price themselves out of their own job. If salaries continue to rise automatically with experience, then, unless this experience has a recognised, calculable value to the organisation, a newer, younger, and therefore cheaper employee will look more attractive. Older workers complain that ageist prejudice does not allow them to compete on equal terms with younger rivals, but 'levelling the playing fields' works in all directions, not only for age but also for salary. On job sites such as Monster.co.uk there are categories for candidate experience required. Monster is slightly skewed because it caters for the low-to-middle end of the jobs market, nevertheless it is revealing. The 'experience' categories go up to fifteen years plus, but there are rarely jobs in any section above five years. So it appears that the thirty years of one employee's experience are not valued more highly than the five years of another employee – most companies simply do not think that those extra twenty-five generic years add to his usefulness. If an individual can demonstrate that his particular additional twenty-five years of experience make him more valuable as an employee, the onus is upon him to do so.

So to avoid the Over-Priced Pete problem, companies need to keep a tight rein on salaries, even in boom times. Instead of inflating over time, ideally salaries should be bench-marked against the rest of the industry at regular intervals, and adjusted accordingly. However, even checking salaries against competitors will not control wage inflation across an industry or across the wider economy. Take the case of a computer programmer or web designer who joined a company during the dot-com bubble in 1999, when his skills were in desperate demand, and salary levels were sky-high. His salary continued to rise, but after the turn of the millennium, as the bubble burst and companies amalgamated, the market was awash with young newly-qualified programmers who had piled into it, attracted by high salaries and plentiful jobs. Over-supply pushed down salaries for new entrants, so the overpaid programmer congratulates himself on locking in his pay at a high rate – but only until he is made redundant, as cost is a valid selection criterion when reducing staff numbers.

This problem will not arise if, instead, employees are paid a base salary which is adjusted according to the market rate for the job, topped up with a bonus linked to pre-agreed performance measures, perhaps in part individual targets and partly overall company performance. In this way, an employee who has been highly valued for his experience, efficient working style or particularly relevant combination of skills could continue to be recognised for this in his total remuneration provided that he continues to offer skills that are still as much in demand as previously. Banks are criticised for their bonuses, but paying a moderate basic wage and then a generous bonus has benefits in terms of employee motivation, as having a high element of performance-related pay ensures that an employee never becomes complacent and that each year he is pleased to gain a high bonus instead of taking his salary for granted. More ruthlessly, however, City-style Salary+Bonus pay structures allow firms to make employees redundant more cheaply, since statutory redundancy is linked to basic salary, and this is one of their main attractions to employers. Nevertheless, in the recent Credit Crunch it has become apparent that substantial bonuses are not merely a performance-related perk but viewed as an integral part of the salary. Outrage that bonuses are still being paid in failed banks is countered with the defence that employees expect to earn these sums. The flexible, financially-motivated workforce is more a reality in the City than elsewhere, but the resultant 'bonus culture' starkly demonstrates the trade-off between job-security and pay.

2. Keeping employees up to date

Companies need to aim to take advantage of any available training allowances and other government initiatives, such as redundancy assistance, which is offered on the learndirect website. Employees must be incentivised to keep their skills up to date, both financially through a performance-related pay scheme and also as part of their ongoing job specification. External retraining can be piecemeal or only loosely relevant, so this should be reserved for the acquisition of new skills by the company, whereas practical on-the-job training should be carried out as far as possible by the internal staff themselves, so that knowledge and skills are tailored and applicable. 'Back to the Floor' days not only update mangers but also demonstrate their commitment to new techniques and working practices.

The Credit Crunch highlighted the disconnect between Company Directors and Managers in the inner sanctum of the boardroom, and the functional specialists whom they are nominally managing. Main Boards should in future, as has always been the case in smaller companies, be supplemented with technical operational experts. Better still, the Operational Board should be considered to be the Main Board, taking all the major decisions in the running of the company, with the Board of Legal Directors relegated to their proper place of advisors in financial and legal technicalities, instead of elevated to the role of financial strategists using game theory and accounting rules to take a company where its operational competencies cannot necessarily follow.

3. Employee Promotion & Retirement

Promotion should not necessarily trigger a pay rise such that employees at the next level down are better value for money. Gradual inflation of pay and job titles should be tightly controlled by HR policy, with all jobs clearly defined by objectively-assessed skills levels. The choice of an appropriate retirement age will soon become crucial, not only to save paying premature pensions to the current glut of middle-managers, but also looking ahead to a serious future shortage of labour from 2020 onwards, once the 1960s Baby Boomers start to retire. If the company already has in place objective job specifications and appropriate tests, then these could be applied on an annual basis after a default retirement age of seventy years. The issue of not being able to ease out Over-Priced Petes should no longer arise once the correct salary structures are in place – and by using objective tests of skills and faculties, there should be no need to have an embarrassing conversation about failing hearing or memory loss. Employment regulations may in future be defined in law at a national – and increasingly EU level - despite the UK opt-out from certain employment legislation - but for the present, each company has wide latitude in its policies towards older employees.

4. Recruitment

External recruitment can trigger pay escalation as the process drags on, and the only candidate upon whom everyone can agree negotiates for a higher salary than specified in the job advertisement. The job specification and salary must be clearly agreed right at the start of the process, before one of the non-executive directors recommends his old protégé. The skills required should be specified in writing along with a robustly bench-marked salary range. These skills should be rigorously tested – not merely by a psychometric black box such as "Myers-Briggs", but also using simple generally-available tests for basic practical competencies in maths and logic. These standard tests can be supported if necessary by bespoke tests applicable to the specific industry or function.

Companies need to campaign strongly against the current trend to legislate to make workers harder to dismiss, as this hinders competitiveness. Instead employees should be encouraged to prepare for the need to move jobs and re-skill, both in career-planning but also in their personal financial planning. Recognising that redundancy is a normal part of working life, tax legislation should be introduced to allow job-seekers to spread income tax over two or more years, as some professions have been allowed to do, to avoid the boom and bust of complete years in or out of employment.

5. Publish essential skills expected of employees at each level

The CBI, IOD, CSB and other bodies, who are eloquent about the lack of skills offered by today's job-seekers, should publish guidelines detailing the essential skills required at each business level with practical worked examples, starting from the most basic level of work, such as punctuality and dress code, to the more sophisticated skills such as calculating the pros and cons of hedging the company's FX requirements and presenting these findings coherently to the Board.

6. R&D

There are already tax breaks for R&D expenditure in pharmaceuticals and other spear-head industries, and indeed the Department for Business, Innovation and Skills claims to have provided more than £3 billion in tax support for R&D in the first decade of the Millennium[108]. But this activity should not be confined to R&D departments. To survive, every company needs to engage in regular intelligence-gathering and innovation throughout their business. This includes constant benchmarking of their competitors, and is most effective when carried out by employees themselves as part of their normal day-jobs. All employees should have included as part of their contract of employment a commitment to demonstrate that they take an interest in the business by reading the national press, the trade press and company newsletters and providing feedback to the company.

What can government do?

Is free trade just exporting western jobs to producers with fewer scruples?
Imported goods are cheap because we benefit from global economies of scale and specialisation, but also because we trade with producers whose workforce are poorly paid relative to our own. So we gain on the swings and lose on the roundabouts – for those of us who are in work, our salary has even more purchasing power, but through competition from cheaper labour abroad a large number of low-to-medium-level jobs have been lost.

And why should we worry that the goods we buy are so much cheaper than we can make them ourselves? Because they are produced in economies which do not bear the costs of wages above subsistence level, do not offer acceptable working conditions and do not make provision to clean up their pollution or replace the raw materials they exploit. From a purely commercial perspective, we are hampering our manufacturers with domestic environmental legislation that is not applied to many of our trading partners. From an environmental perspective, we are doing what we can to protect our own environment – after all, we do not have a say in the environment of the exporting countries.

But we *do* have a say, because it is in making goods for sale to *us* that our trading partners are polluting their own environment. We also have a sense of guilt which prevents us from putting tariffs on goods which are causing pollution elsewhere – we grew wealthy polluting the atmosphere, how can we justify pulling up the ladder behind us? Is there also a third, less admissible reason - that for all our fine words, when push comes to shove, we don't care *enough* about child labour and pollution to embargo unjustifiably cheap goods, if it means suffering a drastic cut in our lifestyle? Whilst angst-ridden parents sit in the kitchen drinking *Fair Trade* tea and coffee, their children are out every weekend patronising a range of inexplicably cheap fashion stores. But if an increasing number of middle-class middle-managers are made redundant, such luxuries as paying a little more for a clear conscience may well be too expensive for the adults, too.

There are three options if we wish to pursue our present social and environmental goals: persuade our less scrupulous trading partners to raise their standards of pay and conditions and reduce pollution; cease to trade with them; or impose tariffs on imports to off-set the pollution/exploitation costs. Either way the cost of our imports will then be their true costs, so economists should be really happy (apart from Ricardo). Because now the cheap economies won't be artificially cheap, our trade will either slow down with them, or we will have to work harder to maintain our lifestyle; at the extreme, if we cease to trade with them altogether, this will freeze our balance of payments deficit with them, though at the cost of losing some increasingly valuable export markets. Consumers will be shocked to find they have to pay the true costs of producing the goods domestically or in one of our environmentally-friendly neighbours, and politicians will need to prepare for the political backlash from the trading partners on whose goods we impose

Career Crunch!

green tariffs, who will no doubt impose reciprocal tariffs on any goods our companies are exporting to them, thus cutting off huge present and future markets. Perhaps we would be wiser not to rock the boat, and instead to concentrate on pursuing our social and environmental goals at home. The only issue that will then remain is the efficiency of free markets, which is already taking into account our luxurious lifestyle in the form of clean air and minimum wages, and ensuring our gradual but inevitable decline down the league tables, along with our salaries, health care and employment prospects.

Unwelcome as government intervention is in the market-place, the sheer scale of global businesses requires coordinated action to get and keep jobs, and ensure that the workforce is appropriately qualified to do them, and governments are best-placed to provide the environment for this – in a world that widely condemns the power of global capitalism, it is interesting to note how decisive a role central governments play in their own national economies, not only at a macro-economic level (i.e. setting taxes and interest rates, as economic theory suggests), but also within individual industries. Older employees are particularly vulnerable to global trends, so it is to the significance of government industrial strategy, both helpful and positively harmful, at home and abroad, that we must briefly now turn our attention.

Government intervention distorts the jobs market

Government has increasingly taken on the responsibility for providing the infrastructure and education to support jobs, but this is often despite the people, rather than urged on by them. Babar the elephant, as a benign dictator, might have faced no planning difficulties when the fishes complained about his decision to construct Celesteville beside their beautiful lake, but nowadays any grand industrial strategy undertaken by the UK government which includes infrastructure build to improve traffic flow or air access takes years to implement. The crucial role of government is grudgingly acknowledged by even the most committed free market economists, but in the UK does it have the latitude, the business acumen, the guts, or even the common sense to implement effective strategies to ensure that Britain as a whole attracts and creates rewarding, enduring jobs in the third millennium?

Growth comes from "creative destruction" - old and inefficient firms are replaced by new growing businesses. However, when government steps in, this does not happen. Incompetent and over-ambitious banks are resurrected to crash again another day; public sector administrative jobs are created and awarded huge pay-offs if they are subsequently found to be unnecessary. We are forcing the market to go, or rather stay, where it naturally would not, and that is why the task is such a challenge – we are trying not to predict or exploit but to *buck market trends*. We are out to prove that in terms of both industry and employment, decline is not inevitable – with planning and preparation it can be deferred or even turned around. Products have life cycles; industries have life cycles; countries and people have life cycles – but even more than for products or industries, countries and people are both in a position to extend their commercial lives by developing new skills or offerings. We need to "plug skills gaps" and commit to a government-supported industrial strategy. Does this sound old-fashioned or even dangerously like central planning?

Is government competent to meddle or should it leave well alone? Will it save our jobs or squander out taxes? In the UK politicians have not sought a major role in industry since the 1970's when James Callaghan pursued a mainly disastrous industrial policy which nevertheless created British Aerospace, now BAE, a major UK engineering group. Government is notoriously incompetent in many areas. Data security is one. IT purchasing is another. Take the case revealed in March 2009 of the government database of offenders[109] that took two years to get so far behind schedule that it was scrapped in favour of several smaller systems at an *increased* cost of £279 million. Britain has grown its state sector disproportionately, by more than half a million jobs since 1997[110].

The nation's accounts could be compared to those of a large business. The business provides goods or services which create wealth, and quite early on it also acquires overheads like accountants, IT programmers, cleaners and HR personnel, who do not earn it any money directly, but are there to help the business run more smoothly. In times of plenty most companies allow their overheads to grow, but these are cut back with glee by the ascendant cost-cutters in leaner times, (all except the accounts departments, who argue that they are of course needed to keep track of the cost-cutting). When a nation's public sector is bloated from the good years, cutting back is far harder. Firstly public sector workers are usually entitled to generous pay-offs, generally worth more than two years' salary, which undermine the short-term benefits of making them redundant, and secondly, with more jobless there will of course be an increased need for staff at job centres and many other public services. Yet as with a company, it is the other departments who actually earn the money, and, as they are weighed down by the costs of overheads, the company declines in profitability until it has no more credit-worthiness with the bank and can no longer borrow money. Cutting the overheads is an issue that the company has ducked for too long, so now that task is left to the receiver as the company goes bankrupt. For a national economy, the fear is that the International Monetary Fund (IMF) will be called in to restructure its debts, thereby undermining its worldwide credibility. Of course this mainly happens to the world's poorest economies, but although we prefer to forget this, the UK had to call in the IMF and ask for a loan when the pound collapsed in 1976. The conditions of the loan were harsh spending cuts and austere economic measures. In 2010 the stronger economies of the European Union imposed similar conditions to address Greece's financial credibility. Taking steps to prevent a similar national economic humiliation for the UK, by cutting the national overheads before the economic situation compels us to, inevitably means more middle-management redundancies. Yet this is the only solution to begin the painful process of 'market correction' which is the underlying driver of the Credit Crunch and therefore the Career Crunch too.

Government Industrial Strategy creates jobs

Governments are increasingly enmeshed in global business. For a start, they set interest rates, which help to determine exchange rates, and therefore dictate how expensive a nation's products and services are to the rest of the world. The Chinese authorities are constantly chided by the Americans for keeping the renminbi exchange rate artificially low, so that their prices are attractive, but there are pros and cons for both sides. American industry has no hope of competing with Chinese industry at such low rates, but American consumers benefit from cheap goods. Meanwhile, Chinese workers are deprived of some of the imported goods they could buy if the exchange rate were higher, but overall their country prospers by selling a lot of exports and earning a lot of foreign currency. The ironic twist is that when the US dollar drops in value due to a shock like the Credit Crunch, which makes people start to wonder how much longer countries like the US (and the UK) can continue to pay for their purchases with borrowed money, all that foreign currency earned and saved up by the Chinese also drops in value at the same time, so, in a rather amoral way, the Americans get the last laugh. In the case of the Eurozone, the single currency requires a centralised monetary policy, which can be too inflexible when some regions are prospering more than other, and yet is still only a half-way house to financial integration compared with the United States because there is no central tax system.

So another influence that governments have is that they also set taxes, which play a part in attracting, or deterring, multinationals. They also enter into trading agreements with, or occasionally, and very inconveniently, declare war on, potential trading partners. They are responsible for the infrastructure of a country, for instance, its transport and communications, and also set the standards for education. They enact all sorts of legislation which is generally intended to keep order. They can act as a kind of 'employer of last resort', by increasing the number of jobs in the public sector, as the UK government did over the last decade, when Britain's unemployment levels were much lower than on the Continent, or even by initiating explicit 'job creation programmes', such as the infrastructure build in the US during the 1930s, designed to mitigate the effects of the Depression.

If your jobs depend on trade on a world-wide basis, then size matters, particularly for heavy industry such as ship-building, which requires massive capital investment in plant and machinery. But economies of scale go beyond the capacity to make big heavy things, or even lots of cheap little things, to more abstract consequences, such as the learning curve when a large number of people in one town are employed in the same sector, and therefore develop widespread expertise in it – for example, in the finance sector in London. Then there are economies of scope from all the spin-off industries and services that find work supplying the big businesses, for example the agglomerations along "Silicon Valley" in the US, or "Silicon Glen" in Scotland. Infrastructure, in the form of roads, rail and broadband connections grow up to support them, and a virtuous circle called the 'multiplier effect' is created. For all these reasons, governments fight to preserve jobs in major manufacturing industries such as motor manufacturing. It was an unholy sight to see staunch advocates of free trade such as the USA rushing to support their failing car manufacturers suffering under the Credit Crunch, alongside such overt nationalists as the French. What was an honest broker like the UK to do, caught in the middle? Nevertheless, whilst genuine global competition, wheeling and dealing in a free market, provides cheap goods and a constant supply of new opportunities, it will not provide a stable long-term source of employment in any one location, against new rivals abroad constantly bidding for the business. At the opposite extreme, there is market manipulation, in the shape of monopolies, or cartels such as OPEC, which are very effective at controlling profits for their members. Far from a simple story of a freewheeling market-place dominated by all-powerful global corporations, world trade has evolved over the centuries as a mish-mash of monopolies, cartels, monopsonies, trading agreements, trade areas, currency zones, national interests and declining, or rising, imperialism, all working alongside genuine free trade, and it is on this uneven playing field that ambitious multinationals and cautious, or bellicose, national governments compete to create wealth and jobs.

Given the acknowledged benefits of international trade, an explicit policy of sharing out industries between the major world economies would lead to greater employment stability. Trade would be less competitive, but more orderly. However, most governments, at least publicly, espouse principles committed to increasing, rather than restricting free trade and competition, and sharing out industries would be little different from setting up cartels and monopolies. As a result, countries cannot explicitly negotiate for their own areas of specialisation. However, many, if not most, countries have energetically appropriated specialised economic activities for their workforce, and defend them vigorously against all competition. Some have acquired a natural advantage through the judicious exploitation of fortuitous geology, such as Abu Dhabi, a dwindling community of pearl fishers until only fifty years ago, when about one twelfth of the entire world's oil deposits were discovered there. The government policies of the OPEC states, actively managing a cartel to regulate the quantity and price of oil supplied, have played a major role in controlling their oil revenues. Lacking its own oil deposits, Abu Dhabi's fellow Arab Emirate, Dubai, invested in developing other industries, first becoming a leader in the banking sector, then a shopping centre and recently a global aviation hub, and it was planning to attract bio-technology expertise, having already successfully cloned a racing camel, though this proud achievement did not hit the headlines with the same significance for the racing industry in the rest of the world as it did in Dubai. Without the secure underpinning of a readily exportable commodity, however, its strategies were revealed to be founded on sand when it, too, was hit by the Credit Crunch and global trade dried up.

The spectacular growth in China from the 1980s, and in India, from the 1990s, began when their governments relaxed their former trading restrictions, freeing up business and promoting certain areas such as Bangalore in India and the Special Economic Zones in China. The Irish government was also effective at encouraging growth, but they overdid their encouragement of some areas, particularly property development, and are set to move to the status of a text book case study of *"Not knowing when to stop"*. Most advanced economies are already explicitly targeting 'knowledge' industries, but in 2008 the World Bank published a report urging the governments of poorer, developing nations to aim to acquire the same technologies themselves:

"The most critical aspect of the catching-up process is building the capacity to absorb, adapt, and adopt technologies already being used in other countries. This is not a passive process and it is not something that simply happens to an enterprise or an economy. Nor is it simply a question of attracting foreign direct investment (FDI) and then waiting passively for foreign

investors to foster the catch-up process. On the contrary, experience suggests that catching up requires conscious, active, coordinated capacity building policies at the level of individual firms, as well as at the level of government agencies, public-private technology development institutions, technical and vocational training institutions, and secondary and tertiary education institutions."

Source: The World Bank[111]

This advice from the World Bank illustrates how the developing countries are being actively encouraged to target the technological know-how of the advanced economies. As different, huge economies converge, the challenge will be for them each to find a niche to slip into before they collide, and an international free-for-all ensues.

Germany has nearly a third of its output in manufacturing. Despite the competition constraints on EU members, Germany is able to offer explicit support to its industries, for instance, allowing the national German postal service, Deutsche Post, to take over the private sector courier DHL, and create "the world's leading mail and logistics Group"[112]. The car industry is another important employer in Germany and France, and as GM searched for a buyer for Opel and Vauxhall in 2009, the German Chancellor, Angela Merkel, personally held talks with potential buyers, offering subsidies to save the jobs of the 25,000 Opel employees in Germany. In this particular case the UK government remained coy about exactly what incentives it was willing to offer buyers to preserve British jobs.

Other types of manufacturing attract subsidies in Germany, too. Even for Rolls-Royce, a British national icon, the former East German state of Brandenburg managed to outbid Her Majesty's government and get a new prime high value manufacturing Rolls-Royce test-bed plant located in Germany instead of the UK in 2007. The German bid was over £3 million higher, and as an 'assisted area with high unemployment' they were also able to offer up to 30% of the capital cost, in addition to helping to train employees. But should government take a risk by providing large sums of taxpayers' money to take a punt on jobs and industries for the future? "Picking winners" is still a sore subject for Labour politicians, forty years after they attempted to build up British industry and mostly failed, and British governments are reluctant to subsidise failing industries such as motor manufacturing, perhaps with memories of the hard battles fought in the Thatcher years, between entrenched trades unions and a government determined to drive the UK into a more free market economy.

Yet Sir John Rose, Chief Executive of Rolls-Royce, has argued consistently that the UK needs an industrial strategy to compete internationally. He compares the UK, where his company has received virtually no net funding, unfavourably with the US. Three-fifths of the huge worldwide Rolls-Royce workforce of nearly 40,000 is based in the UK, including over 5,000 engineers. Over a period of five years it received £155 million from overseas governments, mainly the US, Canada, Germany and the EU, very little of which it will have to repay, compared with £128 million of R&D support from the UK government, much of which it will have to repay. The role of governments is certainly emerging as very influential in securing jobs in global manufacturing.

Energy: A case study in how government can create or lose jobs
Nuclear power supplies France with three-quarters of its electricity because the French government launched a large nuclear energy programme after the first world "oil shock" of 1973, in order to generate its own power to compensate for a lack of oil and gas and dwindling coal. According to the website of EDF (Eléctricité de France), the world's largest nuclear power provider, more than 40,000 people are employed in the nuclear industry in France, including 20,000 EDF staff. It is now exporting its expertise to the British, who were the pioneers of nuclear power in the fifties, having been preeminent in the development of nuclear energy through to the early 1940s, and opened the first commercial-scale nuclear reactor at Calder Hall in 1956, before the British government rejected nuclear power on the grounds of safety and its association with nuclear weapons. China has only eleven reactors at the moment but is already constructing a further twenty, and planning or

proposing to build fifteen times the number it already has[113]. The US already has over one hundred reactors, whilst Russia continues its nuclear programme, with over thirty reactors operating and as many again planned for the future, despite the literal and ethical fall-out from Chernobyl[114], but also aggressively pursues other forms of energy, including its control of gas supplies which it uses as an economic and political bargaining tool with Europe.

In contrast to the comfortable situation in France, in the UK *all but one* of our nineteen nuclear power stations are due for closure by 2023, despite the fact that they currently supply almost a sixth of our electricity, and that it takes about ten years to get a new reactor up and running. Nuclear power was too unpopular in the UK to propose before the alternative was turning off the lights, and as they had no other solution, did successive governments consider it best not to mention energy at all? Every power station built in the UK was meant to be the last - or maybe the first, if opinion changed - so, far from a planned programme of building, each station was built to a slightly different design. France has coordinated nuclear capacity, with its nuclear power stations mainly built to the same design, conveniently for spare parts and staff training. As recently as 2006, the British government insisted that British Nuclear Fuels sold off the second-largest nuclear energy provider world-wide, the formerly American company, Westinghouse, which it had owned since 1999. It did this for reasons best known to itself, but although the high cost and long-term responsibility of storing spent fuel and decommissioning old power stations was probably a factor, the huge profit it made from the three billion pound sale must have been another. Now, with a change of heart in the UK driven by a lack of any credible alternative, Westinghouse would be providing globally-relevant British jobs if we still owned it. So whose responsibility is it to plan ahead for UK needs? On this evidence, one might query whether it is, or even should be the government, since governments are only elected for a maximum term of five years, and energy requirements work on at least a ten-year lead time. But if not government, then who?

Career Crunch!

UK gas supplies are running out. Europe obtains nearly half its supplies from politically volatile Russia. Renewable energy is targeted to provide 15% of our energy needs by 2020 – but even if the UK reaches this receding target, it would still be insufficient even to fill the gap left by our declining nuclear capability, let alone to substitute for coal, gas and oil as well. To make matters worse, a major contribution to our unacknowledged energy needs is provided by dirty coal-fired power stations running factories in far-off places - manufacturing the cheaper goods we are too concerned about the environment to make over here. The different official sources of UK energy are at present approximately: 43% gas (and Britain recently became a net importer of gas for the first time since the 1970s); 34% coal (and about half of our fourteen coal-fired power stations will have to be closed down because their emissions are too dirty to meet the EU large combustion plants directive); 15% nuclear, but this figure is dropping every year; and 8% other, including the minuscule 4% from renewables. The stark choice ahead of us will be easier to address once it is generally acknowledged that the UK's energy needs will not be supplied by a few wind turbines out to sea. In November 2008 wind power was generating 1.3% of UK energy, but was planned to overtake Denmark with over 10% by 2020[115]. This is optimistic.

Finally the UK has started focusing on its urgent energy needs. Nuclear power is now being advocated by various green groups and by James Lovelock himself, the originator of the Gaia theory. The problem he identifies is one of scale - there are over 440 nuclear power stations producing 17% of all the world's electricity, surprisingly, about the same as hydro-electricity, in contrast to other renewables which between them only produce an almost insignificant two per cent. So in April 2009 the UK government announced plans for eleven new nuclear power stations, though the earliest any of these could be in operation is 2017. The nuclear industry also has an ageing workforce and a shortage of skilled employees, but received clear government endorsement in the summer of 2009 from Lord Mandelson, UK Secretary of State for Business, Innovation and Skills, who stated that: *"Nuclear is absolutely vital for our country"*[116]. This should attract in new recruits and investment as it boosts confidence that the industry will survive and be supported by the government. The importance of older workers to use their skills to start up new industries is evident in the wind energy sector, which is hoping to attract across the North Sea oil and gas workforce which uses the same skills. However, as employment in the North Sea itself has been declining, the workforce are on average aged in their mid- to late-fifties, so there is a danger of a skills gap, which will need to be addressed by a long term commitment to develop the workforce.

Funding for such large projects such as the nuclear power industry is also difficult to obtain from commercial sources. As Lord Mandelson explained: "*The return is over such a long period of time that it is very difficult, in the present economic climate, to get the private-sector funding on the scale that you need.*"[117] Government nervousness about intervening into industry was clearly in his mind when he insisted that in general the government's role was to "*provide clear firm frameworks and policies within which commercial decisions can be taken by the private sector.*" Again, government has to tread a fine line between supporting its domestic companies and being seen to be dealing fairly, so he drove home the point: "*We are pro-competition: we are not protectionist, we believe in open markets,*" he insisted. This example sums up the tricky dilemma of governments whose countries benefit from trade in open markets yet whose industries are competing with state-supported rivals. However, in this instance the government finally overcame its dual fears that state intervention will either fail, and be seen to be a waste of public money, or be successful, and be seen by other nations as anti-competitive, and in March 2010 it agreed an £80 million loan to the engineering firm Sheffield Forgemasters to help to fund the huge press needed to make reactor vessels for the nuclear industry.

And is the UK managing to create jobs in the universally targeted 'green energy' sector? Portugal has no oil, coal or gas, and no expertise in nuclear power, but it does have a lot of sun and wind, and over one third of all Portuguese electricity is already from wind and solar power. This compares with Britain's *target* of 15% by 2020, which it may not even achieve. Meanwhile, the European Renewable Energy Research Centres Agency states that solar power is the "renewable energy source with the highest potential," and that by 2040 solar power will account for a fifth of all global energy consumption[118]. It already employs more than 40,000 people in Europe, though they are mainly based in Germany (30,000) and in Spain (6,300), and has grown 50% every year for the past five years. But in the UK only a small number of companies assemble solar panels; almost none produce the silicon required for a PV cell[119]. The UK government already funds programmes such as the £1.2 million project Havemore at the New and Renewable Energy Centre (NAREC) to create more attractive panels.[120] This organisation also works with Lab2line, an EU funded project, which raises the question of whether it would be more efficient to support large industries centrally at a European level, but the need to preserve jobs not simply within the EU, but based within the British Isles, requires support at a national level, too.

So despite ideological reservations, and spectres of past failures, government is the only body in a position to take the lead in a national industrial strategy to ensure employment for most of our extended working lives in the cut-throat global market-place. This does not mean gambling on a business when it is still a twinkle in a mad scientist's eye (a 'New Industry' – *see Chapter Two*). Nor does it mean shoring up failing behemoths in order to preserve mass employment in the short-term (a 'Declining Industry'). Instead, it is at the 'Growth' stage, identified by a rapid expansion in sales and recruitment, that government needs to take a serious look at and assess any new industry's suitability as a flagship. As Felix Dennis notes in his book "*How to Get Rich*", it is easier to expand and make money in an industry that is already growing[121].

But targeting industries should not necessarily entail direct government investment. If the business plan is sound, then investment should be commercially forthcoming from the banks and venture capitalists. Instead, having identified the new industry as a growing source of jobs and wealth, the government needs to act promptly to provide the physical infrastructure support for it, such as rapid transport, access and communications, right up to what might appear to be luxury items, such as fast broadband internet access. Industry also requires the protection of a regulatory infrastructure, such as the legal framework to allow a company to grow and compete on a global scale, and appropriate regulation by government experts in law, finance and promising new technology. Industry thrives in a deregulated jobs market, where the workforce is already trained and appropriately qualified, but, on the other hand, growing industry benefits from assurances of government commitment and continuing unequivocal support, so that investors have the confidence to invest, and workers enter and remain in the industry. Above all, the government needs to resist the urge to interfere counter-productively, by imposing punitive taxes and restrictive regulation for the sake of its own short-term political goals. Of course, it is only real-life examples which illustrate how influential such apparently self-evident government commitments could be: the British nuclear industry mentioned above, or the stop-start government relationship with the UK airline industry, both as a manufacturer, and as a global transport hub, primarily at Heathrow. Such government support, even at a general and non-financial level, can be highly controversial, and easier to promise vaguely than to deliver.

The pattern that applies to careers can be applied to global industry. UK plc has already largely gone 'up-and-out' of a series of important industries – manufacturing of heavy goods such as ship-building (the remote and land-locked Lake Titicaca between Peru and Bolivia still boasts of its ship brought from England over a century ago in pieces and carried up to over two miles above sea level to the Lake on mules); trains (Buenos Aires in Argentina still uses its showcase British underground carriages preserved from the beginning of the last century), coal, which fuelled the Industrial Revolution; nuclear power, in which the UK was the world leader; North Sea oil and gas, which sustained the economy in the latter part of the twentieth century.

Manufacturing no longer provides most of the jobs

The UK has lost about one million manufacturing jobs over the past ten years, thereby also losing brands, intellectual property and routes to market. It is set to shed a further 400,000 jobs in the near future. In Britain those students who harkened to the government cry for more engineers in the '70s and '80s found themselves competing for jobs in a decreasing number of manufacturing companies. Overall employment in manufacturing in the UK dropped like a stone, from 29% in 1978 down to 12% in 2003, and even the apparent increase in older workers in manufacturing is only attributable to the fact that they have stayed on in older manufacturing industries while younger entrants go into the service sector. In terms of major manufacturers of infrastructure, the leaders are no longer British.[122]

It is worth remembering how huge manufacturing still is - the UK exported just under £200 billion of goods in 2008, nearly half our exports, and the fact that we imported well over £250 billion of manufactured goods is another reason to continue manufacturing as much as possible, so that the net deficit of getting on for £60 billion on manufactured goods does not grow any bigger. Perhaps we should stop referring to manufacturing as a dying sector. Contrary to the assumptions of the general public, and even of many commentators, Britain remains the sixth largest manufacturing economy in the world, and has increased productivity by 50% since 1997.

The argument is sometimes put forward that the UK still benefits from manufacturing activity within the rest of Europe. But this is no comfort to a worker in the UK who, simply because there aren't other people working in manufacturing in the country where he lives, is unable to get to work without taking the major decision to emigrate temporarily or permanently. It is geographical – jobs are created in clusters with a benign roll-out effect. If the clusters are a thousand miles away then only a massive economic incentive, such as that which attracted hundreds of thousands of Polish workers into the UK and Ireland in the last few years, will make it viable for workers to migrate large distances for jobs.

Yet despite trade imbalances there is UK growth in sectors such as pharmaceuticals: according to the latest manufacturing report of The Work Foundation, both imports *and* exports have increased in the pharmaceuticals industry[123]. Manufactured goods are quoted in value terms, so that price effects can also disguise increases in production. In 2007 the UK built more passenger cars than in 1977, but their value as a share of GDP is significantly lower because technological developments and increased efficiency have driven prices down[124], especially relative to the less productive services sector, which has until recently also faced less international competition as services were harder to export - over the past decade the price of manufactured goods in the UK has on average *fallen* by 20 per cent whereas the price of services has *increased* on average by 50 per cent. Manufacturing, usually cited as a classic illustration of 'Decline' in the UK, is also an example of adopting a different strategy when an industry has reached maturity. This is now mainly in the form of servicing contracts by such companies as Rolls-Royce, or such leading edge products as blue tooth design, fuel cells, plastic electronics and frontier technologies, biotechnology and nanotechnology. Instead of wholesale abandoning of the industry, its life cycle can be extended by re-inventing its core proposition and focusing on the more sophisticated associated services. These include highly automated production and highly engineered products, and adding value by providing support over the life-time of the more complex and high capital-investment products. In this case, erstwhile competitors can become important customers. In the UK, a growing proportion of the manufacturer JCB's customers are now in India and China, once viewed solely as competitors. Similarly, Rotork, one of the top five UK engineering companies, depends on the continuing prosperity of the developing world to enable those countries to buy its products.

In terms of manufacturing's contribution to the sought-after 'knowledge economy' in the UK, the hi tech element of Britain's manufacturing constitutes over a third of manufacturing exports, a higher proportion than in Germany, which only has about a fifth, though this is because Germany has much greater exports of manufactured goods across the range of technological complexity. Instead of ceding their industrial base to cheaper producers, some economies such as Germany, Japan and South Korea have managed to retain a range of basic manufacturing, which underpins the value-added specialist manufacturing and R&D, whilst Japan, in particular, invested in plants in the UK and the USA so that it became a local employer as well as a major supplier. For the UK, too, The Work Foundation insists that "manufacturing should be seen as a priority sector for the post-recession knowledge-based economy." 'Green' manufacturing of electric or hybrid cars has been encouraged by the UK government, not only in words but also with some investment, and in 2010 this policy also bore fruit in Nissan's plans to manufacture the "Leaf" electric car in Sunderland, in addition to BMW's development of its electric mini in Oxfordshire.

In the service industries, Britain still has various traditional brand strengths, for example in tourism and education, as well as major natural advantages from its near-universal language, and its position as a convenient hub for travel between the Americas and Europe. Retailing has been a feature of the UK economy from Napoleon's scornful dismissal of us as a "nation of shopkeepers" to the modern-day Oxford Street, but only a few stores such as Tesco are on the way to emulating the scale and efficiency of the USA's vast retailer Wal-Mart. The UK also has a world-leading position in the Arts, from sculpture to music and literature, from Shakespeare to J.K.Rowling. Meanwhile the UK has retained its pre-eminence as a world leader in scientific discovery and education. Oxford University was established as a seat of learning in 1167, though studies had already begun in the eleventh century, and is the oldest university in the English-speaking world. Many academic institutions celebrated anniversaries in 2009: St Paul's School has been teaching in London since 1509; Cambridge University is 800 years old. As its website states: "Cambridge affiliates have won more than 80 Nobel Prizes, more than any other institution in the world. Some of the most famous scientific minds in history have studied, researched or taught here. This is the home of Newton and Darwin, Crick and Watson, Babbage and Hawking. However, it is also the place where the first fully 3D computer game was written, where the precursor to the modern webcam was invented, and where some of today's best-known entertainers began their careers".

Career Crunch!

Each nation is in the continual process of carrying out an assessment of patterns of global competition and making appropriate tangible investments for their long-term benefits. In the Credit Crunch the developed countries most reliant on manufacturing export trade in their economies – Japan and Germany, each with a fifth of their income dependent upon exports - suffered the most initially, as purchases of their goods dried up, whereas the UK's pharmaceutical and aerospace industries, for instance, held up relatively well in the recession, in response to which some commentators have inferred that raising our manufacturing from its present 13% of the economy may not be the answer. Certainly, the UK is not large enough to support a wide variety of significant high added-value global industries, so if specific industries are to be encouraged, someone must decide which ones to choose.

Industries to provide the Employment of the future

The government has bitten the bullet and made a commitment to an industrial strategy, supported by a strategic investment fund. In a report entitled "New Industries New Jobs"[125] it outlines key areas of pro-active UK industrial strategy, namely skills, creativity and technological change, and in January 2010 the government made further commitments to invest in UK industrial development."[126] It focuses on such sectors as low carbon technology[127], life sciences and pharmaceuticals, advanced manufacturing,[128] creative industries, and professional and financial services, and many of these sectors have already received government subsidies – in the case of financial services, somewhat more than originally planned.

Up until the Credit Crunch the UK financial sector, the biggest out of the OECD's major economies, had been growing rapidly in terms of value added (although the number of employees remained at about one million). Overall, financial services grew 170% from 1995 and contributed nearly eight per cent to GDP in 2007[129]. They generated a trade surplus of nearly £40 billion[130], worth nearly four per cent of GDP. To put this in context, the total UK GDP, that is, everything we produce, is somewhere over one trillion pounds, or one thousand billion pounds, or one million million pounds. Total exports in 2008 were about £420 billion and imports were about £460 billion, making the total trade deficit for the UK about £40 billion. Finance provided around a third of the UK's knowledge-service-based exports[131], whilst the other two-thirds of the knowledge-intensive income are generated by business services, royalties and licence fees and technical and trade-related services, and manufacturing.

Business services are expected to be a source of growth, and have added 1.7 million jobs over the past twenty years. Meanwhile, the creative industries sector, which includes design, software, publishing, and advertising, has been growing over the past decade. Far from being a rather touchy-feely concept, it contributes getting on for a tenth of GDP and employs an impressive two million people[132]. The area called 'life sciences' employs about 400,000 people in the UK. Exports from two of its largest sections, pharmaceuticals and healthcare products and services, totalled about £26 billion. Currently the UK claims to be Europe's leader in pharmaceutical R&D, though the industry is cutting costs in the face of increasing competition and declining revenue streams from older patents.

New jobs can be created by Innovation

Innovation is seen as a panacea to the world's problems, from energy needs to illness: the UK government's industrial strategy set out in 2009 included a £150 million innovation investment fund. Yet radically new inventions are often initially greeted with cynicism. Personal computers were not introduced to universal cries of "At last! How have we lived till now?" In 1985 I was selling one of the first laptops in the UK to computer dealers, who admired its compact engineering but were doubtful if they could sell many, asking, "....But how many people would want to carry a computer around with them?" In the year 2000, I was negotiating deals for our travel dot.com with enthusiastic suppliers as well as sophisticated investment bankers. The travel trade took the internet threat to their traditional way of doing business very seriously, but the "expert" financiers approached our business plans for ambitious online sales with tolerant scepticism about the technical readiness of the population.

"People will no doubt *research* their holidays on the internet," they conceded, thinking they were very avant-garde to see the internet's information potential, "but ordinary people won't actually *book* their holidays online," they concluded.

Major innovation in an industry comes in a massive step change, and then rapidly becomes fixed and set in stone – Excel is prettier and easier than its predecessor, Lotus 123, but basically the same product as those early spreadsheets, and most of the old commands still work. Yet innovation, like the magic of youth, is too ephemeral and indefinable to pin down, too sure of itself to take cognizance of any suggestions, too iconoclastic by definition to be responsive to training and practice. So how can you specialise in 'innovation'? What type of organisation nurtures innovation? The example usually cited is that of Apple, where employees have been encouraged to work on their own projects alongside the company's, and where the etiquette is to be informally dressed but workaholic. Yet according to The Work Foundation, not all knowledge workers like the kind of organisation in which they work, even if it values innovation: "fifty per cent of knowledge workers said their organisation's predominant feature was innovation, development and being at the cutting edge, but only twenty-four per cent preferred this type of organisation". Can we form an entire nation of mad scientists, and will this pay off?

Across the OECD, whose members should be leading the world in innovation, fewer than one per cent of workers are directly involved in R&D. Meanwhile, the main reason why the NICs (Newly Industrialised countries) and BRICs (Brazil, Russia, India and China) are developing so quickly is that the path has been trod before them – there are supplies of fuel, know-how and capital all readily available on the market, especially in the case of China, where Foreign Direct Investors are desperate to bring their technology into the country. They do not need to start from scratch to invent, fund and engineer the industrial processes they decide to adopt – the More Economically Developed Countries (MEDCs) have already done that for them.

But the spark of genius is only the start of technological innovation. It is the application of technology to daily business operations that is the most productive aspect of technological innovation - as in the text-book case of the giant retailer, Wal-Mart, whose application of computer technology to its stock control is claimed to have been more significant to US economy than the advent of PCs themselves. This is perhaps a more predictable commercial goal for us to aim for. There is no choice – we need to train the labour force, young and old, in the skills required by the high-earning industries we have, and the growing industries we select to target, and visibly encourage and support them with incentivising, not punitive, tax regimes and state-of-the-art physical and technological infrastructure. The entire population, not just the progeny of a successful elite, need to believe that it is worthwhile gaining the skills to survive in a global market which may only begrudgingly pay us a living wage. The role of government in innovation is to join up the thinking of all the different stakeholders in education and training, from the CBI to the workers and students, and incentivise with facilities and financial rewards those willing to acquire and pass on the skills self-evidently necessary to push the boundaries of technology and then commercialise new discoveries to create a virtuous economic circle.

Specialist Training is essential to create and preserve employment

On its website, the major (now-)Japanese nuclear power provider, Westinghouse, addresses the dilemma for workers looking to start a career or possibly to retrain in exactly the kind of specialist area that will be needed in future by reassuring potential applicants that there is more demand for nuclear power workers than supply. It is this kind of reassurance that is needed to encourage UK workers to train or retrain for new industries in the UK, and a government commitment to certain sectors will give workers the confidence necessary. The US giant, GE, makes great play on its website of the fact that it invests one billion dollars every year on training its 300,000 plus workforce who are spread across the world from New York to Bangalore and Shanghai[133].

Trends can certainly be reversed by cash incentives supported by effective government communication, taking the example of the French Government's methods in its successful campaign to reverse its declining birth rate. Teenagers, too, are pragmatic. How many rich scientists are household names? And when top A-Level Grades are essential, why would you choose to study a subject which has been proven to be harder to achieve high grades in than 'media studies' or drama? What incentives are there for students to adopt a war-time spirit and choose to study difficult sciences which will qualify them to be paid a low salary in a smelly, noisy, dying industry, just to broaden the nation's future economic potential? Companies that operate globally cannot justify paying high salaries to encourage the development of scientific expertise in the UK, when they can buy the same expertise "off-the-shelf" more cheaply in fast-developing countries, even if, as for Rolls-Royce, the UK is their country of origin and remains their spiritual, or at least, brand-positioning heartland.

Within a national economy, simple incentive measures to remedy skills shortages can, however, easily be devised and implemented, from providing career information and arranging taster industrial work placements for students studying targeted combinations of A Levels, then providing financial incentives such as paying off the tuition fees of students who achieve good grades in the useful STEM subjects at university, to following through with vocational training and mature employee retraining explicitly agreed with employers in the targeted industrial and service sectors. On a local level, companies also need to be incentivised to retain and retrain older staff, and informed about the mechanics and the benefits of doing so, and need to agree a strategy to address, and in future prevent, the problem of overpaid staff whose salaries do not reflect their true value to the company, either because they have increased over time without extra merit, or because staff have become too remote from new technology to adapt to the next major business shift.

Messages that "*Training is a good thing*" are rather bland – "*Renew or retire*" would be more accurate. How and why do doctors, for instance, keep up to date theoretically and practically as they progress up the medical hierarchy? There is of course a duty to keep up to date by reading medical journals, but in addition it is because they do not completely stop doing the practical side of their work. A GP does not stop seeing patients; a surgeon confines herself to a specialist area and has junior staff to do some of the work but nevertheless continues to practise her own specialism in a literally 'hands-on' (or 'hands-in') manner. This is where ageism at both ends of a worker's career will make or break the MEDC economies. If older workers do not retrain, we cannot employ them, and if we cannot employ them we have to pay their pensions for a very long time; at the other end of the age range, if young people are excluded from productive output by abstract ideals of a super-educated workforce, or pipped to the job centre post by a temporarily under-priced mobile European workforce, we waste our best future resource. When conscientious and capable migrant workers to do more cheaply the only jobs our unskilled workers *could* do, the unfortunate result is that the UK economy loses out twice over – we pay our unskilled workers *not* to work and we lose the opportunity to create a viable employment structure that does not rely on an exploited proletariat at the bottom of the pile.

"Education, education, education"

Education has now become a global obsession: ambitious mothers in some parts of China receive text messages every day on their mobile phones, setting out their child's homework for that night. One of the reasons for China's attractiveness for Foreign Direct Investment, which has levered up its phenomenal growth, is the high educational standard of its workforce. Vietnam is now developing rapidly for similar reasons. Training and education are key to equipping a skilled and flexible labour force who can be employed in our increasingly sophisticated economy. If the system fails, or succeeds in educating only some of the population adequately, then sections of the labour force will be unemployed and the next generation of students will become alienated and disillusioned. Government support is not always effectively targeted: the National Audit Office gave only limited praise to the government Train to Gain scheme, which it did not consider provided good value for money at a cost of nearly one and a half billion pounds[134]. What should the role of government be in terms of its responsibility for employment, and how far should it go to support it? Government will inevitably continue to take the lead on State Education, but it should liaise more with the CBI and other industry leaders, to produce school-leavers with relevant and adaptable basic skills necessary for all workers, and to produce university graduates in industrially essential academic subjects trained to a world class standard. Even better, the government should be at an arm's length distance from the education system, rather in the way the Bank of England is independent of immediate government pressures.

Government-sponsored vocational training in response to our changing work demands in the UK is simply too generic, low level and generalised. It is a step in the right direction to gain your ECDL (European Computer Driving Licence) but this does not actually qualify you for a specific job. Businesses want: "literacy, numeracy, punctuality, communication skills and an ability to be well-presented", according to Colin Willman, Chairman of the FSB (Federation of Small Businesses), but a quarter of small companies reported skills shortages when trying to fill vacancies. Whilst school-leavers are technologically sophisticated, a CBI survey found that more than half of all employers are dissatisfied with sixteen-year-olds' basic English and Maths skills. At the same time the British Chamber of Commerce said that the level of skills among school-leavers was 'a national scandal', and employers are equally dissatisfied with university graduates' preparedness for the workplace. It would appear that we are touting British world leadership in the latest technology when a large part of the next generation cannot add up or write a letter. At least the forty-year-olds should be able to beat the younger generation to the lowest-paid jobs – after all, they can manage to write their own application letters. But then there really will be no-one lined up to pay our pensions.

Yet officially, the UK workforce is better trained and educated than it has ever been. Consider these figures from The Work Foundation: "In 1970 the better educated constituted just over one per cent of the workforce, but by

2005 this had increased to nearly 20 per cent. The less well educated with just basic schooling declined from nearly 60 per cent to about 12 per cent over the same period." The problem is that official international reports (from the World Bank and the OECD) now all equate a better-trained workforce with one that has studied at university. But a university training does not equip graduates to do any job at all straight away without substantial further training, so there is a mismatch between employee skills and requirements. The Work Foundation has identified that "serious underlying structural problems remain around the effective utilisation of skills and science and technology[135]" The CBI and the universities are liaising to see what skills are needed to prepare graduates for work. However, the conclusion of some industrialists is that a traditional university may not be the most appropriate place to prepare most students for the new specialist workplace.

Meanwhile, the very subjects that students are abandoning, the 'hard' pure subjects of Science, Technology, Engineering and Maths (the so-called 'STEM' subjects) are in great demand from employers. Only 5% of UK students apply to study engineering (it used to be nearly 10%), compared with 15% in France and 44% in China. There were more students in the UK taking A Levels in media studies than in physics in 2005, despite the fact that physics-based industry alone employs getting on for two million people in the UK and contributes over £130 billion in export value to the UK economy. Biotechnology is one of the areas targeted by the UK government, in competition with a number of advanced and developing economies, but a long colourful history, traditional hegemony and a nice damp climate alone have not always won out against the ability to offer generous development funding. The UK is targeting nano-technology, yet the university chemistry and physics departments are closing down. Since 1994 one in four universities that previously had significant numbers of undergraduates studying physics has stopped teaching the subject. Is Britain realistic or simply nostalgic when it identifies its skills and core competencies as world class, when the CBI warns that that our new workforce lacks basic literacy and numeracy?

Career Crunch!

Keeping up to date

Logistical or technical improvements, or changes in the rules, can change the nature even of the traditional professions. We have all observed that the traditional general-purpose solo GP surgery is disappearing, as larger practices are formed to allow GPs more flexible hours and also to bring together more specialised doctors to deal expertly with specific ailments. And specialist areas themselves can be rendered unnecessary with progress – we no longer need to treat smallpox (unless we are attacked with biological warfare from the two sources in the world where supplies of the killer disease are stored). Whole industries can disappear: with gas and oil supplies under threat and former coal-mining communities still burdened with unemployment, we can now see that having our own supply of coal would be a reassuring backup for our energy needs; nevertheless we are also all aware that the job of mining was dirty and dangerous, and that, for the environment, so is burning the coal it extracts. So no career or industry will remain the same throughout the course of one person's working life, and we need to take this into account in our planning. Training and education will need to continue throughout workers' lives, right across all stages of economic development, as set out by the World Bank, in a paper which is in fact addressing the needs of developing countries, but which we could well hear in one of our own government speeches:

"Moreover, since the skills required by today's labor market may not be the same as those that will be required in the future, a process of lifelong learning must be built into the education system. And at all levels and life-cycle stages, the education system must work with the private sector to understand and respond to its needs" [136]

Workers should expect only part of their training to be done on-the-job. Learning how to use a new piece of machinery needs to be demonstrated at work, but then workers should expect to devote some of their free time, in the same way that businessmen, and lawyers do, to keeping up-to-date, reading the manuals at home to familiarise themselves with processes and procedures, and applying their new knowledge in the workplace. The onus is on the individual to keep up to date and on the employer to make this duty explicit in all employees' job descriptions, but also to support them with targeted on-the-job instruction and clear direction in annual employee appraisals. A car mechanic is expected to take a general professional interest in new designs of car engines, even if he in turn expects to receive training from his employer in the specific servicing requirements of the latest models.

The change in emphasis from lifelong jobs to lifelong employability has been gaining popularity. It was successfully introduced to IBM by the former CEO Lou Gerstner, as he describes in his autobiography "Who says Elephants Can't Dance", though his turnaround of IBM was launched with swingeing redundancies. Otherwise, redundant middle managers risk going the same way as the old fridges piling up in landfill sites across the globe: only as there are starting to be too many to ignore will "repairability" be discussed. The outdated consumerist innovation of "built-in obsolescence" is now less appealing than the more environmentally-focused "built-in repairability", and similarly, an older employee should not be replaced simply because her skills need renewing – she should be continuously retraining and updating her skills so that they can be reused in other areas. When manufacturers have a commercial incentive to design-in easy repairs instead of selling us a complete new gadget every time it goes wrong, we will all benefit, in the same way as when employers believe that it is worthwhile training up an existing employee, instead of getting a newly-trained one off the shelf, or even better, when employees themselves find that training and constantly keeping up to date pays dividends.

Government, too, has a role to play. Having committed to supporting our growing industries, it will need to encourage and incentivise workers at all levels to take up relevant training, targeting effective basic education in literacy and numeracy but also recognising the high standards that will be required in the harder 'STEM' subjects up to university courses and beyond. Inspiring a new generation is not sufficient – students must have reason to believe that it will be worth their while committing themselves to several years spent acquiring the specialist technical skills and experience necessary to drive the industries of the future, in terms of both job stability and higher salaries to reflect the longer years of harder study – at present any aspiring future scientist is officially warned: "*But don't expect to earn very much money in this profession*". Finally, the UK government has announced measures to attempt to attract young workers into manufacturing and to create more "green jobs" – they should also look to older workers who already possess many of the necessary skills and just need to update them.

Commercial enterprises are at the forefront of the drive to reinvent and progress. What governments and industry leaders need to provide is a favourable environment to *enable* them to evolve – physical infrastructure, large open markets, financial liquidity, and above all demonstrably *useful* basic and higher education, effective training and clear unbiased information. To underpin its messages the government must explicitly set out a coherent industrial strategy, not to protect domestic industries but to invest in them by informing and coordinating the efforts of educators, industrialists and financiers alike, so that all stakeholders have confidence that targeted sectors will be supported. Aligning trading conditions between heavy polluters off-loading their costs on the external environment, and environmentally responsible producers bearing the costs of cleaning up after themselves, will ensure level playing fields, to say nothing of a future for the planet. Finally, successful national governments are already engaged in sending clear signals to their trading partners and rivals that they have made a commitment to a limited number of specific industries and sectors to diversify their investment away from the large but old industries such as car manufacture, kept alive artificially in advanced economies by national governments, and into an internationally complementary range of new activities.

In the future it is clear that what will be *needed* are knowledge workers who can compete globally on expertise and price, far more care workers, and a comparatively large number of highly-specialised scientists to research and innovate in energy, high-end manufacturing and bio-technology and other leading-edge sciences, all working till they are at least seventy. However, what we *have* are unskilled workers and generalist administrators at the top of the global pay-scales under threat from up-and-coming global competition; ambitious City financiers who have gambled on the global economy and lost; a huge and growing public sector with inflexible contracts and pensions which are guaranteed but largely unfunded; and finally too few scientists fighting for support from a decreasing number of University departments. They all still hope to retire at sixty-five. Every employee needs to understand the implications of the global nature of all employment, even apparently localised jobs, and the changes taking place in the traditional lifelong career, and in the traditional human lifespan, so that they can take on the daunting responsibility of planning their own training and finance to keep themselves both sufficiently specialised and at the same time sufficiently flexible to survive in the new *up-and-out-and-roundabout* career pattern of the future.

Conclusion

Up-and-out-and-roundabout Careers

There are no more pre-packaged forty-year careers. As the German academic Ulrich Beck states: *"the 'job for life' has disappeared"*[137]. The most enduring career formats, the 'professions', require continually updated knowledge and experience, but economic crises such as the Credit Crunch still intervene to cut back the numbers of specialists. In the Darwinian world of employment, each employee constantly needs to evolve to be the best fitted to his changing environment. After an initial phase of traditional career progression within the same company, the emerging career pattern is of continual sideways, upward or even downward movement round employers and roles, each time extending, adapting and retraining, formally and informally, to deepen, broaden or update expertise.

But this does not mean that there will be no careers, and no need for study, training or qualifications. Quite the opposite: there will be even more development between your first job and your last. Working lives will, by necessity, last longer, as an increasing proportion of the population remain active into their eighties, but careers will be more fragmentary, and a constant ebb and flow of flexible, skilled and well-informed labour will continually exit and re-enter the market, each time deposited by the current, or by an invisible hand, in a slightly new position. As rates of unemployment remain permanently high across Europe, government regulations relating to hiring and firing will need be made less onerous for employers in any countries determined to solve this problem, interim staff will be employed increasingly, and renewable contracts will be accepted as the norm for many employees. The new winners will no longer be the most loyal, but the most adaptable, and, above all, the most persistent, and *up-and-out* employment patterns will produce *up-and-out-and-roundabout* employees. As they enter the Career Value Gap in their mid-forties, when their perceived value to their employer is overtaken by their constantly rising salaries, employees will be increasingly vulnerable to redundancy, but canny employees will maintain their skills sets and re-enter the market, often via a sideways or downwards move, in order to work their way up again. Alternatively, they will enter a period of *Flex*employment, working on a series of temporary contracts of variable duration and at different salary levels. This style of employment may carry them through until the end of their working life, or they may use their functional expertise to move step by step into a permanent role in a new or expanding sector, or vice-versa, developing new areas of sought-after expertise in their current sector.

Like the disappearing final-salary pension schemes, a successful career will no longer be determined by the position you hold when the music stops, but by a personal narrative spanning several decades in a range of related roles and sectors.

Even with flexible, constantly retraining workers, jobs are not fixed in one place, but move around the world. The current status quo, whereby workers in the poorer developing nations underpin the lifestyle of the rich nations, will soon follow the same pattern of rise and fall as all historical empires. The undisputed hegemony of the 'West', from vast economies such as the United States and Europe, to city-states such as Dubai and Singapore, will not be sustainable, as ambitious workers in developing economies acquire the same skills and technology. As rates of pay begin to equalise internationally, migrant labour will either return home or demand the same rates of pay as their indigenous hosts, and manufacturing abroad will also cease to be the cheapest option, because rising salary expectations and environmental tariffs will raise prices in emerging economies. Only those nations whose governments explicitly commit to and effectively support a coherent strategy which is different from, and complementary to its trading partners, will be able to provide interesting and well-paid jobs for a large part of their workforce.

Career Crunch!

Both as individual employees, and as a nation trading in the world, we can see more competition entering the market at the bottom, whilst we cannot afford to relinquish our position at the top. We can no longer expect to train up when we are young for a secure, predictable future and then to sit comfortably - we will have to compete through innovation, retraining and lifelong flexibility, with the explicit support of a coordinated national industrial strategy, in order to retain our jobs as world-class producers and innovators, responding to, but also setting the direction for, the global economy in the twenty-first century.

Career Crunch!

Coda

There is Time

The inhabitants of the developed world have more quality Time-Left-to-Go than ever before in human history. There is Time for a career break. There is Time to change career direction – once, twice, three times. There is Time to start again. There is Time to retrain and reinvent yourself, your staff, your business. The Romans, who found time to build monuments to last two thousand years, still complained that "*Tempus fugit*", but no longer. You cannot afford to ignore the statisticians – take their numbers to heart and act upon them. Compare your life expectancy with figures from just a century ago. Time has stopped and waited for you. It has presented you with thirty to forty extra years on a platter, bearing an ominous label:

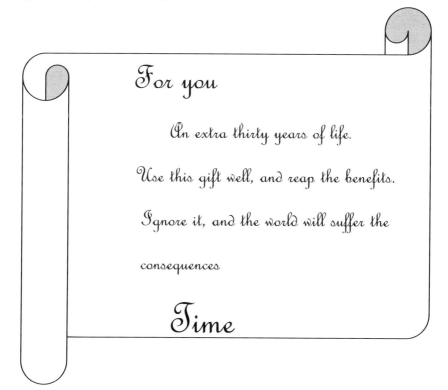

For you

An extra thirty years of life.

Use this gift well, and reap the benefits.

Ignore it, and the world will suffer the

consequences

Time

INDEX

<u>Appendices</u>

<u>Glossary of terms used in this book</u>

Acronyms:

CBI: Confederation of British Industry

FSB: Federation of Small Businesses

LSC: Learning and Skills Council: now replaced by:

    Young People's Learning Agency

    Skills Funding Agency

QCA: Qualifications and Curriculum Authority

CIM: Chartered Institute of Marketing

defra: Trendy lowercase typeface that fools no-one because it still stands for the Government: Department for Environment, Food and Rural Affairs

AIM: alternative Investments Market (a stock exchange for smaller, riskier companies)

EU: European Union (formerly the 'Common Market', then the 'EEC')

LEDC: Less Economically Developed country

MEDC: More Economically Developed country

NIC: Newly Industrialised Country (*or* National Insurance Contribution)

BRIC: Brazil, Russia, India and China – large and rapidly growing economies

GATT: General Agreement on Tariffs and Trade

IMF: International Monetary Fund

H&S: Health and Safety

NEETs: Aged 16-24 and Not in Employment, Education or Training

OECD: 30 developed countries in Organisation for Economic Cooperation and Development

ONS: Office for National Statistics

SPA: State Pension Age – due to go up to 68 years between 2024 and 2046

RPI: Retail Price Index

CPI: Consumer Price Index used as headline "inflation" but often lower than RPI

ECDL: European Computer Driving Licence

CPD: Continuous Professional Development

MBA: Masters in Business Administration (Finance, Accounting, Economics, Marketing, Operations Management etc)

HND: Higher National Diploma

NVQ: National Vocational Qualifications

BTEC: Business and Technology Education Council

STEM subjects: Science Technology Engineering and Maths. Useful subjects rejected as too difficult by most students

SBTC Skill-Based Technological Change

LLB: Bachelor of Law - undergraduate Law degree

ACA: qualified Chartered Accountant

CACHE (Council for Awards in Children`s Care and Education) Diploma in Childcare and Education (formerly NNEB qualification)

BOGOF: Marketing jargon for 'Buy One Get One Free'

FMCG: Marketing jargon for Fast Moving Consumer Goods

OTE: Sales jargon for 'On Target Earnings', basic salary plus commission

T-accounts: book-keeping records set out on the page in the shape of a 'T'

PR: Public Relations, getting free advertising by media coverage

HR: Human Resources (Formerly Personnel): "A damn silly name for a job" to quote Prince Philip

R&D: Research and Development

CEO: Chief Executive Officer – runs the company

MD: Managing Director– runs the company/division

SNCF: Societe Nationale des Chemins de Fer, French railways

LIFO/FIFO: Last In First Out/ First In First Out

SIMS: Computer game where you create virtual homes and inhabitants

Economics jargon:

'Eurozone': ("Euroland"):16 EU members in the European Monetary Union (EMU) i.e. all using the   Euro as their currency: The original 12: Belgium, Austria, France, Finland, Luxembourg, Italy, Netherlands,   Germany, Portugal, Ireland, Greece, Spain; plus Malta, Cyprus and Slovenia and Slovakia. The Eurosystem, headed by the European Central Bank, is

responsible for monetary policy within the Eurozone. Based on 2007 GDP, the Eurozone is the largest economy in the world.

'externality': an effect not intended by the undertaking (usually negative) and something companies will try to ignore unless regulated

'moral hazard': the fact that people will not take such careful precautions against negative results for which they are insured, so there is less incentive to do the right, sensible thing

'public good': something that benefits everyone so no one individual feels personally responsible

'natural monopoly': Water or gas might have been a good example – how can you believe there is true competition when every supplier has to use the same pipes and the same sources?

'monopsony': a market in which there is a single buyer (like monopoly but the opposite)

People:

Adam Smith: famous for being on the £20 note, and before that for founding economic theory, stating that that free markets function without interference as if steered by an "invisible hand"

David Ricardo: early economist advocating Free Trade

Thomas Malthus: Early political economist who believed that war, famine and disease were necessary to limit population growth

Karl Marx: nineteenth century political economist - the father of Communism

Deng Xiaoping: Chinese communist leader who opened up the economy in the 1980s

Charles Handy: Management guru published a number of best-selling books on business organisation

UK Ageism Legislation 2006

Some key points:

Ageism is now illegal. (Though ironically some ageist practices are now compulsory)

Employees have the right to request postponed retirement.

Employers have the right to refuse postponed retirement. They can also refuse training to an employee who has too little time before retirement to make cost-effective use of the benefit.

Job adverts should not specify age, either explicitly or implicitly.

Ageist harassment or prejudice in the workplace is illegal.

Useful websites

www.efa.org.uk The Employers' Forum on Age – clear useful site

www.acas.org.uk/media/pdf/r/j/Age_and_the_Workplace.pdf

> (excellent website specifically addressing ageism legislation)

www.bbc.co.uk/theoneshow/article/2007/09/ct_ageism.shtml

> (useful insights into ageism with video)

www.acas.org.uk guides to employing older workers and other advice.

Your former employers' websites for company information

Websites of each company you target (*especially the "About Us" or "Corporate Information" pages*)

http://www.direct.gov.uk/en/Employment/RedundancyAndLeavingYourJob/Redundancy UK government site with clear, practical advice

www.companieshouse.gov.uk Companies House (*download accounts of companies you might want to work for*)

www.oecd.org OECD website stuffed with global facts and figures

www.statistics.gov.uk and www.ons.gov.uk Office for National Statistics

www.gad.gov.uk Government Actuary's Department population figures

www.parliament.uk Government reports

www.globalsubsidies.org Information on subsidies distorting global markets

http://20plus30.com Marketing Consultancy specialising in marketing to customers aged 50+

epp.eurostat.ec.europa.eu: Eurostat European figures

jobs.guardian.co.uk Guardian newspaper jobs

www.telegraph.co.uk Telegraph newspaper jobs

www.timesonline Times newspaper jobs

www.Totaljobs.co.uk

http://www.businesslink.gov.uk Business Link website advises on running a business

www.Bluesteps.com (*register your CV for recruitment agencies*)

www.askgrapevine.com Executive Grapevine (*local library and website*) *Lists key recruiting firms by sector.*

Skills councils such as:

www.cogent-ssc.com (chemicals, oil, gas etc)

www.euskills.co.uk (energy and utility skills)

www.energinst.org.uk (professional membership)

www.thepensionservice.gov.uk check out the rules for your pension

www.businesslink.gov.uk New business support in England

www.bgateway.com New business support in Scotland

www.businesseye.org.uk New business support in Wales

www.hmrc.gov.uk Information about tax

What training is already available?

Anything you could possibly want! There are millions of pounds of funding for thousands of colleges, universities and Institutes providing hundreds of courses. The following institutions and websites are just a small selection:

Local Colleges

Universities, including evening classes

Open University (see website below)

Companies offering in-house training

Companies offering Day release

Private Training companies

Chartered Institutes – Engineering, Personnel, Marketing and others

Specialist providers such as the Power Academy (will sponsor annually 60 undergraduates to study power engineering)

Useful government and other training and careers sites:

Career Crunch!

www.traintogain.gov.uk

www.aimhigher.ac.uk

www.jobcentreplus.gov.uk

http://jobseekers.direct.gov.uk

www.direct.gov.uk

www.learndirect.co.uk

www.careerserviceni.com

www.careers-scotland.org.uk

www.connexions-direct.com/jobs4u Excellent government careers information for 13-19 year olds – Connexions Service

ypla.gov.uk Young People's Learning Agency

skillsfundingagency.bis.gov.uk Skills Funding Agency

www.careers-scotland.org.uk – Scotland

www.careerswales.com - Wales

www.becomeamechanic.co.uk Example of vocational training information

www.prospects.ac.uk Excellent graduate careers information

www.open.ac.uk Open university

www.fssc.org.uk Financial Services Skills Council (FSSC) About exams in finance

www.barcouncil.org.uk About barristers

www.lawsociety.org.uk About solicitors

http://www.qca.org.uk Qualifications and Curriculum Authority

http://www.dfes.gov.uk Department for Children, Schools and Families

www.apprenticeships.org.uk Details of apprenticeships (these should not legally be age-related so it is worth trying)

Useful organisations for older workers

Age Concern
Age Concern provides essential services and information to people in the UK over 50. It campaigns on issues like age discrimination and pensions.
http://www.ageconcern.org.uk/

Career Crunch!

Age Positive
Age positive are a team working in the Department for Work and Pensions, responsible for strategy and policies to support people making decisions about working and retirement.
www.agepositive.gov.uk

Are you over 50?
Are you over 50? is a practical guide to advice, support and services available through government and voluntary organisations for people aged 50 and over.
www.over50.gov.uk

Centre for Policy on Ageing (CPA)
The CPA is an independent centre of research and reference and aims to inform and influence service providers on the issues affecting older workers.
www.cpa.org.uk

The Employers Forum on Age (EPA)
The EFA is a campaigning organisation made up of an independent network of leading employers. Core members include B&Q, Barclays, BBC, BT, Cabinet Office, Centrica, and the Chartered Institute of Personnel & Development.
www.efa.org.uk

Equal Opportunities Commission (EOC)
The EOC is the leading agency working to eliminate sex discrimination in the UK.
www.eoc.org.uk

Help the Aged
Help the Aged is a charity campaigning for the rights of older people.
www.helptheaged.org.uk

Third Age Employment Network (TAEN)
TAEN is a campaigning organisation, working with the media, employers and government to change attitudes and public policies on older workers.
www.taen.org.uk

Cambridge Interdisciplinary Research Centre on Ageing

CPA Centre for Policy on Ageing

www.ageconcern.org.uk Age Concern

Help the Aged

EFA Employers forum on Age

The Pensions Commission

Career Crunch!

www.primeinitiative.org.uk:

Prince's Initiative for Mature Enterprise, helps 50+ year olds into self-employment

www.saga.co.uk:

 Saga provides online information about starting a business in its Money section

over50.gov.uk: the Direct Gov internet portal has a section dedicated to the over 50s with information on becoming self-employed

www.olderpreneur.net:

The Olderpreneur is a network for those over 50 wanting to start or running their own business

seniority.co.uk: Seniority UK is a forum for people over 50

jobcentreplus.gov.uk: New Deal 50 Plus provides training for people over 50 to become self-employed if they have been on benefit for more than 6 months

Useful places to go to find information:

Your local job centre

Your local Library for free computer courses

Your local Reference Library for basic Business Data

City Business Library

Westminster Reference Library

The Business and Intellectual Property Centre at The British Library, King's Cross (*not the latest Mintel reports but excellent access to online databases*)

Pocket guides:

"The Economist Pocket World in Figures 2007"

"Sustainable development indicators in your pocket", Department for the Environment, Food and Rural Affairs

Job-hunting Checklists - see **www.career-crunch.com**

[1] "The Age of Unreason", Charles Handy

[2] 2006 Ageism Legislation; UK State Pension Age raised to 68 by 2046

[3] Booz & Company New York, May 22, 2007: Study of CEO turnover at the world's 2,500 largest publicly traded corporations. Permission granted.

[4] CEO Succession 2006: the Era of the Inclusive Leader" (2007); Booz & Company

[5] Robert Half researched incumbent chief executives of FTSE 100 and S&P Global 100 companies for its report "UK Chief Executives serve longer than global counterparts" (30th April 2008) Permission granted.

[6] Robert Half, "UK Chief Executives serve longer than global counterparts" (30th April 2008)

[7] CEO Succession 2006: the Era of the Inclusive Leader" published 2007; Booz & Company studied 357 CEOs of the world's largest 2,500 publicly traded companies who left office in 2006

[8] The changing influence of the Chief Marketing Officer, SpencerStuart 2006. Permission Granted.

[9] From CMO to CEO: the route to the top, published by SpencerStuart 2009

[10] ibid: "Only a few marketers will make the transition to CEO. With average tenure somewhere between 2–3 years (depending on the market) the odds are stacked against CMOs progressing into general management and then the top slot."

[11] Office for National Statistics February 2009 Claimant Count Report 11(2)

[12] Office for National Statistics February 2009 Unemployment figures Report 9(2)

[13] "A Midsummer Night's Dream", William Shakespeare

[14] "Complete War Walks", Richard Holmes

[15] As noted by Duncan Hewitt in "Getting Rich First", Chatto & Windus 2007

[16] "Ageism" David Thorp, The Institute of Marketing 5th March 2007

[17] "The Brave New World of Work" Ulrich Beck, Polity Press 2000

[18] Third Age Employment Network, www.taen.org.uk

[19] Court v Dennis Publishing Limited 2007

[20] "Freakonomics" Levitt & Dubner (2005)

[21] Office for National Statistics

[22] SpencerStuart: "2004 CEO study: A statistical snapshot of leading CEOs"

[23] "How to Get Rich" by Felix Dennis, published by Ebury 2006. Used by permission of The Random House Group Ltd. A brilliant book and a must-read for all entrepreneurs

[24] He beheaded two of his wives (Anne Boleyn and her cousin, Catherine Howard), and executed various ministers, including Sir Thomas More, Cardinal Wolsey and Thomas Cromwell.

[25] Source: ThyssenKrupp website

[26] "Getting Rich First", Duncan Hewitt, Chatto & Windus 2007

[27] *Working Longer: The Solution to the Retirement Income Challenge"* Alicia H. Munnell, Steven A. Sass, Brookings Institution Press 2008

[28] The 2008 Interim Management Association market audit report states that that 71% of assignments were completed by men

[29] Alium Partners, an interim management agency with five thousand people on their books. http://www.aliumpartners.com/clients/interim-market.aspx

[30] The ST 100 which ranks the UK's 100 fastest growing private companies on sales value during a three year period

[31] It came 38th in the top 50

[32] Approximately: Brazil 180 m, Russia over 140m, India 1 billion, China 1.3 billion

[33] "Getting Rich first" Duncan Hewitt, Chatto & Windus 2007

[34] ONS statistics: in 2008 24% of all live births in the UK were to mothers who were born abroad

[35] according to the National Insurance Recording System

[36] Accession States are 10 countries which joined the EU on 1st May 2004. They are: Malta, Southern Cyprus and a further 8 known as the A8: Czech Republic, Slovakia, Slovenia, Estonia, Latvia, Lithuania, Poland, Hungary

[37] Only four years previously, in the year 2002-3 there were 115,000 Numbers issued to workers from Asia and the Middle East, but only eighteen thousand from the A8 countries

[38] September 2008

[39] The Economic Impact of Migration, House of Lords 1/4/08

[40] "The Brave New World of Work" Ulrich Beck, Polity Press 2000

[41] Plumbers are in Standard Occupational Classification Group 5134

[42] Goos and Manning (2003)

[43] *Postcapitalist Society,* Peter F. Drucker Oxford 1993, though he first used the term in 1968

[44] Knowledge Workers and Knowledge Work *The Work Foundation* March 2009, website: www.theworkfoundation.com

[45] OECD Factbook 2009

[46] Knowledge Workers and Knowledge Work *The Work Foundation* March 2009, website: www.theworkfoundation.com

[47] 34% earned above the median

[48] "What is a Public Sector Pension Worth?" 1 October 2007, Disney, Emmerson and Tetlow, published by the Institute for Fiscal Studies (Permission granted)

[49] The Gilgamesh Epic written on clay tablets found in the great Library of King Ashurbanipal in Nineveh

[50] Research by Andrew Oswald, Professor of Economics, Warwick University,

[51] B&Q website:
http://www.diy.com/diy/jsp/bq/templates/content_lookup.jsp?content=/about bandq/2004/press_office/company/2006/2006sept_agepositive.jsp&menu=abo utbandq

[52] http://www.nationwide-jobs.co.uk/home/about-us/equality-diversity

[53] Source: 20plus30 Consulting 2007 (Dick Stroud) Reproduced by permission

[54] Professional Engineering 11th June 2008

[55] Professional Engineering 11th June 2008

[56] It is expected that that over the next 10 years the nuclear sector will need to recruit between 5,900-9,000 graduates and 2,700 to 4,500 skilled trades to meet the on-going needs of decommissioning, power generation, the fuel Institute of Mechanical Engineers Press release 25th April 2008

[57] Institute of Mechanical Engineers Press release 28th January 2008

[58] *"The stability of General Intelligence from early adulthood to middle-age"* published in the journal "Intelligence" carried out in 2007 by Lars Larsen from Denmark

[59] *"Step by Step Intelligence Tests"* by C.N.Bissenden, pub. Wheaton 1958-1968

[60] learndirect.co.uk "new skills wanted" 2008

[61] Knowledge Workers and Knowledge Work *The Work Foundation* March 2009 website: www.theworkfoundation.com (Permission granted)

[62] Lundavall and Johnson 1994 and OECD 1996

[63] "Knowledge Workers and Knowledge Work" The Work Foundation: www.theworkfoundation.com March 2009

[64] "Knowledge Workers and Knowledge Work" *The Work Foundation* March 2009 website: www.theworkfoundation.com

[65] Robert Half: "UK Chief Executives serve longer than global counterparts" (30th April 2008)

[66] Robert Half "Over Three Quarters of Newly Appointed FTSE 100 CEOs Have Strong Financial Experience" (23rd March 2009). With permission.

[67] Website of McKinsey & Company 29th April 2010:
http://www.mckinsey.com/careers/what_will_it_be_like_if_i_join/where_mckin sey_can_take_you.aspx

[68] Government Actuary's Department, UK

[69] The Government Actuary's Department projects that the number of pensioners will rise to 21,000 by 2020; by 2056 there are predicted to be 286,000 centenarians out of a population projected to rise from 60 million to nearly 80 million

[70] Office for National Statistics: in 2007 there were 3,345 infant deaths (at age less than one year); in 1951 there were 30 infant deaths per 1000 live births; in 1901 this figure was 151.

[71] Office for National Statistics

[72] ibid: 12% in 1901; 66% in 2007.

[73] 2006 figures from the Office for National Statistics

[74] Based on Period life expectancy figures; this figure implies a higher life expectancy than the average for new babies because it is based on people who have already reached retirement age.

[75] Cohort life expectancy figures (these take future changes into account and therefore at the moment are more positive)

[76] SPA remains at sixty for women born on or before April 1950. For women born after April 1950 it is set to rise from sixty to sixty-five over the decade from 2010 to 2020.

[77] Towers Watson press release March 22 2010, www.towerswatson.com/united-kingdom/press/1418

[78] The FTSE 350 pensions deficit is currently estimated to be around £80 billion

[79] After correcting for over 150,000 staff transferred to the private sector through Private Finance Initiatives, numbers appear to go down by 660,000 or 11%, between 1991 and 1998, but have since risen by 13% to 2005.Source:ONS

[80] http://www.statistics.gov.uk/pdfdir/lmsuk0110.pdf ONS Labour Market Statistical Bulletin, January 2010

[81] 3rd June 2009

[82] Office for National Statistics figures for 2004 downloaded from the website on 11th September 2008: 30% of public sector workers work part-time compared with 24% of private sector workers

[83] The peak is actually amongst those born in 1946/7, so those aged 58/9 in 2005, and in their early '60s today

[84] figures from 2004,from the OECD

[85] OECD Factbook 2009: Economic, Environmental and Social Statistics

[86] 2008 figure

[87] Produced by permission of the Office for National Statistics Webpage: http://www.statistics.gov.uk/CCI/nugget.asp?ID=260&Pos=1&ColRank=2&Rank=320

[88] In 2004, 582,000 people moved into the UK and 360,000 left (ONS)

[89] "Real Retirement Report" for AVIVA, the major insurance and pensions group

[90] From 1994 to spring 2004 the percentage of men working rose from 64% to 72% and women from 60% to 68%

[91] The Decline of Employment Among Older People in Britain, Nigel Campbell, CASE paper January 1999

[92] Figures quoted by Roger Morgan in "Older people and the labour market " in Focus on Older People, Office for National Statistics

[93] Lissenburgh and Smeaton (2003) and Barnes et al. (2002)

[94] The Decline of Employment Among Older People in Britain, Nigel Campbell, CASE paper January 1999

[95] As documented in the book, *Cycles,* by Maddy Dychtwald (Free Press 2003)

[96] In 2006 9.6% of men and 11.1% of women over retirement age were still working. In 2005, the employment rate for men aged 50-64 was 72.4% (overall rate: 74.6%), and for women aged 50-59 it was 68.4%. Academic papers include: Disney and Hawkes: *Declining job opportunities for Older Workers in Britain* (2001)"; "*Why has Employment recently Risen Among Older Workers in Britain*?"(2003)" Ulrike Hotopp of the DTI confirmed that employment rates in the older age group *are* going up.

[97] "Men in their 50s who were self-employed were much more likely than those who were employees to still be working ten years later. In addition, workers over SPA [State Pension Age] were more likely to be employed in small companies with 1 to 10 staff and far less likely to be employed in larger organisations with over 50 staff." (Office for National Statistics)

[98] The Real Level of Unemployment, Professor Steven Fothergill, Sheffield Hallam University, May 2007

[99] Source: "Jobs in the public and private sectors", Duncan MacGregor, Employment Earnings and Productivity Division, ONS

[100] UK Immigration Minister, Phil Woolas

[101] "*How to find work when you're over 50*", Jackie Sherman, howtobooks 2006

[102] "*The Economic Possibilities for our Grandchildren*" John Maynard Keynes 1930

[103] "*Babar the King*", Jean de Brunhoff, Methuen and Co 1936; originally published 1933

[104] "*The Brave New World of Work*" Ulrich Beck, Polity Press 2000

[105] "*The Disposable Worker*" BusinessWeek 18th January 2010

[106] Knowledge Workers and Knowledge Work March 2009 The Work Foundation website: www.theworkfoundation.com

[107] *William Wilberforce*, by William Hague

[108] "New industry, New jobs", http://www.bis.gov.uk/files/file51023.pdf

[109] the National Offender Management IT System

[110] Whilst the south-east only derives just over a third of its income from the public sector, in the north-east it is two-thirds and in Northern Ireland it is over three-quarters

[111] Excerpt from report entitled: Science, Technology, and Innovation: Capacity Building for Sustainable Growth and Poverty Reduction. Edited by Alfred Watkins and Michael Ehst (2008) Downloaded 30th June 2009 Reproduced by permission of the International Bank for Reconstruction and Development, The World Bank.

[112] According to their website: www.deutschepost.de

[113] World Nuclear Association 1st February 2010

[114] In 1986 the world's worst nuclear accident took place at Chernobyl in the USSR

[115] According to Mike O'Brian, Energy Minister

[116] Professional Engineering 8th July 2009. (Permission granted)

[117] Professional Engineering 8th July 2009

[118] Professional Engineering 8th July 2009

[119] PV Crystalox, based in Abingdon makes silicon ingots and wafers used in PV cells based. Romag, based in County Durham, assembles solar cells into solar PV modules that integrate into walls and roofs. Source: Professional engineering 23rd April 2008

[120] Professional engineering 23rd April 2008

[121] "How to Get Rich" by Felix Dennis, published by Ebury 2006. Used by permission of The Random House Group Ltd.

[122] For the railways the leaders are Bombardier, Siemens, Alstom; for power generation it is Alstom, Siemens and GE - nuclear power is dominated by Areva (French), Westinghouse (now Japanese-owned American) and GE; for aircraft it is Boeing and Airbus; and for ports it is Dubai Ports, Hutchison Whampoa , AP Moller-Maersk and PSA Singapore.

[123] Import penetration (as a percentage of UK demand) doubled between 1992 and 2004 (Imports increased from 16 per cent to 33 per cent of UK demand) but over the same period exports measured in the same way went up by nearly half as much again (Exports increased from 29 per cent to 43 per cent).

[124] The Work Foundation: Manufacturing and the Knowledge Economy February 2009 website: www.theworkfoundation.com

[125] published April 2009

[126] "Going for Growth: Our future prosperity" and the website of the Department for Business Innovation and Skills www.bis.gov.uk/Policies/new-industry-new-jobs

[127] Mainly wind, wave, tidal and nuclear power generation

[128] Examples include: aerospace, composite materials, industrial biotechnology, plastic electronics

[129] ONS National Account Blue Book 2008

[130] ONS Balance of Payments Pink Book 2008

[131] The Work Foundation: Manufacturing and the Knowledge Economy February 2009 website: www.theworkfoundation.com

[132] Creative Industries Fact File, Department for Culture Media and Sport

[133] www.ge.com/careers

[134] in its report to the House of Commons on 20th July 2009

[135] Manufacturing and the Knowledge Economy February 2009 A report produced by The Work Foundation www.theworkfoundation.com

[136] www.worldbank.org Overview of Science, Technology and Innovation Report 2008 Reproduced by permission of the International Bank for Reconstruction and Development, The World Bank.

[137] 'The Brave New World of Work', Ulrich Beck, Polity Press 2000

All references to data from the Office for National Statistics reproduced under the terms of the Click-Use Licence, Licence Number C2010000619.

1083255R0

Printed in Great Britain by
Amazon.co.uk, Ltd.,
Marston Gate.